With Best Wishes

George. E. Bartlett.

Fuchsias
THE NEW CULTIVARS

George Bartlett

The Crowood Press

First Published in 2000 by
The Crowood Press Ltd
Ramsbury, Marlborough
Wiltshire SN8 2HR

British Library Cataloguing-in-Publication Data

A catalogue reference for this book is available from the British Library

ISBN 1 86126 338 4

Line illustrations by Cy Baker.

Acknowledgements
The author would like to thank most sincerely those specialist fuchsia nurseries kind enough to send him copies of their catalogues from which much of the information and descriptions were obtained. The names and addresses of these nurseries are printed at the back of this book.

The author is also extremely grateful to the fol-lowing nurseries who kindly provided young plants at the beginning of the year so that they could be grown and photographed:

Brynawel Fuchsia and Garden Centre
Breach Lane Nurseries
Clay Lane Fuchsias
John Smith and Son
Kathleen Muncaster Fuchsias
Littlebrook Fuchsias
Mike Oxtoby Fuchsias
Oldbury Fuchsias
Percival's Fuchsias
Rooster Fuchsias
Silverdale Fuchsias

Without the assistance of these dedicated fuchsia growers it would have been impossible to produce this second guide.

Typeface used: Sabon, main text; Helvetica, captions.

Typeset and designed by
D & N Publishing
Membury Business Park, Lambourn Woodlands
Hungerford, Berkshire.

Printed and bound by Leo Paper Product, China.

Contents

Preface

As a result of the great success of the first book *Fuchsias – A Colour Guide*, it was decided to produce a second volume incorporating many of the newer types of fuchsias. It is in a way unfortunate that books such as this are virtually 'out of date' before they are even printed as more and more new cultivars are introduced each year. However, we can but try our best to keep growers of fuchsias informed about many of the newer cultivars introduced during the last few years.

As readers will appreciate, many of the descriptions contained within this volume are those which have been used by the nurseries in their catalogues. As such it is not possible to obtain all the facts and information that we desire. Every effort has been made to get full information but there are a number of plants where it has not been possible to ascertain the name of the raiser or the date upon which it was first introduced. If such omissions cause any offence, I apologize most sincerely and would be very grateful if the information could be passed to me so that it can be included in subsequent printings.

One of the questions most frequently asked concerns the availability of the various plants. Following the descriptions, I have included codes for the nurseries from whose catalogues the information was obtained (*see* Nursery Addresses – 2000). It is quite possible that such nurseries will, after a few years, no longer be stocking the particular plant you require, but I have no doubt that they would supply you with information about where to obtain such a plant, if requested, or suggest a suitable similar cultivar.

The Author is extremely grateful to all the nurseries who sent their catalogues and particularly to those who supplied plants so that photographs could be taken. Without such assistance the production of a book such as this would have been impossible.

The response to the first book was so complimentary that I am fearful lest the standard of this second book does not match the first. I do not profess to be a photographer – I rely upon the camera to do the thinking and the focusing for me and concentrate purely on the 'making' of the picture. I am delighted, however, to have had the opportunity once again of sharing my love of the fuchsia with you. I still maintain that the growing of fuchsias is a hobby that should be enjoyed and have no hesitation in asking you once again to –

HAVE FUN WITH YOUR FUCHSIAS.

George E. Bartlett

Introduction

History

It seems almost impossible to believe that fuchsias have only been known to the modern world since 1703; and it was not until the 1820s that the nurserymen and hybridists realized the potential of these plants and started to breed new plants from the available species. It is quite amazing that such a vast quantity of cultivars, of so many differing colours and form, has become available to us in so short a time.

Approximately 100 different species have been identified to date. All are native to the southern hemisphere, most growing in the countries of South America although one group is native to New Zealand. As it is from these species that all our modern cultivars have emanated, I feel that it is important to tabulate them giving the areas within which they are found (*see* below).

All the Species of Fuchsias

Section 1. *Quelusia*
(Argentina, Brazil and Chile)

F. bracelinae	F. magellanica var. alba
F. campus-portoi	
F. magellanica var. macrostema	
F. coccinea	F. regia
F. magellanica	F. regia var. alpestris
F. regia var. regia	

Section 2. *Fuchsia*
(Andes and Central America)

F. abrupta	F. ampliata
F. andrei	F. austromontana
F. ayavacensis	F. boliviana
F. canescens	F. caucana
F. ceracea	F. cohabambana
F. concertifolia	F. coriacifolia
F. collata	F. corymbifolia
F. crassistipula	F. cautrecasii
F. decussata	F. denticulata
F. dependens	F. ferreyrae
F. fontinalis	F. furfuracea
F. gehrigeri	F. glaberrima
F. harlingii	F. hartwegii
F. hirtella	F. lechmanii
F. llewelynii	F. loxensis
F. macropetala	F. macrophylla
F. macrostigma	F. magdalenae
F. mathewsii	F. nigricans
F. orientalis	F. ovalis
F. pallescens	F. petiolaris
F. pilosa	F. polyantha
F. pringsheimii	F. putamayensis
F. rivularis	F. sanctae-rosae
F. sammartina	F. scabriuscula
F. scherffiana	F. sessilifolia
F. simplicaulis	F. steyermarkii
F. sylvatica	F. tincta
F. triphylla	F. vargasiana
F. venusta	F. verrucosa
F. vulcanica	F. wurdackii

Section 3 *Kierschlegeria* (Chile)
F. lycioides

Section 4 *Skinnera*
(New Zealand and Tahiti)

F. colensoi	F. cyrtandroides
F. exorticata	F. perscandens
F. procumbens	

Section 5 *Hemsleyella*
(Bolivia and Venezuela)

F. apetala	F. cestroides
F. chloroloba	F. garleppiana
F. huanucoensis	F. inflata
F. insignis	F. juntasensis
F. membranacea	F. nana
F. pitaloensis	F. salcifolia
F. tilletiana	F. tunariensis

Section 6 *Schuffia*
(Central America and Mexico)

F. arborescens	F. paniculata

Section 7 *Encliandra*
(Central America and Mexico)

F. × bacillaris
F. encliandra ssp encliandra
F. encliandra ssp tetradactyla
F. microphylla ssp hemsleyana
F. microphylla ssp microphylla
F. microphylla ssp mintiflora
F. parviflora
F. thymifolia ssp minimiflora
F. thymifolia ssp thymifolia

Section 8 *Jimenezia*
(Costa Rica and Panama)

F. jimenezia

Section 9 *Ellobium*
(Central America and Mexico)

F. fulgens	F. decidua
F. splendens	

Composts

'What is the right type of compost to use when growing fuchsias?' This is a question asked time and time again when visiting major shows. Unfortunately it is a question that has no answer. One tends not to be believed when giving the answer 'Whatever *feels* right to you is probably right for your plants.' And yet that is perhaps the only correct answer that can be given.

There is no magical formula that is necessary for successful fuchsia growing. Perhaps the most important factor is that the compost should be well-drained and open to the extent that the root system can breathe and the compost kept in a just moist condition. It matters very little whether the compost you use is loam-based or peat-based as both will be of equal value to your plants. The cost of the compost is no real guide either as cost usually reflects the amount of nutrient contained within the compost when first purchased. But as we will be adding our own nutrients and moisture to the compost as the seasons progress, what is contained within them initially is of little importance.

Perhaps it might be wise to use a loam- or soil-based compost such as the John Innes composts if you are in the lucky position of having some old-fashioned clay pots at your disposal. The porosity of the clay permits air to pass through to the roots and for excessive moisture to pass out. With the more commonly used plastic pots, which are both lighter to use and less prone to breakage, then a peat or coir-based compost will be quite satisfactory.

I was once asked if I could define a good compost. I was hard put to find a satisfactory answer but decided eventually that a good compost was one in which the plant was happy to anchor its roots and from which the root system could take up any moisture or nutrients that were present. Additional drainage material to open out the compost to assist with aeration and the 'breathing' of the roots was an added bonus.

A compost such as this can be found in all garden centres and DIY stores. The 'general purpose' composts sold by these firms, many at discounted prices, are quite adequate for our purposes and the plants will grow well in them. It is a pity that such bags of compost do not have a 'mixed on' or 'use by' date marked on them as a fresh, recently mixed, compost is what we need. Be wary of buying bags of peat or coir-based composts which feel very heavy when lifted and certainly leave alone any bags where the printing on the outside has become somewhat faded. As seasons progress the amount of compost sold by garden centres will ensure that there is quite a rapid turnover in their stock – perhaps it might be advantageous to develop a friendship with an employee who could direct you towards the latest batch of bags to arrive.

One of the cheapest forms of compost that can be bought is sold as grow bags. These are often referred to as tomato bags and many growers think that that is their sole purpose. I have found that the compost sold in grow bags is ideal for fuchsias – it is perhaps a little coarser than some of the other mixes but this is advantageous in that it gives added drainage. The complaint is sometimes made that the quantity of nutrients contained in grow bags is minimal. That being so, we will just have to start feeding our plants a couple of weeks earlier. If you are using copious quantities of compost in patio tubs and troughs then certainly grow bags contain the type of compost for you.

I have mentioned the necessity for a good well-drained compost. Yes – fuchsias like to have a 'just moist' compost through which their roots can circulate.

Additional drainage can be obtained by adding a proportion of grit to the compost (Cornish or Chichester grit is ideal as it is of a granite-type consistency). The addition of the grit will give added weight to the containers – very useful when growing standard fuchsias in pots – and will also ensure that excess moisture has a quick passage through and out of the pots.

If weight is not a consideration, especially when hanging baskets or pots are being used, then the compost can be 'opened' by using Perlite or Vermiculite. Both of these inert substances have the ability to absorb their own volume in water and yet still maintain their granular shape. The absorption of water assists greatly on those occasions when very hot weather rapidly dries out the compost and it is necessary to re-moisten the compost. Peat-based composts have the tendency to shrink away from the sides of the pots but the addition of Perlite or Vermiculite eases the problem quite dramatically.

I have mentioned coir-based composts as they are a natural replacement for peat-based composts and their use causes less environmental destruction. However, many growers who have tried coir have been unhappy with the results. I feel that this is a shame as a little perseverance and understanding of the compost will bring good results. Because of the very fibrous condition of the compost there is excellent drainage and it is probably necessary to supply water more frequently. The result of using extra water means that the nutrients contained within the compost are going to be leached out rather more quickly. They will therefore need replacing on a very regular basis – no real problem as the recommendation is often to feed the plants each time you water them.

The correct feeding of your plants is perhaps one of the most important factors in achieving the success that you aspire to. Although many growers have problems with regard to the elements necessary for healthy growth there are no real secrets. Plants to grow healthily need to have access to a number of trace elements. Perhaps, though, just three of them are the most important. On any bottle or packet of plant food you will find an analysis which gives an idea as to when it should be used. The three magical letters are (N), (P) and (K) – nitrogen, phosphates and potash. Nitrogen is important to plant development in that it promotes good, strong, upright and bushy growth. Excessive nitrogen will provide luscious growth at the expense of flowers. The phosphates help to build up a very strong root system – a vital element for the development of good plants. The potash helps the plants to assimilate the first two and also to ripen the plant and encourage the formation of buds and flowers. Potash is also obtained by plants from sunlight so during long sunny periods it might be advisable to reduce the amount of potash given to your plants.

It is always advisable not to exceed the recommended dosage as written on the packet or bottle. However, most manufacturers talk about feeding plants just once a week whilst more experienced growers often recommend feeding each time a plant is watered. If the latter advice is taken the amount should be reduced quite considerably – feeding at a quarter of the normal recommended strength. It might also be a good idea to get into the habit of using plain water once a week so that any build-up of salts in the compost can be washed away.

A recently introduced nutrient – sold as a fuchsia food – contains an additional 2 per cent of magnesium sulphate. Commonly known, when used as a human supplement, as Epsom salts this element has the ability of increasing the chlorophyll content of the foliage, helping plants whose leaves have become a little pale to regain their natural vibrant greenness.

Regularity of feeding and watering is of great importance when growing fuchsias. It is tempting, when a feed has been forgotten, to give a double helping the following day. Please resist the temptation – I suppose it would give the plant the equivalent of indigestion.

To sum up – my personal feelings are that the compost is of little direct importance but the subsequent feeding and watering of your plants is vital for good, strong and healthy growth.

Watering

In describing the types of compost available today, mention was made of the need to ensure that the compost is 'well drained'. As all plants need quite large quantities of water in order to be able to live and grow, the question is often asked, 'How often and how much?'

The first part of the question is very difficult to answer. It would be very easy to say 'whenever they need it' but that really begs the question. Plants will show you when there is a dire need for moisture as the leaves will become very flaccid and the sepals of any flowers will start to droop. Get to know the weight of each pot by constantly handling them. If the symptoms described above are evident, then lifting the pot up will indicate if it is short of water as it will feel very light in weight. The remedy will be to give the compost a thorough soaking: this can be achieved either by pouring water into the top of the pot and allowing it to seep through the compost, by pouring water into a saucer in which the pot is standing; or by immersing the whole pot in a bucket of water until all air bubbles cease to rise from the compost.

Unfortunately, many of the peat-based composts tend to shrink away from the sides of the pot as they dry out, and water poured into the top will find the easy route out and escape down the sides without moistening the compost to any great extent. Filling a saucer with water will have the desired effect of moistening all the compost by capillary action, but this takes time. There is also the possibility that the plant will be left standing in water so the compost becomes saturated and the air spaces disappear. After a period of time this will result in the root system being starved of air, and cause the plant to die by drowning. Immersing the pot in a bucket is perhaps the safest and quickest way of ensuring that the compost is thoroughly moistened.

There is also considerable debate as to whether tap water or rainwater should be used. Rainwater contains many minerals collected from the air and so is undoubtedly the best, but when supplies run out, as they invariably do during hot summer weather, then we will need to use water from the tap. If possible such water should be allowed to stand for a couple of hours before use to allow the chlorine content to disperse; if it is not, however, and watering is carried out directly with the use of a hosepipe, no harm will come to the plants. Watering overhead with a hosepipe does mean that the leaves will have a residue of chalk on them in hard water areas of the country.

When large numbers of plants have to be watered in a relatively short space of time then a hosepipe is the only real solution. However, bearing in mind that our plants sometimes also need feeding, it may be necessary to carry out this task by using a watering can. It is so easy to forget that during a long spell of hot weather, the plants will suffer with the continual leaching out of the nutrients when the watering takes place.

Plants indoors on windowsills will probably be standing in saucers to protect the woodwork. Watering of these plants should be carried out either by taking them to a sink where the water can be allowed to drain through the compost, or by watering into the saucer. If this is done, the recommendation is that the plant should be allowed to take up as much moisture as possible in about a quarter of an hour and then any excess water should be removed from the saucer.

Bear in mind that a damp sponge will always pick up more moisture than a dry one, and that very dry compost will take a great deal of patience before it contains the requisite quantity of moisture.

Overwatering

The symptoms which are present when the plant is dry and needs watering are unfortunately the same as when the plant is too wet and is 'drowning'. However, by lifting the pot you can quickly determine if the pot is too light or too heavy, and if it is very heavy then it is important to take immediate action to reduce the quantity of moisture in the compost.

Remove the whole of the rootball from the pot: if it is very heavy the compost will look dark and soggy; there might also be a rather unpleasant smell coming from it. Stand the rootball on an upturned flowerpot and allow it to drain for several hours. If there is still no improvement to the look of the plant then more drastic action might be necessary, and as much of the old compost must be removed from the root system as is possible. The state of the roots can then be determined: white roots are alive and active, whilst brown gnarled roots are probably dead. If repotting is necessary then the plant, when repotted, should be placed in a shaded position until recovery is complete.

Treatment in Hot Weather

Often during periods of extremely hot weather, plants will give the impression of wilting even when there is sufficient water in the compost, the roots being unable to take up water in

sufficient quantities to maintain the turgidity of the leaves. This excessive transpiration can be rectified by spraying the foliage at intervals during the day. Fuchsias are happier in shaded conditions so we must endeavour to give them this type of situation.

Fuchsias in the Home

When talking to visiting members of the public at shows a criticism of fuchsias often received is that plants purchased in full flower often drop their flowers and buds after a few days indoors. Although most of the enquirers are prepared to accept that it is possibly something that they have done incorrectly, others blame the fuchsia.

Actually neither the fuchsia nor the purchaser are entirely to blame. It is a pity that the supplier of the plant does not point out that fuchsias need a slightly humid atmosphere around them in order to grow healthily. Unfortunately, we like a dry atmosphere in our homes. If we think about the places where fuchsias are found growing naturally then we would realize that the moisture-laden atmosphere of the lower wooded foothills of South America is somewhat different from that in our houses. I am always very doubtful about recommending fuchsias as house plants for this very reason. It must be very disappointing to buy a superb flowering specimen only to witness the dropping of the flowers and the buds shortly after purchase. But the sudden change in humidity from greenhouse to home interior is to blame.

I like seeing fuchsias indoors but I prefer to think of them as being temporary visitors only – just in for a day or two and then back outside in a slightly more humid atmosphere. I was once told by a nurseryman that unless moss and ferns were able to grow alongside his fuchsias in the greenhouse the conditions were not right.

So how can we get the best of both worlds and enjoy the beauty of our plants indoors? These remarks apply in equal measure to those who wish to use fuchsias as table decorations as to those who like to grow fuchsias and other plants in conservatories. As we do not want to have high humidity in the whole of the room we must restrict it to an area immediately around each plant. Let us use the method recommended by growers of Saintpaulias (African violets) for they too need fairly high humidity around the plants to get the best results. Plant pots standing in a large saucer containing moist pebbles or large grit will have the higher humidity created by the moisture passing through the foliage. Perhaps though a word of warning, or a gentle

reminder, might not come amiss. The compost in the pots should never be allowed to become a wet mass. The compost should always be kept in a 'just moist' condition. In order to be able to thrive a plant needs to have roots that are alive and active; roots completely immersed in water will rapidly rot and die. Roots need to be able to breathe and the only way in which air can enter the root ball, apart from entering from the top, is through the drainage holes in the bottom of our plastic pots. (Yes – limited air can enter through the sides of clay pots so perhaps these might be the best containers for plants growing indoors.) The base of the pot should, therefore, be above the level of the water in the tray or saucer – that is, the pot should be standing on the pebbles and not in them. Regular attention needs to be given to the watering of the compost to retain that just moist condition, but do not allow the water in the tray to rise above the base of the pot.

These remarks apply mainly to those plants which have been purchased or to those plants which were originally growing in your greenhouse. But what about plants that have known no other home than the one in which you now wish to display them? Plants which have been raised as cuttings on the windowsill (probably with the aid of a reflecting box to maintain straightness and evenness of growth) will be accustomed to the drier atmosphere and will therefore grow quite strongly for you. However, I would still advise the reader to stand the pots on pebbles to get the best results. If you have your plant pots standing in individual saucers then it is highly likely that you will be watering the plants by filling the saucer and allowing the root system to take up all the moisture it requires. The saucer should be filled with water and the plant given about fifteen minutes to absorb as much as it needs. After that time any water that is left should be thrown away and air will be able to enter the drainage holes once again. As there is likely to be quite a loss of moisture through transpiration it will probably be necessary to water plants growing in these conditions each day and maybe even more frequently. Get to know your plants by handling them regularly so that you will immediately recognize the symptoms when leaves start to lose their turgidity and become a little limp. Regular handling will also give you an idea of the weight you would expect – lightness will probably indicate dryness and a need for watering whilst heaviness will suggest that further watering is unnecessary. If there are flowers on your plants then it is the condition of the sepals that will give you the first indication that a drink of water is required. The sepals should be quite turgid and will be standing out and away from the petals in the corolla.

Plants growing permanently indoors still need to be fed and inspected for signs of attacks by aphids. Feeding with liquid feed at the same time as watering is quite satisfactory although perhaps better results are achieved if slow-release fertilizers are placed in the compost. It will be necessary, if pests such as greenfly or whitefly are found, to take the plant outside to give it a good spraying with insecticide or soapy solution. A regular freshening of the foliage to remove the inevitable dust particles that abound in dry conditions will also be very beneficial to your plants. Putting the plants outside during a rainstorm will carry out this task very satisfactorily.

To reiterate, I would not really recommend fuchsias as houseplants, but for those people who have no alternative then it is quite possible to achieve some considerable success and a great deal of satisfaction.

The Hardy Border

Fuchsias really do show themselves off to their best advantage when they are being grown in the garden border. The extra space available to them to make a superb root system means that top growth can grow luxuriously. The beauty of growing fuchsias in this way is that so little needs to be done, following the initial preparation of the ground, to ensure many years of fantastic flowers.

One of the major criticisms often heard is that the number of different types of fuchsias that can be grown in the open is minimal. Because of their delicate charm it is often thought that they must have a very delicate and tender constitution and will therefore need to be taken under cover during the winter months – that is not so. Another criticism is that hardy fuchsias are all red and purple in colouring – a visit to a national collection of hardy fuchsias will soon dispel that myth.

There are two basic ways in which fuchsias can be used in our garden borders – either as temporary occupants that will be taken up at the end of the season or as permanent members that will become firmly established and provide us with flowers over a number of years. The method of growing plants for using as temporary residents in the border varies very little from the method used to grow plants in large pots that will decorate the patio.

As with all things in gardening a certain amount of forward planning is necessary to ensure that the ground is in good heart and ready to receive the plants, and that the plants themselves are of sufficient size. I would suggest that by the end of spring it will be necessary to have good bushy plants growing very strongly in 3½in (9cm) or 5in (13cm) pots. It is therefore important that the young plants be started off as cuttings in the autumn prior to the year in which they will be permanently planted. You can take these cuttings yourself and overwinter them on the windowsill of a spare room or purchase some from a nursery or garden centre in early spring. Such plants will have been grown from cuttings taken in the autumn of the previous year. If you decide to buy in young plants then it will be necessary to grow on sturdily in the size of pot mentioned. Do not be tempted to place these plants in their final positions until the end of spring when all risk of frosts should have passed.

The preparation of the border can also be carried out during the autumn. Bearing in mind that once planted these fuchsias will remain *in situ* for a great many years then it is important to ensure that the ground is in good heart. Deep digging incorporating well-rotted compost will be of the greatest benefit to the plants as the root systems can forage amongst the water-retaining humus. A sprinkling of a fertilizer such as bone meal or Grow More and raking it into the surface will also be beneficial. Fuchsias prefer not to have perpetual sunshine throughout the day, dappled shading being the ideal. However, provided that the root systems can be kept moist throughout any hot dry spells, they will thrive virtually anywhere.

With the vagaries of the climate, it is possible that even in late spring there will be nights of quite severe ground frosts. However, it is important to give our plants as much time as possible in their first year to build up a good strong root system before the onset of early autumn frosts. So, when you consider that the risk of frosts is minimal, plant out your strongly growing plants but be prepared to cover them with horticultural fleece or some other insulating material if the weather forecasters talk of frosty mornings.

Four months of strong growth will produce those vital root systems. It is from the roots that, even when the top growth has been killed during the winter, fresh young shoots will produce for us a rich bounty of flowers in the summer. It is important to remember that fuchsias only flower on shoots that have grown during the current season.

Planting out fuchsias and the depth at which we place the roots is of considerable importance. There is no better insulation against sharp frosts than planting our fuchsias deeply in 'mother earth'. Usually, when planting from pots it is recommended that the level of the compost in the pots should be level with the surface of the surrounding soil. I would suggest that, with fuchsias, a much deeper planting would be an advantage. If the surface of the compost in the pot is 2–3in (5–7.5cm) below the surface of the surrounding soil then extra protection from frosts will be given. One suggestion is that a saucer-shaped indentation should be made in the soil so that the centre of the indentation is about 3in (7.5cm) lower than the surrounding

Hardy Border Calendar*		
WINTER	Dec Jan Feb	• check plants in hardy border and indoors
SPRING	Mar Apr May	• protect young growths from late frosts • purchase young plants at the end of spring and plant in garden • feed with a balanced fertilizer
SUMMER	June July Aug	• cut back old stems • feed with a balanced fertilizer; water • check for pests and, if necessary, spray with a systemic insecticide • remove old flowers
AUTUMN	Sept Oct Nov	• take cuttings and nurture them in a cool room • prune plants in the hardy border and prepare bed

* for the Northern Hemisphere

soil – the plant is then removed from its pot and planted in the indentation. During the course of the summer the saucer-shaped indentation will fill in and the plant will be at the required depth.

The temptation when first planting is to place the plants fairly close together. This is a mistake as plants grow very strongly and can attain bushiness with a diameter of 3–4ft (1–1.25m) during the second and subsequent years. If you intend planting one each of a number of differing cultivars then it would be best to place them about 18in (45cm) apart. Perhaps a better display is obtained if a group of three plants of the same cultivar are planted fairly close together. In this case, 9–12in (23–30cm) would be quite satisfactory and will give a glorious mound of foliage and flowers.

Once planted it is important to encourage good strong growth of both roots and tops during the first summer. Do not allow the root systems to dry out and an occasional feeding with a balanced liquid feed will ensure good strong growth. The training of the plant into a bushy form will have been carried out before planting so there will be no need to consider taking out the growing tips of the shoots to encourage further bushiness. It is important though to keep an eye open for any attacks by pests especially if your plants are in fairly close proximity to trees. Whiteflies are less of a problem in the open garden but attacks by greenflies and capsid bugs can be a nuisance as they nibble at the growing tips of the shoots causing blindness and distortion. A regulars praying with a combined

insecticide/fungicide should keep these pests at bay. Plants in the hardy border are less likely to suffer from the disease 'rust' but nevertheless keep a wary eye open.

The first winter is the most important one for our hardy plants so we must make sure that they are given all the protection necessary. However, the amount we need to do is minimal especially if the plants were planted deeply. Following the first few frosts the bushes will probably be completely defoliated. Do not be tempted to remove the dead-looking stems as they will be useful in giving protection during the winter and will also act as a reminder of the position of the plants. By all means trim them back, perhaps by about a third, so that they are relatively tidy. A mulch of bark chippings around the crown of each plant will give further insulation from the frosts. Be prepared though to add to this mulch during the winter should birds be tempted to scratch about in it.

In the spring new growths will be seen pushing their way up through the mulch from the root systems. Be ready to protect these young shoots with horticultural fleece should severe frost threaten. When the shoots are growing strongly then the dead branches from last year can be removed by cutting them back to ground level. Even if new green shoots appear from the old branches (and this will happen if we have a mild winter), I would still recommend cutting out all the old stems as it is from the growth made during the current season that we get our new flowering branches. I like to see foliage and flowers from as low down as possible and prefer not to have quite long lengths

11

of bare stems. However, if the plants are being used as hedging, then it is possible to be a little less ruthless when cutting the leading stems back to strong growing shoots.

Throughout this second year it will be wise to continue feeding your plants with a balanced fertilizer. Watering in dry weather will assist in keeping the foliage turgid and the flowering continuous. If, after three or four years, the plants have made such growth that they are becoming somewhat overcrowded then it might be advisable to thin them out. I would suggest that the best time of the year to do this is during early spring when the first new growths are beginning to show. The root system will have become quite extensive so it will be necessary to remove a very large block of roots and soil. If you intend to move the plant to a fresh site then make sure you have a large hole prepared and ready to receive it. It might be easier to take cuttings from the plants you wish to move during the autumn and to dispose of the old plant.

Selecting the plants that you will be using to make up your new border can be assisted by sending off for the catalogues prepared by specialist fuchsia nurseries. The height and spread expected of each cultivar is usually mentioned so that it should be possible to plan your border or bed with the taller growing plants situated at the rear. The colour, form and size of the flower is also mentioned so that the colour scheme that you require can be implemented.

Within the descriptions of plants later in this book an indication will be given of the hardiness of each plant together with the height and spread likely to be achieved.

Growing Fuchsias in Baskets and Half Baskets

A criticism sometimes levelled at plants growing in the hardy border is that the flowers cannot be seen in all their glory as they are too low down. The suggestion is often made that plants growing outside should be mainly those that carry an upward-looking type of flower. My mental picture of a fuchsia is of long arching branches from which the flowers hang pendulously. Many of our fuchsias fulfil this criteria but even greater success can be achieved in 'showing off' our fuchsias if we can grow them in such a position that the viewer can look up into the flowers.

Here then is where hanging baskets come into their own. The plants can be encouraged to form longer trailing branches from which the flowers will naturally hang down pendulously.

From the decorative point of view there is no need to worry at all about the type of container in which you grow your trailing plants. For show purposes various regulations are laid down so that all competitors start from the same line. These regulations usually cover the type of container, the shape of the basket, and the diameter and depth. Basically though, any container that can be suspended and will hold a reasonable quantity of compost that can be maintained in a well-drained condition, will be ideal for our purposes. Open mesh containers will need a liner of some type to hold the compost in position. This lining can be pre-formed layers of moss, or a sheet of polythene (old compost bags are ideal for this purpose). The most important requirement is that there should be drainage holes in the lining to prevent the drowning of the root systems.

The type of compost used for hanging containers is entirely up to the grower's preference. I prefer to use one of the lightweight composts made from peat as I find that a moist loam-based compost creates quite a strain on the hanging basket. A good all-purpose compost will be ideal and, bearing in mind that when hanging, baskets are open to the elements and tend to dry out quite quickly, it might be useful to add some of the newish water-retaining gels to the compost. It is also beneficial to mix in some slow-release fertilizers.

Although it is possible to keep baskets full of fuchsias from one season to another, the plants will be getting progressively larger, so most of us prefer to make up new baskets each year. It will therefore be necessary to think ahead so that plants of the required size will be available when needed. The earlier a basket is put together, the better and more floriferous it will be. A basket made up from small fuchsia 'plugs' purchased in April or May are unlikely to make an eye-catching display in the first season. However, cuttings taken in the autumn of one year will produce plants of the required size for the following spring. You can therefore take your own cuttings or purchase young plants from garden centres or specialist nurseries in very early spring (try looking in your garden centre during January and I am sure you will be amazed at the selection available to you in that wintry month). You will need six plants of the same variety to completely fill a 15in (37cm) or 16in (40cm) diameter basket. Although it is possible to use mixed varieties within the same basket they never look quite so good as a complete ball of flowers all being produced at the same time.

Such plants will need to be grown on steadily and sturdily but this can be done quite easily on the windowsill of a spare room, especially if a simple reflecting box is used. Good bushy plants will be required for March or April so the necessary 'pinching out' of the growing tips in order to get bushy plants should be undertaken each time that two or three sets of leaves have formed on each young branch.

By March or April the plants should be growing strongly in 3in (7cm) or 3½in (9cm) pots and should have a very vigorous root system. To make up a basket is quite a simple operation. Place the basket on a large flower pot or bucket for stability. Having put the liner (with drainage holes) in the basket, a small quantity of the prepared compost (with water-retaining gel and slow-release fertilizer – if required) is placed in the base of the basket. You will now need six pots of the same size as that in which the plants are growing. Place these empty pots on the compost in the positions that you wish the plants to occupy. Five around the edge of the basket and one in the centre would be ideal. Carefully fill the whole of the basket, including the empty pots, with your compost firming it by gently tapping it on the bench. There is no need to use your fingers for this firming. Fill the basket with compost until it is level with the tops of the positioning pots. When you remove the central pot you will find that you are left with an indentation in the compost the exact shape and size of the root systems of your plants. Remove the first plant from the pot and place it in the 'formed' hole. Continue with the remaining plants until all have been used. Your basket is now complete

although you might decide to use the compost in the pots used as 'formers' to add to the height of the compost in the basket. Always leave a sufficient gap below the top level of the basket to assist in later watering of the plants.

Baskets made up during March and April cannot be placed outside as the risk of frost is always present. Give them as much light and warmth as possible in a greenhouse or conservatory to encourage strong and rapid growth of the branches. On very mild days it is possible to place these baskets outside so that a good watering and overhead spraying can be given, but be ready to take them inside before the temperature drops at night. Regular feeding with a balanced fertilizer and watering to maintain moistness but not wetness around the root systems will assist in this rapid growing. Keep an eye open for pests and diseases (white- and greenflies in particular) and deal with them as quickly as possible should they appear.

From about the middle of May it should be possible to place these baskets in their final positions on their hanging brackets – but always be ready to take them in should a frosty night be forecast. It should not be necessary to do any further 'pinching out' of the growing tips, but allow the laterals to grow strongly and to cascade over the edge of the basket.

By the end of June your patience should be rewarded with a hanging container overflowing with glorious flowers. Enjoy them but make sure that they continue to grow in good health by regularly feeding and watering them. Continuity

Preparing a basket. Note the 'formers' used.

of flowering can be assisted by regular removal of any flowers before they set seed.

As autumn and winter approach it will be necessary to consider how you intend to overwinter your baskets. A second season of flowers is quite possible, but it will be necessary to ensure that the complete container is kept in a frost-free position throughout the cold seasons. Some growers prefer to leave their plants *in situ* whilst others like to remove them from the basket, separating them and treating them as individual plants (making up the basket anew the following spring).

If you decide to leave the basket as a complete unit then it will be necessary in late autumn or early spring to take the whole of the root ball out of the basket, remove a couple of inches of compost from the base (an old bread knife is ideal for this purpose), replace with fresh compost and then return the remains of the root ball. This will give the old root systems some fresh compost into which they can send new young, white roots.

There are a great many fuchsias with a trailing habit from which you can make your selection. A whole galaxy of colours is open to you. Look through the descriptions for those plants which have a 'trailing' habit or are 'lax' in their growth. I am sure you will be delighted with the success that you can achieve as you look up into the blooms and admire the 'ballerina' appearance of these dancing flowers.

Propagation and Propagators

The question is often asked as to how one can increase the number of plants in a collection or how one can raise new varieties.

With regard to the raising or discovering of new fuchsias there are two basic methods. The first is to obtain seeds from a plant and to raise new plants from them. This can be a random collection of seedpods or can be as a result of cross-fertilization of two plants of your own choice. The intention of any hybridizer is to improve upon the stock of plants already available or perhaps to introduce new colour variations. Unfortunately if some of the modern cultivars are used for this cross-fertilization there can be no guarantee as to what colour or type of plants will result. In fact from one seed pod it is possible to get many young seedlings all with different form, habit or colouring. Since the introduction of fuchsias in the early eighteenth century many crosses have been made

using the species available at the time and also the results of those crosses. It would be interesting to discover whether some of the newer plants being produced each year are as a result of F_1 or, perhaps, F_{20} crosses. Unfortunately, as a result of the weakening of the strain, many of the newer introductions do not have the strength and stamina to last more than a few years and, as a result, disappear from the nursery catalogues.

Fortunately some of our modern hybridists have realized this fact and have been returning to our 'roots' and using the species crossed with species (F_1) to get new colour breaks. These 'inter-specific' hybrids have presented us with some very interesting new colour and form breaks.

Nevertheless, it is still possible to get something really exciting, 'a complete breakthrough', as a result of pure luck and the crossing of two favourite fuchsias.

Another of the methods by which new cultivars can be found is by simple observation. Very frequently a plant that may have been growing in the garden or in a large pot starts to produce branches that carry flowers or foliage completely different from those on the rest of the plant. This is referred to as 'sporting'. If cuttings are taken from the branch which is showing this variation then it is possible that the resultant plants will also have the same variation. It will be necessary to continue to grow these new plants for a number of years to ensure that the change of colour in the flower or the foliage has been 'fixed'. It is surprising how often plants of the same cultivar will, in wildly differing parts of the country, produce such 'sports' in the same season. Nobody seems to understand why this phenomenon occurs.

If it is our intention to simply increase the number of plants that we have of a specific cultivar then we need to take 'cuttings'. A cutting is a small piece removed from a plant and given the right conditions for the formation of roots. Once the young plant has its own set of roots then we have a new plant which will be identical to the one from which the cutting has been taken. A cutting taken from a plant such as 'Snowcap' will produce another 'Snowcap' and can be named as such. That is why it is possible to purchase plants of the cultivars we choose from many differing sources around the country and for us to know the type of flower and growth that we will get. We should not forget though, when taking 'cuttings' from our plants, that strength will beget strength and cuttings taken from a weak and ailing plant are unlikely to have a great deal of vigour.

14

So what will we require in order that all the cuttings that we take from our plants will root and become new plants in their own right? Fortunately there is no need for any sophisticated equipment or even to be the proud owner of a greenhouse – a windowsill will serve our purpose just as well. We will need a propagator of some sort within which it will be possible to maintain humidity (types of propagators will be discussed later). We will need small pots or strips of pre-formed trays and a suitable compost or other material which will retain moisture. Further equipment required – a sharp knife or razor blade, plant labels and a waterproof marking pen. Finally we will need the plants from which cuttings can be taken or a supply of cutting material received from another grower.

Propagators

These can be as simple as possible and can be a 2lb jam or pickle jar, a coffee jar or a plastic sweet jar, a small flower pot with a plastic bag of sufficient size to enclose the pot, a flower pot and a cut-down lemonade bottle that will fit in the top or a simple ice cream tray into which a rooting medium can be placed. In fact any transparent container, capable of being sealed so that the high humidity required for the successful rooting of the cuttings can be maintained, will be ideal.

It is of course possible to become far more sophisticated and to purchase a heated windowsill propagating tray onto which can be placed small trays of cuttings. A larger type of electric propagator within which the temperature can be thermostatically controlled can also be used. Ordinary seed trays with plastic domes will also give the necessary conditions for rooting to take place.

As will be seen from the list the main criteria for successful propagation is the provision of a humid atmosphere around the cuttings – the humidity will keep the severed cuttings turgid until rooting commences.

Compost or Other Rooting Mediums

If it is your intention to root your cuttings in compost then it is necessary to provide a material that will retain moisture. I use my ordinary peat-based multi-purpose compost to which I add an equal portion of Vermiculite. The Vermiculite opens out the compost but at the same time, since it is capable of absorbing its own volume in water, retains moistness around the base of the cuttings and the developing roots. In fact any medium can be used which is able to retain moistness. The compost does not need to contain any nutrients as the cuttings are incapable of taking up food until a root system has been formed. It is with this in mind that I would suggest a further medium into which you can root your cuttings – that is, the florist blocks of

In their own humid mini-climate the cuttings will root quite easily – but shade them from the sun.

15

Individual cuttings in their separate rooting modules will root easily. Label individually.

(Below) Types of cuttings from a single stem.

OASIS. A 1in-thick slice of well-moistened OASIS placed in the ice cream tray and standing in a small quantity of water will hold a number of cuttings, the root system forming within the OASIS. Not really very scientific perhaps – but it works.

With our 'propagators' and the medium into which we will be placing our cuttings ready, we can take our cuttings. Perhaps the most important thing to ensure success is to have parent plants that have been well watered several hours prior to removing the cuttings so that every part of the plant is fully charged with moisture. There are numerous differing types of cuttings that can be taken and I have tried to show these in the illustration. Perhaps the easiest and most successful cutting is the 'soft green tip cutting'. This is the very tip of each of the branches and will consist of a piece approximately 1in long (25mm) and will have a pair of semi-mature leaves and a growing tip. I remove this small piece by severing it from its parent by cutting just above the next lower pair of leaves. A good clean cut will ensure that there is no bruising to the base of the cuttings – any bruising might well lead to the onset of botrytis (rotting) and the loss of the cutting. The small cutting will be pushed gently into the compost that has not been firmed in any way. Once inserted, the cuttings should be 'watered in' using a fine rose on a watering can or a bottle with a screwed on 'bottle top

waterer'. The young cuttings should be labelled and the propagator top placed in position. The propagators should be placed in a position in light but not in a place where the hot rays of the

'Soft green-tip cuttings', being charged with growth hormones, will root easily.

sun can come through a window and through the propagator. If this happens, it is likely that the cuttings will be 'cooked'. Really, the cuttings should be kept as cool as possible, a temperature of about 60°F (16°C) being ideal for the rooting process to take place. If there is the possibility of sunshine falling on the propagators then some type of shading will be necessary.

If you are using OASIS then it will probably be necessary to make a small hole with a cocktail stick in the OASIS so that the cutting is not damaged. With soft green tip cuttings there is no need to use hormonal rooting powders or liquid but if it gives you added confidence then by all means use them. Make sure that you place a label alongside each cutting so that you will not forget the name of the plant at a future date. When you have taken sufficient cuttings to fill your propagator or OASIS (making sure that no two cuttings are so close to each other that they are touching) then a slight watering with a fine rose on a watering can will settle the compost around the cuttings. This will be the only watering that your cuttings will receive until they are removed, well-rooted, from their propagators.

If rooting in OASIS there will be no need to cover the container with a plastic bag to retain humidity as the layer of water in the base of the tray will have that effect. Make sure that the water does not evaporate or the OASIS become dry. No harm will come if the tray is enclosed within a plastic bag.

After three or four weeks the young cuttings will be showing the first signs of growth. The centre shoots will be taking on a lighter green appearance and the leaves will develop a sheen. Do not be in a hurry to remove them from the propagators just yet – perhaps a further week would be advisable. You might however start the process of weaning the young plants from their high humidity. Allowing fresh, drier air to enter the propagators for a few minutes and gradually extending the period of time over the next few days will be beneficial.

With the plants beginning to grow quite strongly it will be necessary to plant them in larger pots containing your normal multi-purpose

Cuttings inserted into wet OASIS will root very easily. Keep the OASIS moist by having water in the base of the container.

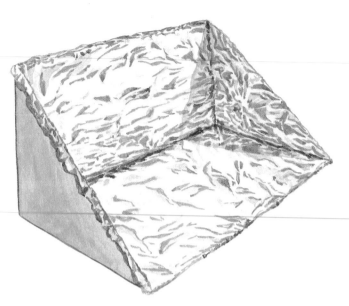

compost. I would suggest that they should first be placed in a 6cm square pot as they take up less room on the windowsill. Again make sure that each plant pot has its own label – do not rely on your memory. These small square pots can be placed in a home-made reflecting box which can be placed on the windowsill (*see* illustration above). These simple reflecting boxes will assist the young plants in growing sturdily and straight as they will have light coming from all directions and not just through the glass of the window. More care will need to be taken over the individual watering needs of each plant, so regular daily inspection will be necessary.

Cuttings rooted in OASIS need to have slightly different treatment. When roots are visible through the sides of the OASIS the opportunity can be taken to get the new young plants used to the type of nutrient they will experience when they start foraging in the compost. To this end the recommendation is to pour away the 'pure' water in the base of the container and replace it with a solution made up with a liquid fertilizer at about a quarter of the normal recommended strength. If this process is carried out a week or so prior to 'potting' up then the plants will suffer no setback when they are transferred to their compost. We will not need to remove the OASIS from around the root system but will cut a block of OASIS containing the roots and plant the block in the compost. Make sure that no part of the OASIS is above the surface of the compost as the exposed portion will become dry and will leach out the moisture from the rest of the small block. I feel

that young plants started in OASIS need to have compost in slightly moister conditions than those planted directly into the compost.

Cuttings of fuchsias can be taken at any time of the year, but I find that I get the greatest success in early spring and in the autumn when I have far greater control over the temperature. Moisture and moderate warmth (not heat) is all that is required to root cuttings. However, it is possible to take a different type of cutting in the autumn of the year with a minimum of effort and with a great chance of success. Hard wood cuttings, up to 1ft (30cm) or more in length, can be removed from plants growing strongly in the garden or in large pots. All the foliage should be very carefully removed making sure that the dormant eyes in the leaf axils are not damaged. It can be advantageous to wound the base of each cutting by gently tapping the bottom inch or so with a sharp knife or razor blade. This will just cut through the surface of the skin. The base of the cuttings can then be dipped into hormonal rooting powder or liquid before insertion into a 3½in (9cm) pot or in the corner of a cold frame. The pots can be placed in a cold greenhouse but ensure, during the winter, that the compost does not dry out. Rooting might take a little while although it is possible that the buds in the leaf axils will develop and start to produce green shoots even before rooting commences. Although these plants will never make good specimen plants (useful though as plants in a hardy border) they will provide a good supply of young 'green tip shoots' for use as cuttings during the spring.

When roots are seen emerging through the sides of the OASIS, change the water in the container to a dilute liquid feed.

(Below) When rooted, separate the cuttings so that the root systems are still contained within their individual blocks of OASIS.

(Below right) Bury the blocks of OASIS in the compost so that no part of the OASIS is above the surface of the compost.

The ease with which pieces taken from fuchsia plants will root is amply demonstrated by a comment recently heard. Following a relatively mild winter, when the frosty periods lasted for a very short time, the old stems removed from the plants in the hardy border in spring were found to be quite green and moist with sap. These pieces were slightly reduced in length, were given a clean cut at the base, and pushed into the soil (in the same sort of way that cuttings of currants would be taken). Each of these long hard wood cuttings rooted and provided a very attractive low screen full of flowers during the following summer.

There is no real reason why you should not get 100 per cent success when taking cuttings of fuchsias. Practically any part will root given the correct conditions. Experiment with different types of cuttings, different types of composts or mediums and different types of propagators – I know you will not be disappointed.

Fuchsias as Bonsai Subjects

There has been a great deal of interest in recent years in the growing of fuchsias as bonsai specimens. Please do not feel alarmed at the prospect of having to tend your bonsai plants for many decades as it is possible to produce a 'bonsai-type' plant in just a couple of seasons.

There are two main ways of starting – the first is to find a plant that has been neglected and upon which the branches are growing rather unevenly. The second is to start from scratch with an unrooted cutting and develop the bonsai plant from that.

Preferably you should make your choice from those plants that have small foliage and small flowers as a far more balanced and natural look will be achieved. Some growers are drawn towards plants of the Encliandra-types – those with long, thin, wiry stems, small foliage and minute flowers. My personal feelings are that the growth of this type of plant is too rampant and that they would be put to far better use as 'topiary' subjects being trained around wires to form fascinating shapes – but that is a personal preference. Undoubtedly I will be proved wrong and some magnificent 'Encliandra' bonsai plants will be achieved.

Growing fuchsias as miniature bonsais is yet another facet in the growing of fuchsias.

The beauty of a bonsai plant is very much in the eye of the beholder so there are no rules and regulations that you have to slavishly follow. The most important aspect must be in obtaining good proportions within the plant and with the container. Shallow dishes with very little space for the root system will give the impression of maturity and if it is possible to raise the plant so that some of the root system is exposed then that appearance of antiquity is accentuated.

Let us start with a mature plant. It would be very strange if in every greenhouse there is not one or more plants that have escaped attention and have, as a result of becoming pot-bound, taken on a rather old and gnarled appearance. Such plants are ideal subjects for use as bonsai subjects. Look preferably for a plant that has a single stem rising from the compost and decide at what sort of angle you wish to have that stem growing. It is the 'windswept' look that we will be seeking. Reduce the amount of growth on the plant by judiciously removing or reducing most of the branches. A stem placed at an angle of about 45 degrees to the soil level will encourage upward growth and will give a very attractive appearance. When you are happy with the positioning of the branches the root ball should be removed from the pot and all the old compost teased away. Severe pruning of the root system will be necessary in order for it to fit into the space available in your new small tray-like pot. To obtain the exposed root appearance, partially fill your bonsai pot with a slightly gritty compost remembering to cover the drainage hole with a piece of gauze or some such material that will enable excess moisture to pass through. A small stone can be placed in position on the compost (keep clear of the centre of the pot). The reduced root system can now be carefully draped over this stone and spread over the compost. Ensure that the trunk of your plant is at the angle you desire and fill the pot with more compost. At this stage, if the stone was positioned so that it was slightly above the edging of the pot you will find that some of the roots will still be exposed. Continue to add compost so that these roots are covered – you will find that you have a mound of compost that will gradually be washed away when the plant is watered later. We do not want the roots that will eventually be exposed, to be open to the elements just yet or they are likely to dry out and possibly die. In view of the fact that the plant is leaning at an angle it will probably be rather 'top heavy' and it will be best to secure it in the position you require by using thin wires around the pot.

The plant will have suffered quite a shock from having had both the root and top pruned

The attractive windswept
appearance in early spring *(right)*
and flowering in summer *(below)*.

(Below)
Bonsai *Magellanica alba*

This small-flowered and small-leaved cultivar will give the right proportions for bonsai-type growth. Even though this cultivar is hardy it will need winter protection.

so it will be wise to keep it in a shaded position for a few weeks so that it can become established. Watering should be carried out very carefully either by using a spray or a very fine rose on a small watering can. There will be sufficient nutrient in the fresh compost that you have used to last for a few weeks but when you do start to feed, keep clear of any nutrient containing a high nitrogen content. A balanced or even a high potash nutrient will be ideal for our purpose.

Overwintering these plants will consist in keeping them in a frost-free position and not allowing the root system to completely dry out. Subsequent spring activities will be a question of maintaining the desired shape by selective pruning and

21

Bonsai 'Antie Jinks'

Another small-flowered cultivar which looks right when grown as a miniature bonsai.

Bonsai 'Baby Bright'

Make use of the trailing habit of this superb fuchsia to get a good bonsai effect.

repotting and root pruning when it is considered necessary. The restriction on the root system will, we hope, ensure a slight reduction in the size of both leaves and flowers.

It is possible to grow a bonsai fuchsia from a freshly rooted cutting. When rooted, the plant should be placed in a small pot and the root system should be regularly examined and kept within bounds. The young supple growth can easily be trained to take on the shape that you require and can be held in position using small sticks, wires or the type of wire obtainable from bonsai shops.

After two or three years such plants will take on the appearance of being far more ancient. Perhaps it is the choice of containers that helps to create the beautiful windswept picture so admired by enthusiasts. Placing your plants off centre and using the pot to counterbalance the top growth of the plant certainly gives a very pleasing effect.

Growing plants in this sort of way will prove just how much enjoyment can be obtained from cultivating fuchsias.

Fuchsias for Containers

No matter how large or small your garden, or even if you have no garden at all, it is still possible to enjoy the pleasure of growing fuchsias.

Fuchsias are perhaps the perfect plant for growing in all sorts of different containers. A visit to any garden centre will open your eyes to the great variety of containers available. Let your imagination wander and see if it is possible to make use of some of the discarded objects that you have accumulated over time. Pots can come in all shapes and sizes and can be made of many different types of material. Old wheelbarrows, chimney-pots or drainpipes can all be used to make attractive features. After all, it is not the container that will eventually catch the eye but the cascading and beautiful effect of the plants contained within it.

It is not necessary for hanging containers to be made of wire mesh. Any receptacle that can hold compost and has drainage holes will be quite satisfactory. Containers made of wood to any shape or size you require can be suspended from brackets so that your plants trail downwards in an eye-catching display. Thought must always be given to the means by which they are suspended from a wall, and brackets used should be of sufficient length and strength to support the weight of the container when it is full of moist compost.

Pots can be displayed on tiered staging and can be very decorative when the plants are in full flower. Consideration though will need to be given to ensuring that the pots are stable in windy conditions – the sight of a well-grown plant rolling around on the ground can be very distressing. It is possible to purchase wrought iron stands especially made for holding six or more pots. Such features dotted around on the patio can be very attractive.

Perhaps the most important feature about growing plants in containers is their mobility. One can very easily change the positioning of each container to present a different picture and a different perspective.

Even with patio containers it is important to use the height of some plants to remove the appearance of flatness. The use of fuchsias grown as standards is certainly very beneficial for this purpose. One standard fuchsia in the centre of a container can very easily be surrounded at the base with other, lower growing or trailing, fuchsias or with other types of plants. Again, plants from the Pelargonium family, especially those with delightful coloured foliage, can be used. Begonias, both tuberous and fibrous rooted can be used as also can the 'busy Lizzies'. The plants used to complement the fuchsia must again be a very personal choice but consideration should be given to the harmonizing of the colours.

Window-boxes can be used to great effect to display a colourful selection of fuchsias but perhaps it would be better to concentrate more on the lower-growing or smaller-flowered type of plants. The cascading effect of some fuchsias over the edge of a window-box can be extremely rewarding. Within these boxes it is possible to use some of the dwarf cultivars available to us. Try the 'Thumb' family – 'Tom Thumb' with its red and purple flowers, 'Lady Thumb' (a 'sport' from 'Tom Thumb') with its red and white flowers. As each of these plants only grows to a bushy height of 9–12in (23–30cm), they will not obstruct the light passing through the window. Again such containers can have other low-growing plants complementing the fuchsias – lobelia, alyssum, fibrous begonias all come to mind.

Making hanging baskets or other containers with fuchsias and other plants can follow the same procedure. The smaller trailing plants, such as lobelia, can be pushed through the lining of the basket so that they will help to disguise the container. It is possible to be very generous with the number of plants that are placed in a mixed basket although it will be necessary, as the summer season progresses, to remove the spent flowers of each of the plants to ensure the continuity of flowering. Regular watering and feeding of the plants will help to maintain strong healthy growth. These containers will benefit from having water-retaining gel and slow-release fertilizers mixed with the compost.

Growing Fuchsias Indoors

Fuchsias are not really house plants as they require a humidity in the atmosphere that is not usually present in our living quarters. However, it is possible to use fuchsias as temporary visitors to the home by placing the pots on a tray of moist pebbles. The humidity rising through the pebbles and through the foliage will encourage the plants to retain their buds and their flowers that otherwise might drop. Do not have the pots standing *in* water but merely resting on pebbles that have a level of water beneath them. It is important at all times for the drainage holes at the base of pots to be kept clear of water so that air can enter the compost.

Plants that have been raised as cuttings on the windowsill and have known no conditions other than the dryness of our dwellings can give quite a satisfactory display with a minimum of effort.

Be alert for pests such as greenfly and whitefly that seem to appear from nowhere on indoor plants. If there are signs of infestation then the plants should be taken outside and given a good spraying with a soapy solution or an insecticide.

Fuchsias look extremely nice as table decorations especially those plants grown as miniature standards (those with a clear stem of 6–10in (15–25cm)). These miniature standards can be grown quite easily in a few months.

Overwintering your Fuchsias

Perhaps the question most frequently asked at major shows is about the overwintering of plants that are being purchased. It would be very simple to ask the enquirer why they should wish to bother about looking after plants through the winter when it is possible to purchase new plants early in the year. As these plants will grow into strong flowering specimens by quite early in the summer success will have been achieved with a minimum of effort. It is very tempting to say 'Let the nurseryman have the anxiety and expense of keeping plants growing through the winter', but that begs the question.

In its simplest form the question can be answered by merely saying that there are two main requirements for successful overwintering. Keeping the plant in a frost-free position, and not allowing the root system to completely dry out. The frost-free position can be a large box with the plant inside and surrounded by insulating material such as polystyrene chips. If you have a shed, garage or greenhouse that can be kept frost-free at minimum expense then this will be an ideal situation. The most important part of the plant that will require protection is the root system – pots wrapped in bubble film will be quite snug. The old branches will probably die, or will certainly be reduced drastically in size in the spring, so a covering with horticultural fleece will serve very well. Plants that are growing in large patio tubs can be taken under cover and again the pots can be covered with some insulating material to protect the root system. Again it is advisable to reduce the size of the 'head' of the plant, removing all of the leaves and any debris that mighty have accumulated on the top of the pot, before covering it up. If we bear in mind that we will be encouraging our plants to form fresh shoots and branches in the spring then we will not have too much anxiety about the top growth. Remember that fuchsias only flower on wood that they make during the current season so removal of the old wood to encourage 'new' wood will be necessary later.

When overwintering 'standard' fuchsias we need to be rather more circumspect. After all it will have taken a number of months or even years to get to the shape it now enjoys so we do not want to lose it by having failed to give it adequate protection. There are three places where protection is necessary – the root ball, the stem and the head. We do not wish to lose any of these. The root ball (still contained within its pot) can be wrapped in an insulating material, but it will be necessary to leave access to the compost so that some watering can take place through the winter. The stem can be protected by wrapping it in an insulating material or by surrounding it with a tube of the foam material sold for insulating pipes. The head can be protected by covering it with several layers of horticultural fleece.

Some growers prefer to keep their standard fuchsias ticking over during the winter. It is quite possible to keep them in green leaf if you have the facilities to maintain a temperature in excess of 40°F (5°C) through any cold spells. In order to get fresh young growths it will be necessary to prune the head of your standard quite severely in early autumn. Cut each branch back to a half or even less of its original length. Carefully remove all the old foliage from the remaining parts of branches and give the whole of the head a good spraying with a combined insecticide/fungicide spray. This will dispose of any lurking pests and diseases. It will also have the effect of softening the young buds that are in the

old leaf axils and they will be encouraged to start growing. With this sort of treatment it should be possible to have a fine covering of young green shoots over the whole of the head within a month.

The standards should be placed under cover before the first frosts arrive. Maintain the temperature at the level recommended and you will have no anxieties regarding uneven breaking of new growths in the spring as they will be in position for you throughout the winter. It is not our desire during the winter months to have rapid growth of the new shoots – we merely want them to be ticking over and not growing. If we give them too much heat during this period when the light intensity is very poor then we will encourage long, thin, straggly shoots as opposed to the strong, short jointed ones that give strength to the 'head'.

Take every opportunity during the winter months when the outside temperature is sufficiently mild, to open the doors and vents of the greenhouse or even to take the plants outside for an airing. Regular spraying of the head with water (with the chill taken off) will keep the foliage fresh and vibrant. Keep a careful watch out for any signs of pests. It is amazing how both greenfly and whitefly still manage to survive the colder weather. But the ideal conditions that we are giving our plants will also be ideal breeding conditions for them.

Plants that are growing in the hardy border will need very little attention from us during the winter. The dead-looking stems that the plants produced last year will be left in position and will provide a modicum of protection to the root ball in addition to reminding us of the exact locations of the plants. If the plants were planted deeply then 'mother earth' will be providing very ample insulation for the root system, but we can give a little assistance by adding a mulch of bark chippings or peat-free compost around the necks of the plants. Keep an eye on these mulches as the winter progresses as birds find them to be very useful scratching places in their search for food. In the spring, when fresh growths can be seen coming through the surface of the soil around the old stems, remove all of the latter to ground level.

So with a little bit of thought and careful planning it has been possible to get our old favourites through the winter. However, a visit to a specialist fuchsia nursery in the early months of the year will be enough to get the enthusiasm flowing once again. These young plants, raised from cuttings taken in the autumn and carefully protected by the nursery throughout the winter months, can be tended quite easily in a cool room within our own house – on the windowsill and preferably in a reflecting box – but we must not be tempted to share with them the type of heat that we enjoy.

Buying Fuchsias by Post

Without doubt the best possible method of buying your new fuchsia plants is by going to the place where they are being grown and selecting those that you wish to have. But even this method can be fraught with some difficulties. How do you decide on which plants to choose when faced with a great number of the same variety. The majority of specialist fuchsia nurseries or even garden centres will be offering young plants growing strongly in 6 or 7cm pots. I have described these as young plants as opposed to rooted cuttings because that is really what they are. Plants purchased in the very early spring will most likely have been rooted at the nursery during the autumn of the previous year. In order to have bushy plants the growing tips will probably have been removed and each plant will have four or five strongly growing young branches. (Incidentally, it is probable that the growing tips will have been removed at the nursery for two main reasons – the first, as already mentioned, being to present you with a well-branched young plant and the second, so as to provide the nursery with a batch of cuttings that, when rooted, will form the next group of saleable plants.)

Always decide before setting off to visit a nursery or garden centre on the number of plants that you will be needing. It is so easy to get just one or two more even when the space is going to be somewhat at a premium later in the season. You will also need to have a clear picture in your mind as to the way in which you will be using your plants. If you intend to make up several baskets of fuchsias then it will be necessary to purchase five or six each of the cultivars you have chosen. If plants are required for growing on as standards then you will need to select plants from which the central growing tip has not been removed.

However, it is not always possible to visit a nursery or garden centre to obtain the plants of your choice and you may have to resort to buying plants through the post. The majority of specialist fuchsia nurseries, many of which advertise in gardening papers/magazines, carry out a postal service and produce very useful catalogues of their fuchsias at the beginning of each year. It is also possible to purchase collections of young fuchsias from some of these nurseries but unfortunately such collections are usually delivered

Plants received by post should be unpacked as soon as possible.

rather too late in the year to be of much use during the current season and will often require growing on through the winter in order to get good-sized plants for flowering during the following year. In the Appendix to this book you will find the names and addresses of nurseries who specialize in fuchsias, many of which offer a postal service. Following the description of each plant you will find a code indicating the nurseries from which the cultivars can be obtained.

So what do we do with the fuchsias that we purchase early in the year? The purchases should be made as early as possible for they will take up very little room while they are small and can be nurtured through the final weeks of winter on the windowsill of a spare room or in a small heated part of a greenhouse. The electrically and thermostatically controlled propagators that can be purchased have sufficient space for quite a large number of young plants in small pots.

I have been very surprised in recent years at how early the garden centres have their young fuchsias. They are sometimes even available in the first half of January. These are autumn struck cuttings and will make excellent plants

Gently tease out the root systems and let fresh compost trickle through and around the roots.

(Below) New young plants can grow strongly in pots up to about 3½in (9cm) in diameter.

(Left) Shade the newly potted plants from the hot sun until they have become established in their pots.

for use in baskets, in pots or in the open garden for the current year. If you are visiting a nursery and purchasing plants this early in the year please ensure that they will be protected from the cold whilst being transported to your home address. An insulated large cardboard box will be ideal for this purpose. In the early months we will not be seeking rapid growth from our plants as, with the low light intensity, any growth will be rather thin and spindly. To this end keep the plants as cool as possible and give them as much light as possible either within the greenhouse or contained within a reflecting box on a windowsill indoors. Take the opportunity to examine the root systems as soon as possible and if the roots are completely filling the small pots then it will be necessary to move them into slightly larger ones.

Plants received through the post need to be given rather careful attention as soon as they are received. Bearing in mind that they will probably have been deprived of light for a couple of days and will have been in rather cramped conditions they will need a little pampering. Gently take the plants from their packaging making sure that no labels become dislodged. If they have been sent in miniature pots then there will be little need to do anything other than that already mentioned in the preceding paragraph. Do not place the plants in direct sunlight too quickly, but an overhead spray with clean, slightly tepid water will freshen up the foliage and give them a chance to recuperate from their incarceration. If the root systems have been removed from their initial pots and the rooted cuttings are sent with their roots wrapped in paper then it will be necessary to place them in fresh compost in small pots as quickly as possible. Treat each cutting as an individual and again make sure that the label is with the plant. Gently tease the root system of each plant from its 'ball' of roots placing it in the new small pots and allow fresh 'just moist' compost to trickle around and through the roots. Take your time about this, do not firm the compost, but tap the pot on the bench occasionally to ensure that there is compost between all of the roots. When all have been potted (again don't forget the label), an overhead spray and placing in a shaded position will ensure that the young plants recover quite quickly from their traumatic journey.

Once the plants are growing strongly it will be time to consider the purpose for which you wanted them and to start their training accordingly. Always bear in mind that any small tips removed from the plants to encourage bushiness can be used as small cuttings to increase your stock of those plants.

Young plants purchased in the first three months of the year can be encouraged to grow strongly so that they will flower in 5in or 6in (13cm or 15cm) pots from about July onwards. Plants used in baskets will fill a basket with healthy foliage and a cascade of flowers throughout late summer and early autumn. These young plants will also have developed strongly enough to be used to make a permanent bed of fuchsias during the month of June in the outside hardy border. Flowers will be expected from July onwards of the first year and will grow in size and abundance in each successive year.

To summarize – the best method of obtaining new plants is by selecting your own at a nursery or garden centre. However, if that is not possible or if the particular cultivar you require is only available from another source then it will be necessary, with good chances of success, to purchase plants through the post.

Pests and Diseases

Although it often seems that the reverse is the case, fuchsias do not suffer greatly from many pests and diseases. As early identification of any problem is of vital importance regular inspection and handling of plants will prevent any build-up or infestation of the plants.

Pests

WHITEFLY AND GREENFLY

These perhaps should have been placed under the general heading of Aphids as the same treatment will keep attacks by all sap-sucking insects under control. Both whitefly and greenfly are very visible so it is possible to treat attacks at a very early stage. In the early part of the season a few isolated adult whiteflies found on the undersurface of the leaves can be eradicated by gentle pressure with finger and thumb. If the numbers increase considerably it will be necessary to resort to chemical sprays. There are quite a number on the market and they can be seen on the shelves of all garden centres. Read the label carefully to ensure that the spray of your choice is suitable for use with fuchsias. Always use sprays mixed precisely to the dilution rates suggested by the manufacturers. Do not spray any plants under cover when the strong rays of the sun are shining through the glass – the droplets of moisture will be magnified and the leaf will suffer from severe scorch marks.

Whitefly.

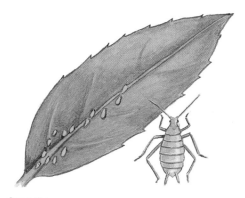

Greenfly.

27

For those growers who are against the use of chemical sprays, methods used by some of the Victorian gardeners are still as useful today as they were in the nineteenth century. Sprays made by using soft soap or some of the milder detergents, for example Stergene, appear to have very beneficial effects.

Regular use should always be made of any type of spray as they kill the adults only. Repeat sprayings, perhaps every three or four days, will also kill any adults emerging from eggs laid in earlier days.

The use of the natural predator *Encarsia formosa* can be used to great effect in greenhouses when the temperature and conditions are correct for the development and activity of the predator. The predator lays its eggs in the 'scales' of the whitefly thus preventing adult whiteflies from emerging. Unfortunately, as the predator will itself die out when all of its food supply has been removed, some whitefly are left so that the predator's source of food, the honeydew exuded by the whitefly, is still produced. However, the population of the whitefly will have been reduced considerably.

Insecticides, both contact and systemic, should be used carefully. In order to prevent a build-up in the resistance of the pests to these chemicals it is important to use a number of differing insecticides in rotation. When plants are in flower, overhead spraying would cause severe marking to the flowers so it will be necessary to use systemic insecticides watered into the compost and taken up into the sap stream through the plants' plumbing system. Insecticide sticks that are coated with chemicals are used in the same way.

RED SPIDER MITE

Not really a 'spider', but it is certainly one of the worst pests as far as fuchsias are concerned. They are very difficult to detect in the early stages as they are virtually invisible to the naked eye. Plants that have been attacked by 'red spider' can be recognized because the foliage turns to a bronzy colour and becomes extremely brittle. In the latter stages of a severe attack very fine webs can be seen spreading from leaf to leaf. The pest will likewise rapidly spread from plant to plant in a greenhouse.

The mite thrives in hot dry conditions, so if your plants are growing in a warm and moist environment they are less likely to suffer severe attacks. Affected plants should be isolated and thoroughly sprayed with a good systemic insecticide. Following an attack all plants in the greenhouse should be sprayed regularly.

CAPSID BUGS AND THRIPS

Both these pests are likely to attack plants that are growing in the open garden. They unfortunately attack the small growing tips, causing disfiguration of the young leaves and, in severe cases, causing blindness thus preventing the formation of flower buds.

Usually found when plants are growing in close proximity to trees, they can be kept under control by regularly spraying the plants with a good systemic insecticide both over the foliage and in the ground in proximity to the root ball. I am afraid that it is very easy to forget the plants that are growing, the hardy border until the first signs of an attack are noticed. Perhaps a regular pattern of spraying all plants would be beneficial.

LEAF HOPPERS

This is another insect that attacks outdoor plants. The results of an attack will leave leaves looking damaged and brown where the top surface of the leaf has been eaten by these fast-moving insects. Use of a systemic insecticide will help to reduce subsequent damage. Unfortunately the disfigurement of the foliage leaves the whole plant looking rather untidy and unhealthy.

VINE WEEVILS

A lot has been said and read recently about the scourge that is affecting fuchsias and many other plants – the vine weevil. The impression is given that great armies of these insects are marching along the motorways in search of susceptible plants. Bearing in mind the life cycle of the vine weevil and the three stages of its life history it should not be impossible to keep them under control.

The adult vine weevil is a nocturnal insect which crawls (rather swiftly) from plant to plant. It cannot fly although the fact that it often infests hanging baskets gives the impression that it might be able to do so. Their presence is first

Red Spider Mite.

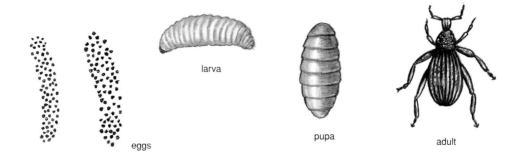

eggs

larva

pupa

adult

Vine Weevil.

noticed when notches are found along the edges of leaves.

Being nocturnal it needs to find places within which to shelter during the course of the day. Under the staging of greenhouses or in debris left on staging is the ideal hiding place. Having removed all debris we can set traps for these pests by providing them with shelters that we can examine daily. The insides of toilet rolls filled with shredded paper or dried grass, or rolled up pieces of corrugated cardboard, make ideal places. If left on the staging they will be used during the day by the weevils which can then be disposed of when discovered.

There are products that are attractive to vine weevils and that will kill them even though designed for other pests. Nippon ant gel is extremely effective when a line of it is placed on the staging. Likewise they are attracted to, and are killed by, wood-lice powder.

The adult vine weevils – that are all female and capable of laying large quantities of eggs – have discovered that the nice soft peat-based composts that we now use are ideal for egg-laying. We can therefore dissuade them from so doing by covering the surface of the compost with a layer of fine chippings. As this will also be beneficial in keeping moistness in the compost during very hot weather it serves a dual purpose.

The eggs, if laid, are virtually invisible to the naked eye but they will in a relatively short space of time hatch out into the little white larval grubs that cause the damage to the root systems. If we can prevent the eggs from hatching then we will again have broken the life-cycle chain. This can be accomplished quite simply by watering a solution of Armillatox into the compost within each pot. A dilution rate of 1/250 is sufficient to render any eggs that may be present sterile. Sterile eggs will not hatch into the root-eating larvae.

Now to the villains of the piece – the larval grubs. Each grub is something like ½in (1cm) in length – half-moon shaped, white with a brownish head. The only real remedy is to seek and destroy. Perhaps this is best done in the autumn of the year. Before placing your pot-grown plants in their winter quarters it might be as well to remove and replace all the old compost. If you are able to keep your plants just ticking over in a semi-heated greenhouse this is probably the best solution. The plants are taken out of their pots and all the old compost completely removed. Whilst carrying out this operation it will be possible to see if there are any larvae present. All the compost removed from the pots, and the larvae, should be placed in sealed bags and taken to the corporation tip. Do not be tempted to spread the compost onto your garden as the larvae will continue to thrive, will pupate into adults and the cycle will restart. A concerted effort will reduce the population of vine weevils quite quickly.

Diseases

BOTRYTIS

Sometimes called 'damping off', this disease usually occurs when the growing conditions are less than perfect. Overcrowding, overwatering, insufficient ventilation and poor hygiene (leaving rotting leaves on or around the pots) can all be contributory factors.

General cleanliness, care when watering and good ventilation (doors and windows left open as often as possible) will help prevent the problem. Regular use of fungicides, either powder or liquid, will help to keep the problem at bay.

RUST

One of the major diseases experienced in recent years is 'rust'. Pale yellowish spots appear on the upper surface of leaves and an examination of the undersurface will reveal orange pustules. The automatic reaction when seeing these pustules will be to call them 'rust' as it has the same appearance as rust on metal. Fortunately we no longer say that plants affected by rust should be taken out and destroyed. Careful removal of the affected leaves (the copper spores are very light and are easily transmitted by air movement or on hands) and destroying them is all that is necessary. Plants, both those from which the affected leaves were removed, and also all others in the greenhouse, should be given a spraying of a fungicide such as Nimrod T on a regular basis, as a preventative.

Good, strong growing and healthy plants are less likely to fall prey to most of the pests and diseases so, in addition to regularly handling and inspecting your plants, a good feeding programme needs to be undertaken.

Feeding, at a dilution rate of a quarter normal strength, with a good balanced fertilizer will keep your plants growing strongly and will ensure the continuity of shoot production and flowering. If you are feeding your plants as per the maker's recommendations, just once a week, make sure that the root ball has been well moistened first. Never feed a dry plant as damage to the root system could easily occur.

Please do not be dissuaded from growing fuchsias as a result of having read this chapter. Fuchsias do not suffer badly from pests and diseases. Bearing in mind the old maxim that prevention is better than cure, be ready to stop any attack of pests or diseases before they can get a foothold.

Understanding the Descriptions

The descriptions of species and cultivars which follow are, of necessity, very brief. In order to achieve some degree of uniformity a certain format and various abbreviations have been used, an explanation of which is given here.

Tom Thumb   This is the name of the plant. The name in normal print (as here) indicates that the plant is a 'cultivar' (a cultivated variety). If the name is printed in *italics* then the plant being described is one of the species, e.g. *F. arborescens*.

Single H3 Bush   This line of information is quite important, not only to aid identification but to give you an indication of whether the plant will suit your purposes.

Single, **Semi-Double** or **Double** indicates the type of flower that is produced by this plant.

Single means that the flower has four petals.

Semi-Double means that the flower has five, six or seven petals.

Double means that the flower has eight or more petals. Some plants produce very small petals called petaloids, which increase the size of the flower and are taken into account in determining the type of flower.

H1 H2 H3   These letters and figures indicate the hardiness of the plant. Such indications can only be a guide, however, as the hardiness of a plant can vary considerably according to the locality in which it is grown.

Types of flowers.

| Single | Semi-double | Double |

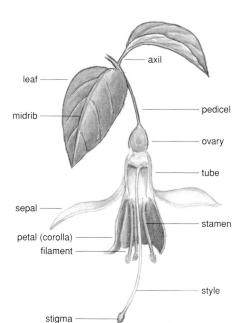

leaf — axil
midrib — pedicel
— ovary
— tube
sepal —
petal (corolla) — — stamen
filament —
— style
stigma —

Trailer indicates a lax, trailing growth. Such plants are best suited to being grown pendulously from hanging containers.

Some plants fall somewhere between these two types, and are described as either a lax bush or a stiff trailer, depending on which is the dominant tendency.

The main part of the description will give an indication of the colour of the flowers and of the foliage. Throughout the descriptions references are made to *tubes*, *sepals*, and *corollas*. The *corolla* is the term used for the petals of the flower irrespective of the number involved; a better indication of the parts of the flowers being described can be obtained from the diagram (*right*). It is very difficult to give exact references to sizes of flowers or foliage as these measurements vary considerably according to the type of cultivation given and the size of the pot in which the plant is grown.

Height and Spread (H. & S.)
If a plant has been shown as H3 – that is, a hardy plant for use in the garden – then an indication may been given as to the Height and Spread which would be expected. Such measurements can be only a very rough guide, as the positioning of the plant and the fertility of the soil can make a considerable difference. When established for a number of years, greater height and width would normally be expected.

(**'Jackie Bull'** × **'Annabel'**) Where possible, the names of the plant's parents are given and appear in parentheses (as here) before the raiser's name.

(**Kennett, USA, 1965**) The name of the raiser of the cultivar, or the name of the person who first described the species, is always given in parentheses (as here). The nationality of the raiser or finder is given next, together with the date when this event occurred. Many growers find this information very useful especially when a decision has been made to make a collection of plants raised by a certain hybridist, or to collect plants which are over a certain age. There are unfortunately a number of instances where such information is not available or cannot be guaranteed. The plant's parents are given where possible, and appear in parentheses before the name of the hybridist.

H1 indicates that the plant is rather tender and is 'frost-shy'. To grow to perfection, the protection of a heated greenhouse will be necessary and it is advisable to maintain the temperature above 7°C (45°F) throughout the year. Plants of the **Triphylla types** are particularly frost-shy and need this level of protection.

H2 indicates that the plant requires protection during the winter but can safely be grown outside the greenhouse during the rest of the year or can be used as a temporary resident in the outside border. Probably it is best to describe them as half-hardy.

H3 indicates that the plants are hardy and can be planted permanently in the garden, and will withstand normal winter weather without lifting. Such plants should be planted, initially, fairly deeply so that there is ample insulation around the root system. The top growths of such plants are usually killed by severe frosts, but fresh growths emerge from the root systems in the spring.

Bush or **Trailer** This indicates the type of growth normally associated with each cultivar or species.

Bush indicates a very strong and upright growth, readily forming branches. These plants will be useful when growing bushes for pots, patio tubs or borders.

A–Z of Species and Cultivars

A

Aalt Groothuis
Single H2 Bush
Tubes and flyaway *sepals* white. *Corollas* violet and saucer-shaped. Growth is upright and strong. Early nipping helps branching. Showy in any situation. *Foliage* medium green.
(Beitje, Holland, 1997) (MO)(PER)(GOU)(HYDE)

Abbey Hill
Single H2 Bush
Tubes cream blushed with pink. *Sepals* cream blushed with crêpe pink and tipped with green. *Corolla* petals dark violet maturing to violet. The medium-sized flowers are freely produced. *Foliage* medium green.
(Foster, UK, 1999) (WAR)

Abigal
Single H2 Bush
Tube dull red with a darker stripe. *Sepals,* held horizontally, a darker dull red with light green reflexed tips. *Corolla* fully flared bright purple with white at the base of the petals. *Foliage* medium green. The medium-sized blooms are held in a semi-erect position.
('Bon Accord' × 'Whiteknights Amethyst') × 'Ting a Ling' (Springer, Germany, 1989) (WV)(ROO)(GLE)

Abigayle Reine
Single H2 Bush
A variegated 'sport' of 'Rose Fantasia' with a beautiful golden edge to every *leaf. Tube* and *sepals* deep pink. *Corolla* petals pink with a hint of mauve. This beautiful new variety has retained its vigour and free-flowering style.
(Eric Hunton, UK, 1998) (ARC)(PER)

Abundance
Single H3 Bush
Tube and *sepals* of the medium-sized flowers rich cerise. *Corolla* petals purple with small cerise petaloids. The flowers are freely produced in self-branching bushy plants.
(Todd, UK, 1870) (BRI)

Achilles
Semi-Double H2 Bush
Tube short, greenish and white. *Sepals* pale pink and fully recurving. *Corolla* petals dark rose. The flowers are large, bell-shaped, and freely produced. *Foliage* mid-green. Strong upright and vigorous-growing plant that has the advantage of being self-branching.
(Goulding, UK, 1989) (CLI)(RIV)

Adagio
Double H2 Trailing
Tube and *sepals* rosy red. *Corolla* petals claret red. The flowers are of medium size and are produced freely on trailing or semi-trailing branches. *Foliage* mid-green.
(Tiret, USA, 1961) (WV)(LOK)

Ada Perry
Double H2 Trailer
Tube fairly short and scarlet. *Sepals* scarlet on top with an even deeper scarlet underneath. *Corolla* petals blue-purple streaked with cardinal red and maturing to rose. *Foliage* dark green with serrated edges. The large flowers are freely produced. Growth is rather stiff for a trailer but will make a good basket and also a bush if given the necessary supports.
('Seventh Heaven' × 'Hula Girl') (Stubbs, USA, 1983) (CLI)(FEN)(SMI)

Ada's Love
Single H2 Bush
Tube pink. *Sepals* white tipped with green. *Corolla* petals rose pink. *Foliage* medium to light green. An excellent medium-sized single with slightly upward-looking flowers. Very floriferous.
('Shelford' × 'Cambridge Louie') (Delaney, UK, 1992) (ALD)(BLA)(KM)

Adelaide Hoodless
Single H2 Bush
Tube and *sepals* of these medium-sized flowers white flushed with pink and tipped with green. *Corolla* petals lilac pink flushed with white at the base. Upright self-branching habit.
(ROU)

Adinda
Single H1 Bush
Terminal-flowering triphylla-type fuchsia. Large clusters of salmon-coloured slender *tubed* blooms, carried on the many branch ends. *Sepals* and *corolla* petals also salmon-coloured. *Foliage* sage green. Medium upright and self-branching growth. Show type.
(Dijkstra, Holland, 1995) (LB) (FOX)(MO)(CHA)(PER)(GOU) (ROO)(HYDE)(ISL)

Admiration
Single H3 Bush
Tube and *sepals* bright red tipped with yellowish green. *Corolla* petals Indian Lake. The medium-sized flowers are fairly long. *Foliage* mid- to light green. Growth is as a rather lax but self-branching bush. H: 15–18in (37–45cm); S: 30in (75cm).
(Wood, UK, 1940) (SIL)(FEN)(RKY)(RIV)(BRY)

Adrien Berger
Single H2 Bush
Tube fairly long and light pink. *Sepals* salmon. *Corolla* petals carmine. The flowers are held in a semi-erect position. *Foliage* is mid-green. Growth is naturally strong and upright with a good self-branching habit. A vigorous grower.
(Lemoine, France, 1901) (RIV)

Agnese Schwab
Single H2 Trailer
Tubes and *sepals* of these medium-sized flowers red. *Corolla* petals robin red. *Foliage* medium green. A natural trailer will make a very attractive basket quite quickly.
(Schwab, Holland, 1995) (HYDE)

AALT GROOTHUIS

ADA PERRY

ADA'S LOVE

ADELAIDE HOODLESS

ADINDA

ADMIRATION

Airball
Single H2 Bush
Tube white. *Sepals* magenta on top and slightly darker underneath. *Corolla* opens magenta and matures to fuchsia purple. Flowers medium-size. *Foliage* light green. Growth is upright and bushy.
(L. Hobbs, UK, 1984)
(BRY)

Alabama
Single H2 Bush
Medium-sized flowers. *Tube* and *sepals* whitish pink. *Corolla* petals cerise. Upright bushy growth. There are some doubts about the correct naming of this one as it could well be 'Arabella' raised by Banks in 1866.
(RIV)

Alabama Improved
Single H2 Lax Bush
The same confusion exists with this as with the previous cultivar. (It could be 'Arabella Improved'.) It is described as having a creamy-wax (whitish pink) *tube* and *sepals*. *Corolla* petals rosy cerise. The small blooms are produced in abundance. The bushy growth is rather lax and this plant may also be used in baskets.
(Lye, UK, 1871)
(FEN)(ASK)(SMI)

Alan Dyos
Single H2 Bush
Tube rich pink. *Sepals* broad and upswept, also rich pink. *Corolla* with its short and flared petals has the same colouring. Could be described as a rich pink 'self'. *Foliage* medium green. Very floriferous, the flowers being small and well held out. Upright growth, vigorous and bushy. Excellent for bush or Standard.
(Dyos, UK, 1984) (RIV)

Alan Titchmarsh
Single/Semi-Double H2 Bush
Tube and *sepals* a delightful rose. *Corolla* the palest pink with distinctive petaloids. Extremely

floriferous. *Foliage* mid-green. Excellent for pot and patios. Introduced at the British Fuchsia Society Diamond Anniversary celebrations at Borde Hill, Sussex, in 1998.
(Weston, UK, 1998)
(LB)(PER)(ISL)(SIM)

Albertina
Single H2 Bush
Tube and *sepals* white flushed and striped with rose. *Sepals* white. *Corolla* lavender rose. Medium-sized flowers. *Foliage* medium green.
(Netjes, Holland, 1988)
(ISL)(ROO)(HYDE)(FUC)(OLD)

Albertus Schwab
Single H1 Triphylla-type
Terminal-flowering single. *Tubes*, *corolla* petals and *sepals* bright orange-red, the latter also green-tipped. *Foliage* mid-green with a slightly furry appearance. Growth is upright and self-branching. Best in tubs.
(Schwab, Holland, 1995)
(CL)(ISL)

Alde
Single H2 Bush
Tube and *sepals* pale orange. *Corolla* with pleated petals, apricot. Smallish plump flowers. *Foliage* medium to dark green. The strong, sturdy growth makes this an ideal plant for temporary outside bedding. H: 12–18in (30–45cm); S: 18–24in (45–60cm).
(Goulding, UK, 1988) (SIL)(WAY)
(EX)(WV)(GOU)(ROO)(CLI)

Algerine
Single H2 Bush
Tube and *sepals* pale pink edged with rose. *Corolla* deepest magenta purple. *Foliage* medium green. Medium-sized flowers. Vigorous grower well suited for using as Standard.
(Dyos, UK, 1995) (LB)

Alice Doran
Single H3 Bush
A very strong upright-growing and hardy cultivar. *Tube* and *sepals*

pinky red. *Corolla* petals of the medium-sized flowers burgundy. ('Empress of Prussia' × 'Rose of Castille')
(Doran, UK, 1996)
(CL)(LB)(ROO)

Alice Sweetapple
Double H2 Bush
Tube and *sepals* pink. *Corolla* opens red purple maturing to magenta. Large flowers with flared petals, distinguished by bud length and bloom colour. Strong, upright growth producing a well-branched bushy plant.
('Cheers' × 'Ruby Wedding')
(Forward, UK, 1993)
(WV)(FUC)(GLE)(ISL)

Alice Travis
Semi-Double H2 Trailer
Large flowers freely produced for their size. *Tubes* and *sepals* carmine. *Corolla* petals deep violet blue. *Foliage* medium green.
(Travis, UK, 1956)

Alipat
Single H2 Bush
This is a 'sport' from 'Alison Patricia'. *Tube*, *sepals* and *corolla* all pink. The flowers are small but growth is strong and upright. The short-joined stems make the growth very bushy.
(Baker, UK, 1993)
(BAK)

Allegro
Double H2 Trailer
Tube and reflexing *sepals* medium rose-coloured. *Corolla* petals rose bengal, loose and flaring. The large flowers have a very open 'blown' look about them and yet they seem to retain perfection of form. The natural growth is long and arching making this a perfect plant for growing in larger hanging containers. Heat-tolerant. *Foliage* light to mid-green.
(Schnabel, Paskesen, USA, 1960)
(FEN)(RKY)(RIV)

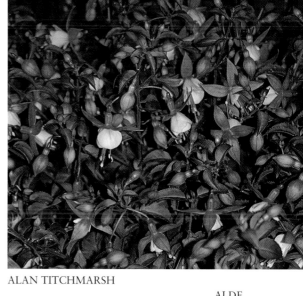

AIRBALL

ALAN TITCHMARSH

ALBERTINA

ALDE

ALGERINE

ALICE DORAN

Allure
Double H2 Trailer
The lax growth of this cultivar
makes it very suitable for use in
baskets. *Tubes* long and thin,
ivory white. *Sepals* spreading,
white flushed with pink. *Corolla*
clear pink. Preferable to grow in
semi-shade.
(Moerman, Holland)
(FEN)(RKY)(CHA)(WV)(HYDE)

Alma Hulscher
Double H2 Trailer
Tube and *sepals* fully recurved
and bright red. *Corolla* pink with
red veins. Excellent in full baskets
for garden display.
(Stoel, Holland, 1988)
(WV)(RIV)(HYDE)

Alsace
Double H2 Bush
Medium-sized flowers. *Tubes* and
sepals red. *Corolla* petals rosy
white. Growth is upright and
bushy. A variety well worth
seeking out.
(Boucharlat, France, 1913) (ISL)

Alsa Garnet
Double H2 Trailer
Tube white. *Sepals* white, tipped
with green and slightly flushed
with pink. *Corolla* petals rich
garnet red. The fairly large
flowers are freely produced.
Foliage medium green. Growth is
naturally cascading and fairly
rapid.
(Thorne, UK, 1965)
(ROO)(FEN)(BAK)(RIV)

Alyce Larson
Single H2 Trailer
Tube and *sepals* of this medium-
sized trailing fuchsia white tipped
with pink. *Corolla* petals white.
Foliage medium green and the
plant is self-branching. An
excellent cultivar for hanging
pots.
(Tiret, USA, 1972) (WAY)

Amazing Mary
Semi-Double H2 Bush
Tube long, light red. *Sepals* arch
back and are also light red.

Corolla petals very dark red. The
foliage dark green. Tall, upright-
growing plant suitable for
Standard work.
(Wright, UK, 1980)
(BRY)

Ambassador
Single H2 Bush
Tube and *sepals* rose madder with
a white flush. *Corolla* violet
purple fading to paeony purple.
Large flowers freely produced.
Foliage mid-green. Upright and
bushy growth.
(Machado, USA, 1962)
(FOX)(ROU)(RKY)(STM)
(CHA)(WV)(BAK)(RIV)(BRY)
(CLI)(ASK)(GLE)(OLI)

American Dream
Double H2 Trailer
Tube and *sepals* dark rose.
Corolla petals purple flushed with
rose. The large flowers are freely
produced. Excellent for basket
work.
(ARC)(RIV)

American Flaming Glory
Double H2 Stiff Trailer
Tube and *sepals* pink. *Corolla*
purple toning to flame red.
Foliage fairly large and medium
green in colour. The largish
blooms are produced quite
freely. Although described as
a trailer it will require the
assistance of weights to cover
a basket. Supporting canes
will make a good bush-type
plant.
(Martin, USA, 1958)
(SIL)(ARC)(BRI)(ROO)(RIV)
(HYDE)(BRY)(CLI)(ISL)(OLI)

Amethyst
Double H2 Bush
Tube and *sepals* pale red. *Corolla*
petals purple. *Foliage* is mid-
green. The flowers are large and
very freely produced for their
size. Good, strong, upright and
self-branching growth. Appears to
be identical in every way with a
plant raised by Brown (UK) in
1845.
(Tiret, USA, 1941) (HYDE)

Amke
Single H2 Bush
Tube and *sepals* robin red, the
upper face of the latter being a
little lighter than the lower.
Corolla dark violet fading to
robin red when matured. Good,
strong, upright and self-branching
growth.
(Bogemann, Germany, 1984)
(ROO)

A.M. Larwick
Double H3 Bush
Sepals and *tubes* rich carmine.
Corolla purplish mauve. Free-
flowering, medium-sized flowers.
Foliage mid-green. Upright and
bushy growth. Accepted by the
BFS as a show bench hardy. H:
18in (45cm); S: 24in (60cm).
(Smith, New Zealand, 1940)
(SIL)(RKY)(BAK)(RIV)(BRY)

F. Ampliata
Species H1 Bush
The flowers are produced in
whorls. *Tubes* orange, of medium
length. *Sepals* short, orange and
spreading. *Corolla* petals bright
orange. Rather sporadic in its
flowering. Shrubby, self-branching
growth. Quite easy.
(Bentham, Equador, 1845)
(CL)(GOU)(HYDE)

Amy Lye
Single H2 Bush
Tube cream. *Sepals* white tipped
with green. *Corolla* petals coral
orange. The medium-sized flowers
are produced early and very
freely. *Foliage* dark green with a
distinctive crimson mid-rib.
Growth is very spreading and
vigorous although rather lax. Will
make a good standard.
(Lye, UK, 1885) (SIL)(FOX)
(RKY)(KM)(BRE)(EX)(ARC)
(BRI)(CHA)(BAK)(ROO)
(CLI)(ASK)(SMI)(LOK)

Amy Ruth
Double H2 Bush
Upright-growing bush. *Tubes* and
sepals deep pink. *Corolla* petals
white pink.
(WV)

ALLURE

ALMA HULSCHER

AMAZING MARY

AMERICAN FLAMING GLORY

A.M. LARWICK

AMY LYE

F. andreii
Species H1 Bush
An attractive and easy-to-grow
species with flowers being held at
the ends of the branches. The
long *tube*, short *sepals* and
corolla petals bright and waxy
orange. *Foliage* dark green and
glossy. Growth is strongly upright
and self-branching.
(Southern Ecuador and Northern
Peru, 1925) (CL)(KM)(GOU)

Andrew
Single H2 Bush
This is an easy-to-grow and free-
flowering plant. *Tubes* white.
Sepals pale rose madder. *Corolla*
petals pale purple. Upright and
self-branching. The medium-
sized blooms are freely
produced.
(Watson, UK, 1967) (KM)(ARC)
(CHA)(BAK)(ROO)(RIV)(ASK)
(FUC)(GLE)

Andrew Carnegie
Double H2 Bush
Tube and *sepals* crimson. *Corolla*
white and very heavily veined
with cerise. Largish flowers with
a very tightly packed corolla
formation. Medium-sized bush
with a good lax upright and self-
branching habit. *Foliage* medium
green. Produces the best results
when grown under cooler
conditions.
(Demay, France, 1865)
(WV)(LOK)

Andromeda
Single H2 Bush
Small to average-sized flowers.
Tubes light red. *Sepals* stand out
horizontally and are also light
red. *Corolla* petals lilac with red
veining. *Foliage* mid-green.
Growth is upright, self-branching
and bushy.
(*F. regia* (var. *typica*) × 'Upward
Look')
(De Groot, Holland, 1972) (BRY)

Angela's Lilac
Double H2 Bush
Tube and *sepals* mid-pink. *Corolla*
petals mid-lilac. A beautiful pastel-
coloured combination. *Foliage*
mid-green. The medium-sized
flowers are carried in profusion. A
good, strong, upright-growing
plant that is self-branching and is
useful for any tall or upright
training.
(Hobson, UK, 1985)
(BRY)

Angelina
Single H2 Bush
Renamed 'Jubilee Quest'. For
description and picture please
refer to this name.
(KM)

Angel's Eyes
Double H2 Trailer
Tube and *sepals* white shading to
dark rose. *Corolla* petals rose
edged with white. *Foliage*
medium green. Lax upright
growth or can be used in baskets.
(McLaughlin, USA, 1991)
(EX)

Angel's Flight
Double H2 Trailer
Tube long and white. *Sepals* pink
with slightly deeper colour at the
base and curling right back
against the tube. *Corolla* white
with pale pink veining. *Foliage*
medium green. A natural trailer
that is self-branching and very
vigorous. Grows best in cool
conditions. Could be used as a
bush but would require staking.
(Martin, USA, 1957)
(BAK)(BRI)(RIV)(HYDE)(BRY)
(SMI)(OLI)

Annabelle Stubbs
Double H2 Trailer
Tube light pink. *Sepals* coral
pink. *Corolla* reddish purple. A
very full double. *Foliage* medium
green. A natural trailing habit.
(Riley, USA, 1991)
(FOX)(FEN)(ROU)(BRE)(EX)
(CHA)(PER)(RIV)(HYDE)(CLI)
(ASK)(FUC)(GLE)(ISL)(SMI)

Ann Ainsworth
Single H2 Trailer
Sepals and *tubes* flesh pink with a
distinctive white flush. *Corolla*
petals lilac pink with cerise
edging. The small single flowers
are borne in profusion. Growth is
vigorous, arching and self-
branching. A fairly compact plant
that rapidly fills a basket with its
beautiful flowers.

Anne Buchan
Single H2 Bush
This delightful flower is from
the same grower who produced
'Baby Bright'. *Tube* pale empire
rose. *Sepals* carmine on the
upper surface and lighter on the
lower. *Corolla* petals pale
fuchsia purple with a slightly
deeper edging. The *foliage* is
mid-green.
(Bright, UK, 1998)
(WAL)

Anne Strudwick
Double H2 Trailer
The short *tube* and arching
sepals pale salmon. *Corolla*
petals a darker shade of salmon
marbled with lighter tones.
Foliage medium green. The lax
growth makes it suitable for
basket work.
(Goulding, UK, 1998)
(GOU)(HYDE)

Ann Lee
Double H2 Bush
Tube and long *sepals* red. *Corolla*
petals a rich violet blue. A very
rich-coloured fuchsia that flowers
very freely. *Foliage* is mid-green.
Growth is naturally upright and
very bushy.
(E. Holmes, UK, 1970)
(BAK)(RIV)

Anthea Day
Double H2 Bush
Tube and *sepals* a rich waxy red.
Corolla petals of these medium-
sized blooms blush pink. The
flowers are produced very early
and continue in a very free way
throughout the season. Growth is
upright and bushy.
('Pink Cloud' × 'Pink Quartet')
(Day, UK, 1981)
(LOK)(EX)(BRI)(WV)

F. ANDREII

ANGELA'S LILAC

ANDROMEDA

ANNE STRUDWICK

ANNABELLE STUBBS

Apache
Double H2 Bush
Tube and *sepals* rosy red.
Corolla petals lilac oversplashed
with pink. The medium-sized
blooms are freely produced for a
double. Growth is upright and
bushy.
('Blue Lagoon' × 'Phyllis')
(Hobson, UK, 1973) (BRY)

Apple Blossom
Single H2 Lax Bush
This flower could almost be
described as 'self-flowered' as the
tube, *sepals* and *corolla* petals
are all shell to coral pink in
colouring. The small flaring
blooms are very attractive.
Foliage dark green. Although it
can be described as a bush the
growth is rather low and
spreading. It is a very vigorous
plant and is heat-tolerant.
(Schnabel-Paskeson, USA, 1953)
(KM)(ROO)

Appollo
Single H2 Trailer
Tube and *sepals* salmon orange.
Corolla rather unusual colour
combination being pink on the
upper half and magenta on the
lower. *Foliage* medium green. A
natural trailer so will make an
excellent basket.
(Dresman, UK, 1987)
(OLD)(FEN)(RKY)

Aquarius
Single H2 Bush
Tube and *sepals* light pink with
green tips. *Corolla* bell-shaped
with pink petals. Upright and
bushy growth. *Foliage* has a
distinctive serrated edging.
Growth is strongly upright, self-
branching and bushy.
(Soo-Yun, USA, 1971)
(RIV)(WHE)

F. arborescens zempulai
Species H1 Bush
A very strong, upward-growing
species that carries its flowers on
large terminal panicles. *Sepals* of
this variant rose-coloured.
Corolla small with lavender
petals. *Foliage* lustrous, large

and green. Needs to be given a
big root run in order to thrive
and must never be allowed to
dry out at the roots. This one
with *F. arborescens* and *F.
paniculata* are well worth trying.
(Date of finding and location
unknown) (HYDE)

Arcadia
Single H2 Bush
Tube thick, of medium length
and red cerise. *Sepals* long and
broad, slightly upturned, and
cerise. *Corolla* petals a true
magenta colouring. Largish
flowers. *Foliage* pale green,
serrated. Upright growth that
will make a good well-branched
bush quite quickly.
(Tolley, UK, 1979)
(RKY)(WAR)(RIV)

Arcady
Single H2 Bush
Tube and *sepals* pink suffused
with salmon, the latter being
green-tipped. *Corolla* petals deep
rose and edged with salmon.
Foliage medium green. The
natural growth is as an upright
bush that is helped by its free-
branching habit.
(Dr Colville, UK, 1968)
(LOK)(WV)

Arend Moerman
Double H2 Trailer
The long thin *tube* and the *sepals*
red aubergine. The full double
corolla dark aubergine. *Foliage*
mid-green. The natural habit of
this plant is to produce long
trailing branches. It looks good
in a hanging pot and rather
unusual.
(Weeda, Holland, 1994)
(MO)(HYDE)(ISL)

Arendsnestje (Could be **Bert's Arendsnestje**)
Single H2 Trailer
The long thick *tube* and the
sepals light pink. *Corolla* petals
rose red. *Foliage* medium green.
The large striking blooms look
well in a hanging pot.
(Pelgrims, Holland, 1994)
(BRE)(MO)(HYDE)

Ark Royal
Double H2 Bush
Tube is bright red. *Sepals* also
bright red and tipped with white.
Corolla petals white and splashed
with red at the base. The blooms
are large and are very free for
the size of the bloom. Upright-
growing, self-branching and
bushy.
(Dyos, UK, 1980)
(BRI)(BLA)(BRY)

Arlendon
Semi-Double H2 Bush
Tube and *sepals* bright red. *Corolla*
petals white, veined with cerise.
Previously known as 'Snowcap
Improved'. Named by the raiser
after his three sons – Arthur,
Leonard and Donald. Strong,
upright-growing plant that
branches quite naturally.
(Green-Horce, UK, 1974/5)
(WV)(BRY)

Arthur Baxter
Single H2 Bush
Tube and *sepals* pink. *Corolla*
petals pale purple. Excellent for
bush or patio purposes.
(Stiff, UK, 1992)
(BAK)(ROO)

Arthur Cope
Semi-Double H2 Bush
Tube long and white. *Sepals* waxy
white. *Corolla* petals spiraea red
flushed with rose red and splashed
with white. *Foliage* medium green.
The natural habit is vigorous and
spreading. The large flowers are
carried quite freely. Best colour in
the shade.
(Gadsby, UK, 1968) (BRY)

Ashley
Single H2 Bush
Almost considered to be a
Triphylla-type. *Tubes* (fairly long),
sepals and *corolla* all orange/red.
Smallish flowers but fairly free-
flowering. *Foliage* fairly large and
medium green.
(Djikstra, Holland, 1992)
(PER)

APACHE

APPOLLO

AREND MOERMAN

ASHLEY

Ashley and Isobel
Single H2 Bush
Tube and *sepals* creamy white.
Corolla petals cardinal red with
orange splashes. The medium-
sized flowers are very attractive
but rather thin. Growth lax
upright but will make a very
good hanging pot or basket.
(D. Clark, UK, 1990)
(STM)(WV)(RIV)

Ashley Jane (1990)
Double H2 Bush
Tube and *sepals* bright red.
Corolla petals palest pink veined
with red. *Foliage* dark green,
glossy, against which the medium-
sized blooms stand out well. This
is a free-flowering upright, bushy
plant that was a seedling from
'Dusky Beauty'.
(Hutchinson, UK, 1990) (ALD)

Ashmore
Single to Semi-Double H2 Bush
Tube and *sepals* red. *Corolla*
petals open as purple veined with
red and mature to purple. Smooth
petal edges. *Foliage* medium green
on the supper surfaces but
yellowish green on the lower. The
veins are light olive green. Growth
Semi-Double H2 Bush is as a
self-branching lax upright. Will
need supports if bush-trained but
will make an excellent subject for
hanging containers.
('Golden La Campanella' ×
'Autumnale')
(Mrs M. Dowson, UK, 1991)
(FOX)(CHA)(GLE)

Atlantica
Single H2 Bush
Tube red. *Sepals* pink. *Corolla*
petals white and red. Flowers are
of medium size and freely
produced. Growth is naturally
upright, bushy and self-branching.
(F. Holmes, UK, 1986) (RIV)

Atlantic Crossing
Semi-Double H2 Lax Bush
Tube and *sepals* pink. *Corolla*
petals blue. As a seedling of
'Annabel', it is well worth
growing. If it emulates its parent

this one should be ideal for
growing as a bush, a basket or a
Standard.
(1996) (ROO)

Atomic Glow
Double H2 Lax Bush
Tube pale pink. *Sepals* pale
orange, tipped with green. *Corolla*
glowing pink with an orange tint.
Foliage medium green. Medium-
sized flowers appear in flushes
throughout the season from an
early start. The lax growth can be
used as a bush or a basket.
(Machado, USA, 1963) (BAK)
(STM)(ARC)(BRI)(ROO)(BLA)
(RIV)(HYDE)(BRY)(OLI)

Aubergine
Single H2 Bush
Tube, *sepals* and *corolla* of this
very attractive flower all dark
aubergine. *Foliage* medium to
dark green. Growth is rather lax
so might be used, with training,
as either basket or bush.
(de Graaff, Holland, 1989)
(FOX)(LB)(EX)(CHA)(WV)(RIV)
(SMI)(LOK)

Aubrey Harris
Semi-Double H2 Bush
Tube and *sepals* of this upright
growing plant are white and pink.
Corolla petals magenta rose. The
medium-sized flowers are freely
produced. *Foliage* is mid-green. A
naturally bushy plant.
(Pacey, UK, 1989) (FEN)(RIV)

Audray
Single H2 Trailer
Tube very short, green. *Sepals* long,
thin and spinel red shading to
neyron rose with white markings
and tipped with green. *Corolla*
petals spectrum violet edged with
imperial purple. Medium-sized
tubular-shaped flowers are freely
produced. *Foliage* light green,
medium-sized with serrated edges
and pale veins. Growth is naturally
trailing so will make a good
subject for use in hanging
containers. Will also make an
excellent weeping Standard.
('Deben Rose' ×)

(Dunnett, UK, 1982) (ISL)(BRE)
(CHA)(RIV)(ASK)(GLE)

Audrey Booth
Double H2 Trailer
Tube and *sepals* pale pink.
Corolla petals a darker shade of
pink. The laterals are strong and
arching. Best suited to large wall
and fully round baskets.
(Goulding, UK, 1995) (GOU)

Auntie Bertha
Double H2 Trailer
Tube and *sepals* of this medium
to large-sized flower red. *Corolla*
petals waxy white. The natural
growth is as a trailer and will
therefore make an excellent
subject for a hanging container.
(POT)

Auntie Kit
Single H2 Trailer
Tube and *sepals* crimson. *Corolla*
petals cyclamen purple veined
with crimson. A prolific flowering
cultivar that, with its natural
trailing ability, will make it an
excellent plant for use in hanging
containers.
(R. Holmes, UK, 1997) (OLD)

Avon Celebration
Semi-Double H2 Bush
Tube white and quite short.
Sepals also white with green tips;
they are broad and well reflexed.
Corolla petals white at the base
blending to aster mauve. *Foliage*
light green/yellow heavily
variegated. Strong upright
growth. The medium-sized
flowers are freely produced.
(J. Lockyer, UK, 1988) (LOK)

Avon Gold
Single H2 Bush
Tube pale pink. *Sepals* pink and
tipped with green. *Corolla* petals
pale lavender pink. The colour
combination is delightful. This
variety has medium-sized blooms
and is very profuse. *Foliage*
beautiful creamy gold. Makes a
strong shapely bush. Good for
show work.
(J. Lockyer, UK, 1985) (LOK)

ASHLEY AND ISOBEL

AUDRAY

ATOMIC GLOW

AUBERGINE

AUNTIE KIT

A.W. Taylor

Single or Semi-Double H2 Bush
Tube white. *Sepals* white, pink at
the base and tipped with green.
Corolla petals pale lilac blue
maturing to rosy lavender. *Foliage*
bluish green. A delightful colour
combination on an upright bushy
plant.
('Brentwood' × 'Party Frock')
(Thorne, UK, 1969)
(BAK)

Axel of Denmark

Single H1 Triphylla bush
This Triphylla-type fuchsia has a
dark green oblong ovary. *Tube*
long, fat and deep red. *Sepals*
small, sharp-pointed and the
same deep red. *Corolla* petals
almost hidden and reddish
orange. The blooms hang in
racemes or clusters. Buds long
and bullet-like with very pointed
ends. *Foliage* dark green. Growth
is very upright and quite stiff but
the plant has the attribute of
holding its flowers for a very long
time. Not dissimilar to
'Leverkusen'.
(Denmark, circa 1980)
(HYDE)(CLI)

Azure

Single H2 Bush
Tube and *sepals* pure white.
Corolla petals blue with white at
the base of the petals. Unlike
others with the same colouring
there is very little fading. A filtered
light is best for obtaining the nicest
colouring. *Foliage* medium green.
Natural growth is as a strong
upright and self-branching bush.
(Rozaine-Boucharlat, France,
1888) (ROO)

Azure Sky

Semi-Double H2 Bush
Medium-sized flowers. *Tubes*
white. *Sepals* held horizontally
also white. *Corolla* deep lilac blue
fading very slightly with age.
Foliage medium green.
(Johns, UK, 1990)
(KM)(CL)(JAK)(ISL)(SIM)

B

Babette

Double H2 Bush
Tube short and pale pink. *Sepals*
long, white tipped with green and
slightly flushed pink. *Corolla*
petals lilac pink at base maturing
to light purple. The blooms are
longish and the colouring is
delightful. Short-jointed and
bushy growth.
(Johns, UK, 1988)
(KM)(BRE)

Babs

Double H2 Bush
Tube creamy pink. *Sepals* wide
and white – pink at base on
upper surface and blushed light
pink on the lower. *Corolla* petals
very pale pink veined with pink.
Foliage dark green on the upper
surface and medium green on the
lower. The veins are green and
the stems red. Good, strong,
upright grower – suitable for
Standard. Does best in filtered
light.
('Torvill and Dean' × 'Groene
Kan's Glorie')
(Bell, UK, 1991) (ASK)

Baby Beverley

Double H3 Bush
Tube and *sepals* pink. *Corolla*
petals creamy white. *Foliage*
medium green. The natural
growth is as an upright bush. The
medium to large flowers are freely
produced.
(EX)

Baby Girl

Single H2 Bush
Tube and upswept *sepals* pinkish
white. *Corolla* also a delightful
pinkish white. *Foliage* olive
green. Growth is strongly
upright.
(Fleming, UK, 1995) (BRY)

Baby Rose

Single H2 Bush
Tube, thick, waxy and white.
Sepals short and white, tipped
with green. *Corolla* petals pale

orange pink. Medium to small
single flowers. Strong, upright
growth. *Foliage* dark green
flushed bronze.
(Hooper, UK, 1995) (JAK)

Baglan Bay

Double H2 Lax Bush
Tube and *sepals* of this medium-
sized fully double flower red.
Corolla petals a delightful
fluorescent purple. *Foliage* mid-
to darker green. The lax growth
makes this suitable as a bush
when given some supports or in
a hanging container.
(EX)

Bagworthy Water

Single H2 Trailer
Tube long and salmon-orange.
Sepals with same delightful
colouring curl right up and
around the tube. *Corolla* petals
claret rose fading to neyron
rose. A delightful arching habit
of growth that makes it an ideal
subject for use in hanging
containers. The medium-
sized blooms are very freely
produced.
(Endicott, UK, 1972) (LOK)

Baker's Tri

Single H1 Triphylla type.
Tube long, tapering and
geranium lake. *Sepals* finely
pointed and Venetian pink.
Corolla petals, partly hidden, are
spinel red with pink stamens.
Foliage lightish green. Lax trailer.
Not vigorous – can be rather
fussy concerning both watering
and overpotting.
(H. Dunnett, UK, 1974)
(BAK)(RKY)

Balcon Queen

Single to Semi-Double H2 Bush
This little known cultivar is a
single to semi-double cerise/lilac
flower similar in many respects to
'Heidi Ann' but with differing
foliage. *Tube* and *sepals* cerise
and *corolla* petals lilac.
(Introduced by Underhill
Nurseries in 1986) (BRY)(OLI)
(*See* photograph on page 47.)

AXEL OF DENMARK

AZURE

AZURE SKY

BABETTE

BABY GIRL

BAGLAN BAY

Bali Hi
Double H2 Trailer
Tube broad and white. Upturned *sepals* also white. *Corolla* petals start violet blue, open to mauve blue. The medium-sized blooms are produced in profusion. A natural trailer so this plant will help to make an excellent basket.
(Tiret, USA, 1955) (HYDE)

Balkon
Single H2 Trailer
Tube and *sepals* pink. *Corolla* petals deep pink. *Foliage* mid-green. The small to medium flowers are very freely produced. The natural cascading growth makes this a very suitable plant for hanging pots, baskets and window-boxes. With supports makes an excellent pot plant.
(Neubronner, Holland)
(WV)(BAK)(RID)(OLI)(LOK)

Ballerina
Single H2 Bush
Tube and *sepals* ivory pink. *Corolla* petals clear pink with rose edges. The medium-sized blooms are profuse. Growth is vigorous but somewhat brittle.
('Rolla' × 'Display')
(Niederholzer, USA, 1939)
(RKY)(FUC)(SMI)(OLI)

Balmoral
Single H2 Bush
Tube and *sepals* of the medium-sized blooms white. *Corolla* petals also white. This plant makes a very attractive bush as it is upright-growing and self-branching.
(RIV)

Bank's Peninsula
Single H1 Bush
A recently discovered apetalous (no petals) inter-specific hybrid. *Tube* green matures to yellowish orange with a bright yellow stigma. The stems of new growths are spotted. Flowers are held in a semi-erect position in the early stages. *Foliage* small and heart-shaped. The stems are trailing and the pollen, as is usual with natives of New

Zealand where this one was found, is blue.
(*F. procumbens* × *F. exorticata* or *F. perscandens*)
(Hutchison, UK, 1980) (KM)

Barbara's Gem
Semi-Double H2 Bush
Tube and *sepals* red. *Corolla* petals reddish purple maturing to a rich red. Blooms are of medium size and slightly flared. The flowers are produced in quantity. The growth is slightly lax so will make a good pot plant with some supports but will also make a good subject for use in hanging pots or baskets. It is worth trying as a hardy.
(J. Allsop, UK, 1998) (ROO)

Barbara Windsor
Single H2 Bush
Tube and *sepals* bright pink. *Corolla* petals violet pink. An extremely floriferous and vigorous cultivar with long-lasting blooms.
(1998) (FEN)(BRE)(WAY)
(STM)(EX)(JAK)(BEL)(ROO)
(ALD)(HYDE)(CLI)(WHE)(FUC)
(ISL)(SMI)

Barnet Fair
Double H2 Lax Bush
Tube short and bright red. *Sepals* also bright red. *Corolla* petals the palest pink with red veining. Medium-sized blooms and very free-flowering for a double. Growth is rather lax with arching branches. Will make a good pot plant with some supports and an excellent plant for a hanging pot or basket.
(Dyos, UK, 1984) (OLI)

Baroness van Dedem
Single H2 Lax Bush
Tube red. *Sepals* red, short and folding back to the tube. *Corolla* aster violet, saucer-shaped when mature. Small to medium-sized flowers. *Foliage* small and mid-green. Excellent for small pots or hanging baskets.
(de Groot, Holland, 1980)
(SIL)(BRE)(BLA)(ISL)

Bart Simpson
Single H2 Trailer
Tubes long, thin and pink turning to rosy red. *Sepals* a darker shade of pink also maturing to rosy red. *Corolla* petals short and red. A spreading habit makes it a suitable candidate for hanging pots.
(Michiels, Holland, 1995)
(HYDE)

Basketful
Double H2 Trailer
Tube and *sepals* pink. *Corolla* white and pink. *Foliage* mid-green. Medium-sized blooms produced quite freely. Excellent for all types of hanging containers.
(Rainbows Fuchsias, UK, 1981)
(SIL)(FEN)(RKY)(ARC)(OAK)
(RIV)(BRY)(OLI)

Beacon 'Annie Elsie'
Single H2 Bush
This 'sport' of 'Beacon Rosa' has splashes of aubergine randomly on the petals and in some conditions even on the *sepals*. The random splashing on the clear pink of the *corolla* and the darker pink of the *sepals* adds a whole new depth to this beautiful plant with no two flowers being identical.
(Steward, UK, 1998)
(ARC)(MO)(BLA)

Beatrice Burtoft
Single H2 Bush
Tube and *sepals* red. *Corolla* deep rose. Flowers are held semi-erect and produced on stiff bushy growth. *Foliage* medium green.
(Bielby/Octoby, UK, 1992)
(KM)(BRE)(BUR)(WV)
(BEL)(CLI)(ISL)

Beau Nash
Single H2 Bush
Tube of medium length and very pale pink. *Sepals* are long and of a much deeper pink. *Corolla* petals fuchsia-purple. The smallish flowers are very freely produced early in the season. Growth is strong, upright and bushy. A small and neat impression is always given.
(Mrs E. Holmes, UK, 1976) (LOK)

BALCON QUEEN

BALI HI

BARBARA'S GEM

BARONESS VAN DEDEM

BASKETFUL

BEATRICE BURTOFT

Beautiful Bobbie
Double H2 Lax Bush
Tube and *sepals* pink. *Corolla*
petals lavender splashed with
pink and white. The good-sized
flowers are produced in
profusion. The lax growth will
make it suitable as a shrub (with
supports) or in a hanging basket.
(Allsop, UK, 1998) (LB)(ROO)

Beauty of Prussia
Double H2 Bush
Tube and *sepals* scarlet. *Corolla*
petals scarlet lake, veined with
scarlet. Medium-sized blooms
freely produced. *Foliage* dark and
shiny. Strong, upright and bushy
growth.
(Homes, UK, 1966)
(SIL)(WV)(ROO)(LOK)

Beauty of Trowbridge
Single H2 Bush
Tube thick, waxy creamy white.
Sepals recurved and also waxy
white. *Corolla* rosy cerise. *Foliage*
long medium green with serrated
edging. The fairly strong upright
growth makes this cultivar
suitable for training as a larger
structure.
(Lye, UK, 1881)
(FEN)(CL)(BRE)(ARC)(BRI)(WV)
(WAL)(CLI)(ISL)

Becky Jane
Single H1 Triphylla
A miniature Triphylla-type –
single flowered fuchsia. *Tube*
neon pink approximately ½in
(1cm) long. The small *sepals* and
the petals in the *corolla* also neon
pink. This plant carries miniature
flowers (slightly larger than those
generally recognized as
Enclandra). *Foliage* small and
medium green in colour. Will
produce a fine miniature
Standard.
(Pike, USA, 1985) (SIL)(ROO)

Bedfords Park
Single H2 Bush
Tube very short and white with a
tinge of pink. *Sepals* long, narrow
with the same colouring. *Corolla*
petals baby pink. Medium-sized

and very floriferous. Upright and
bushy growth very suitable for all
types of training.
(Rout, UK, 1988) (WV)

Belinda Jane
Single H2 Trailer
Tube and *sepals* waxy white.
Corolla salmon orange. A very
vigorous variety with a delightful
medium-sized single flower
displaying a true cascading habit.
(Fisher, UK, 1994) (STM)(HYDE)

Bella Madina
Single H2 Lax Bush/Trailer
Tube long and orange-pink.
Sepals rose cerise with yellowish
recurved tips. *Corolla* petals rose
cerise orange maturing to
mauvish-rose orange. *Foliage*
yellowish. The natural growth is
lax and it is a very easy grower.
The laxity of growth makes it an
ideal subject for all types of
training be it for bushes, baskets
or Standards.
(Weeks, UK, 1986) (BRY)

Bell Bottoms
Single H2 Bush
Tube light salmon. *Sepals*, that
are long, thin and curl back, are
pale orange to salmon. *Corolla*
petals open at first as purple with
a coral base but fade to smoky
orange. The medium-sized
blooms are very freely produced.
Foliage very light green turning
slightly darker in the later stages.
Growth is strongly upright and
bushy.
(Castro, USA, 1992) (CHA)(PER)

Belstead
Double H2 Bush
Tube white faintly shaded with
pink. *Sepals* horizontally held,
pinkish white with darker pink
tips. *Corolla* a deeper shade of
cerise pink with beautifully folded
petals. *Foliage* mid-green.
Upright, strong and bushy habit.
(Ted Stiff, UK, 1998) (PER)

Belvoir Lakes
Single H2 Bush
Sepals spinel red, tipped with

green. *Corolla* petals imperial
purple. There is a rose purple
colouring at the base of each
petal with red veining. A compact
bushy shrub growth that, with its
floriferousness, makes it an ideal
plant for the patio tub or the
show bench.
(Pacey, UK, 1980)
(WAY)

Ben de Jong
Single H1 Triphylla-Type
Triphylla-type with single flowers.
Tubes rose red. *Sepals* green.
Corolla bright orange. *Foliage* a
soft green. Flowers are produced
in terminal clusters of three or
four.
(Van den Burgh, Holland, 1994)
(LB)(BRE)(MO)(EX)(ROO)
(BLA)

Benjamin Pacey
Single H2 Bush
Sepals white, heavily tipped with
green. *Corolla* petals amethyst
violet. Medium-sized flowers
exceptionally freely produced.
Good bushy and upright growth.
(R. Pacey, UK, 1989) (FEN)

Ben Gunn
Single H2 Bush
Tube and *sepals* red. *Corolla*
petals aubergine. The miniature
flowers are produced in great
quantity. It is an excellent
cultivar to use when considering
growing fuchsias as bonsai
subjects.
(Ted Stiff, UK, 1996)
(LB)(PER)(HYDE)

Ben Jammin
Single H2 Bush
Tube pale pink. *Sepals* pink
flushed with pale aubergine.
Corolla dark aubergine. *Foliage*
medium to dark green. Medium-
sized flowers freely produced on
short-jointed plants. Very
distinctive colouring.
(Carless, UK, 1993)
(LB)(FOX)(RKY)(CL)(BRE)
(MO)(BLA)(EX)(CHA)(WV)
(PER)(GOU)(ROO)
(HYDE)(ISL)(LOK)

BEAUTIFUL BOBBIE

BEAUTY OF TROWBRIDGE

BELINDA JANE

BELSTEAD

BEN DE JONG

BEN JAMMIN

Ben Turner
Double H2 Bush
Tube and *sepals* soft flesh pink.
The petals in the very full *corolla*
are rich mauve. Strong upright
grower – makes a fine Standard.
('Ruby Wedding' × 'Dusted Pink')
(Forward, UK, 1996)
(WV)(FUC)(GLE)(ISL)

Beranger
Double H3 Bush
Tube and *sepals* deep cerise.
Corolla petals violet-blue
splashed with cerise/purple.
Small to medium flowers.
Foliage mid-green with a slight
brown vein. Small upright bush
good for the hardy border. H:
12in (30cm); S: 18in (45cm).
(Lemoine, France, 1897)
(SIL)(BAK)

Berba's Happiness
Double H2 Trailer
Large double flowers. *Tube*
greenish white. *Sepals* white,
flushed with pink. *Corolla*
cyclamen purple. Natural
trailing cultivar suitable for
baskets. *Foliage* fairly large and
mid-green.
(Bats, Holland, 1988)
(SIL)(EX)(BRI)(WV)(RIV)
(HYDE)

Berba's Trio
Semi-Double H2 Trailer
Tube and *sepals* pinkish white.
Corolla petals can be either white
or purple or a mixture of both.
Growth is lax so will make a
good hanging basket. Although
the flowers are quite large the
plant is very floriferous.
('La Campanella' × Bridesmaid')
(Wesseling, Holland, 1986)
(BRE)(WAY)(EX)(BRI)(ROO)
(BLA)

Bergerac
Single H2 Bush
Tube white with pink stripes.
Sepals white with small green
tips and flushed pale pink at the
base. *Corolla* petals ivory white
with pink veins. The large
blooms are freely produced. Like

all whites the best and purest
colour occurs when growing in
semi-shade. Rather lax bush so
will need some supporting or
will make a good subject for use
in hanging pots and baskets.
(Van den Bergh, Holland, 1993)
(ROO)

Berliner Kind
Double H2 Bush
Tube and *sepals* cerise/scarlet.
Corolla white veined with pink
at the base of the petals. Small
flowers very freely produced.
Low and small bushy growth.
(Eggbrecht, Germany, 1882)
(SIL)(WV)(BAK)(CLI)

Bermuda
Double H2 Bush
Has large, striking flowers.
Sepals velvety red. *Corolla* petals
dark purple with red flecks.
Growth is strong and upright.
(Lockerbie, Australia, 1960)
(SIL)(FEN)(KM)(WAY)(EX)
(ARC)(WV)(HYDE)(BRY)(OLI)

Bernadette
Double H2 Bush
Tube and *sepals* of these
medium-sized blooms pale rose.
Corolla petals veronica-blue.
Foliage small and dark green.
Growth is upright and bushy
with rather stiff laterals.
(Schnabel, USA, 1950)
(BRI)(WV)(BRY)

Bernard Rawdin
Single H2 Bush
Tube and *sepals* rose red.
Corolla cyclamen purple. Wide
bell-shaped blooms freely
produced. *Foliage* medium
green. Prefers to grow in partial
shade.
('Upward Look' × 'Caroline')
(Gadsby, UK, 1968)

Bernisser Stein
Semi-Double H2 Bush
Tube, *sepals* and *corolla* petals
all aubergine. *Foliage* mid-green.
A good strong bushy plant.
(Weeda, Holland, 1996)
(CLI)

Beryl Shaffery
Single H2 Bush
Tube and *sepals* pale pink. *Corolla*
upward-pointing, saucer-shaped are
pink with a hint of magenta.
Foliage is mid-green. Sturdily
upright in its growth and with its
self-branching habit will make an
excellent plant for the border, as a
show plant, or in patio tubs.
(Shaffery, UK, 1997)
(GOU)(PER)(ROO)

Beryl's Jewel
Single H2 Bush
Tube and *sepals* red. *Corolla* petals
purple. Foliage mid-green has some
variegation. Although the raiser is
unknown this plant was first
introduced by Lechlade Garden
Centre, Lechlade in 1985.
(Raiser unknown circa 1980)
(BRY)(OLI)

Betty Boots
Double H2 Trailer
A large-flowered cultivar. *Sepals*
long, slim and elegant white.
Corolla magenta pink. *Foliage* very
strong and healthy. Naturally a
trailer so will make an excellent
basket.
(Hutchinson, UK, 1997)(ALD)

Betty Jean
Double H2 Trailer
Tube and horizontally flared *sepals*
white. The numerous petals in the
corolla lavender blue with pink
marbling. Extremely floriferous.
The spreading growth and self-
branching habit make it an ideal
plant for hanging baskets or pots.
(Goulding, UK, 1998)
(GOU)(HYDE)

Big Charles
Double H2 Trailer
Tubes immensely long, thin and
white. *Sepals* shorter, arched and
white above a pink reverse. *Corolla*
frilly with mixed mauves and pinks.
Growth rather sparse. *Foliage*
medium green. Looks best in
hanging pots where the length of
the tubes can be appreciated.
(Moerman, Holland, 1988) (GOU)
(HYDE)

BERBA'S HAPPINESS

BERBA'S TRIO

BERYL SHAFFERY

BERYL'S JEWEL

BETTY JEAN

BIG CHARLES

Big Nellie
Single H2 Bush
Medium to large flowers. *Tube* and *sepals* deep red. *Corolla* petals white, veined with red. Very floriferous. Upright, bushy growth naturally branching as might be expected from a seedling of 'Mieke Meursing'.
(D. Downs, UK, 1987)
(BUR)

Big Slim
Single H2 Lax Bush
Tubes exceptionally long, thin and pale tangerine. *Sepals* smaller, spreading and also pale tangerine coloured. *Corollas* much darker orange. Growth is thin and requires early nipping and some support. A novelty.
(Sloots, Holland, 1994)
(GOU)(ROO)(HYDE)

Black Beauty
Double H2 Bush
Tube and *sepals* dark red. *Corolla* petals very deep purple. Large blooms. Growth is upright and very vigorous.
(Fairclo, USA, 1952)
(SIL)(WV)(CLI)

Blackberry Ripple
Double H2 Lax Bush
Large-flowered fuchsia. *Sepals* pink. The multi-petals in the *corolla* are violet. The fairly upright growth is rather lax so will make an excellent pot plant with supports and will also make an excellent basket.
(BEL)

Blackmore Vale
Double H2 Bush
Tubes and *sepals* rose, blushed red. *Corolla* petals red streaked with dark rose. The full flared petals and the delightful texture to the sepals make a very attractive flower. Growth is strongly upright and bushy. An excellent choice for large containers on the patio.
(Forward, UK, 1993)
(WV)(FUC)(GLE)(ISL)

Black Prince
Single H2 Bush
Synonymous with 'Gruss aus dem Bodethal'. *Tube* and *sepals* red. *Corolla* very deep (almost black) purple. *Foliage* medium green. An excellent cultivar for the show bench. Can be trained with weights for a basket.
('Cupido' × 'Creusa')
(Sattler and Bethga, Germany, 1893) (SIL)(ROU)(RKY)(WAR)(BRE)(MO)(BUR)(WAY)(STM)(EX)(ARC)(CHA)(BEL)(RID)(BRY)(CLI)(ASK)(FUC)(GLE)(ISL)(OLI)

Blackwell's Mr Potter
Double H2 Trailer
Tube and fairly long *sepals* of this very vigorous growing plant bright red. *Corolla* petals darker red. In spite of the size of the bloom the flowers are very freely produced. Growth is naturally trailing but is rather stiff and may require some assistance to cover the sides of a basket.
(Blackwell, UK, 1990) (BLA)

Blau Gotteburg
Semi-Double H2/H3 Bush
Sepals of this early flowering plant red. *Corolla* petals blue. Growth is rather short but compact, self-branching and low-growing. H: about 18in (45cm) and could be useful in the hardy border.
(FUC)

Blaze Away
Double H2 Trailer
Tube and *sepals* of this medium-sized double flower vermilion red. *Corolla* petals of the same glorious colour. The natural desire of this plant is to trail and it will therefore make an excellent hanging container.
(Sinton, UK, 199?) (FEN)(ROU)(BRE)(WAY)(STM)(EX)(WAL)(FUC)(GLE)

Bliss
Semi-Double H2 Bush
Tube light pink veined with

green. *Sepals* light pink on the top, slightly crêped light pink on the undersurface with long, apple green tips maturing to rose. *Corolla* petals open very pale lavender veined with darker lavender and a white blush at the base. Upright self-branching plant that flowers continuously.
(Shaffery, UK, 1998)
(ROO)

Blondchen
Tube of this little known German raising reddish pink. *Sepals* also of the same colouring. *Corolla* petals white. The blooms are of medium size and are fairly freely produced on self-branching upright growth.
(Mrs L. Rapp, Germany, 1982)
(BRI)

Blood Donor
Double H2 Bush
The medium-sized flowers contain interesting colour combinations. *Tube*, *sepals* and *corolla* petals all red in varying tones. *Foliage* mid-green and heart-shaped. The plant has exceptional flowering ability starting early in the season and continuing right through to the end. Named to commemorate the anniversary of the formation of the blood transfusion service.
(Bielby/Oxtoby, UK, 1996)
(KM)(FEN)(RKY)(MO)(BAL)(JAK)(ALD)(RIV)(ISL)

Blue Eyes
Double H2 Lax Bush
Tube and *sepals* pale pink. *Corolla* petals bright blue. The flowers are fairly large but are freely produced. Growth is bushy but rather lax. It will therefore need supporting if grown as a bush but will do well in a hanging container. Does not object to frequent 'stopping'.
(Reedstrom, USA, 1954)
(ISL)(FOX)(FEN)(BRE)(STM)(CHA)(PER)(BEL)(FUC)(GLE)(OLI)

BIG SLIM

BLAZE AWAY

BLACK PRINCE

BLOOD DONOR

Blue Haze
Double H2 Bush
Tube and *sepals* pink. *Corolla* petals wisteria blue overlaid with pink. Medium-sized half-flared blooms with a beautiful colour combination. An easy plant to grow. Good, strong, upright plant.
(Sharpe, New Zealand, 1987) (ISL)

Blue Mirage
Double H2 Trailer
Tube and *sepals* white with a pink flush. *Corolla* pink through to blue – full and compact. Growth is strong and self-branching. *Foliage* dark green. Suitable for hanging pots or baskets.
(Bellamy, UK, 1984) (SIL)(FOX) (FEN)(ROU)(RKY)(WAR)(CL) (BRE)(WAY)(STM)(EX)(BRI) (CHA)(WV)(WAL)(BEL)(RID) (RIV)(HYDE)(BRY)(CLI)(ASK) (GLE)(ISL)(SMI)(OLD)(OLI)

Blue Mist
Double H2 Trailer
Tube and *sepals* rosy pink. *Corolla* petals blue and pink. A natural trailing variety that will make a good basket. Flowers medium-sized.
(Tiret, USA, 1964) (BAK)(RKY)(RIV)

Blue Peter
Double H2 Bush
Tube and *sepals* of these large-flowered plants pinkish white. *Corolla* imperial purple. Very attractive and eye-catching flowers. *Foliage* mid-green.
(M. Porter, UK, 1985) (EX)(RID)(LOK)

Blue Petticoat
Double H2 Trailer
Tube and *sepals* white with the palest blush of pink on the inside of the sepals. Corolla petals a beautiful shade of silvery lilac-lavender, turning to orchid pink with age. Medium-sized blooms. Best grown as a trailer.
(Evans and Reeves, USA, 1954) (BRI)(LOK)

Bob Armbruster
Double H2 Bush
Tube and *sepals* brilliant bright scarlet. *Corolla* petals dark blue violet. The large-sized flowers are freely produced. *Foliage* bright green and leaves are slightly lighter on the underside. Good, strong, upright and bushy plant. ('Clio' × 'Voodoo')
(W. Walker, USA, 1981) (FEN)

Bobby's Girl
Single H2 Bush
Tube and *sepals* carmine. *Corolla* petals orchid blue. Good, strong, upright grower.
(Raiser unknown) (RKY)(POT)

Bobolink
Double H2 Bush
Tube and the upturned *sepals* flesh pink. The petals in the large *corolla* intense blue violet. The petals fold together rather loosely. The flowers are very freely produced. Growth is naturally upright on strong self-branching stems.
(Evans and Reeves, USA, 1953) (WAY)(ARC)

Bob's Choice
Single H2 Bush
White *tube*. *Sepals* white with china rose flush, tipped with green. *Corolla* white with rose/purple veining at base of petals. Large flowers. Free-flowering on strong, upright growth.
(Pacey, UK, 1982) (EX)(BRI)(WV)(ASK)

F. boliviana var. **Pink Trumpet**
Species Variant H1 Bush
Tube very long and pale pink. *Sepals* pinkish white. *Corolla* bright red. Strong and vigorous growth. *Foliage* very large, sage green with white velvety sheen and softly hairy.
(J.O. Wright, UK, 1981) (ASK)

Bonnie Bambini
Single H2 Bush
Tube and *sepal* crimson. *Corolla* petals mallow purple. *Foliage*
lime green with two definite variations in colour. 'Sport' from 'Bambini'. The flowers are small, almost miniature but very floriferous. The plant is ideal for use in small pots or as a bonsai. Growth, although small, is short-jointed and vigorous.
(R. Dering, UK, 1997) (OLD)

Bonny
Double H2 Bush
Tube and *sepals* rosy red. *Corolla* petals white. The medium-sized blooms that are fairly free-flowering, have a ruffled appearance, have some petaloids and are veined rosy red. Growth is as an upright and compact bush. Excellent for use in pots for the show bench.
(E.M. Holmes, UK, 1978) (LOK)(EX)(WV)

Bookham Beauty
Double H2 Trailer
Tube and *sepals* pale pink. *Corolla* petals pale beetroot colour. A small-flowered double that will be excellent for hanging pots.
(Meier, UK, 1998) (LB)

Bora Bora
Double H2 Trailer
Tube white, faintly pink. *Sepals* white. *Corolla* purplish blue, fading to pinkish purple with small green petaloids. *Foliage* light green. Excellent for baskets given suitably ventilated conditions. Very bushy trailer, self-branching and free-flowering. Prefers shade.
(Tiret, USA, 1966) (SIL)(FOX)(FEN)(RKY)(KM) (EX)(BRI)(CHA)(WV)(BAK) (OAK)(RIV)(HYDE)(BRY)(CLI) (GLE)(ISL)(OLI)

BLUE MIRAGE

BLUE PETER

F. *BOLIVIANA* VAR. PINK TRUMPET

BONNIE BAMBINI

BOOKHAM BEAUTY

BORA BORA

Borde Hill
Double H2 Bush
Tube and *sepals* of this good-sized flower deep rose. *Corolla* petals blue violet. It is likely to make an excellent plant for the hardy border. Introduced on the occasion of the 60th Anniversary celebrations of the British Fuchsia Society, held at Borde Hill, Haywards Heath, Sussex in 1998. (Dyos, UK, 1998) (LB)(SIM)

Border Princess
Single H2 Bush
Tube short, thin and pink. *Sepals* pink on the upper surface and rose veined darker rose on the underside. *Corolla* petals white with pink veining near the base. A 'sport' of 'Border Queen'. (Collins, UK, 1988) (SIM)(CL)(RIV)

Bornemann's Beste
Triphylla-Type H1 Bush
A very strong growing plant. *Tube*, *sepals* and *corolla* all orange red. Flowers are produced in terminal clusters. *Foliage* largish and green with slight purple reverse. (Bonstedt, Germany, 1904) (SIL)(FOX)(ROU)(RKY)(KM) (CL)(LB)(BRI)(MO)(CHA)(OLD) (WV)(PER)(BAK)(BRY)(CLI) (ASK)(WHE)(GLE)(ISL)(SMI) (SIM)(LOK)

Born Free
Double H2 Bush
Tube and *sepals* a delightful creamy white. *Corolla* petals magenta white, flushed with pink at the base. The medium-sized blooms are freely produced. Very similar to 'Rosy Frills'. Growth is upright and bushy. (Raiser unknown, introduced by Underhill Fuchsias, UK, 1980) (ROU)

Bosom Pals
Single H2 Bush
Tube and *sepals* of this delightful flower blood red. *Corolla* petals violet. A very attractive self-branching bush that flowers profusely. (R. Homes, UK, 1998) (OLD)

Boson's Nora
Single H2 Bush
Tube long and salmon orange. *Sepals* also the same attractive salmon orange. *Corolla* petals salmon. The medium-sized flowers are almost 'self-coloured'. The most important feature is the long tube. A naturally upright and self-branching growing plant that makes a very good bush. (Granger, UK, 1979) (RIV)

Boy Blue
Double H3 Bush
Tube and *sepals* bright red. *Sepals* reflex to hide the tube. *Corolla* petals deep blue. The small star-shaped flowers very prolific. A good miniature hardy. *Foliage* mid-green. Upright, bushy and compact but only attaining a height of approx 6in (15cm). One of a series of miniature hardy fuchsias introduced by Tabraham in 1987. (Tabraham, UK, 1987) (BEL)(HYDE)

Boy Marc
Single H1 Triphylla-Type
This triphylla-type fuchsia has long *tube*, short *sepals* and *corolla* petals that are all orange. The flowers are bright and long-lasting. The habit is robust, self-branching and compact. The lax growth make it one of the few triphyllas suitable for hanging pots and tubs. (Stannard, UK, 1995) (GOU) (RKY)(CL)(ROO)(PER)

Boy Tom
Double H2 Lax Bush
Medium-sized flower. *Tubes* and *sepals* red. *Corolla* petals purple. The lax growth makes it suitable for use in hanging pots, or in tubs if given some supports. (Raiser unknown) (BEL)

Breach Lane Lady
Single H2 Lax Bush
'Sport' of 'Lady Kathleen Spence'. *Sepals* pale pink, tipped with green. *Corolla* a delicate lavender shade veined with pink at the base. *Foliage* golden, and very attractive. Its rather lax growth makes it ideal for growing as a bush (with supports) or in a hanging container. Very heat-tolerant. (Haskins, UK, 1997) (BRE) (*See* photograph on page 59.)

Brenda Megan Hill
Single H2 Bush
Tube short and blush pink. *Sepals*, which are held in the horizontal position, blush pink on the upper surface and coral pink on the underside. *Corolla* petals deep lavender with pink undertones. The medium-sized flowers are freely produced. *Foliage* mid-green. Best colour of flower is found when the plants are grown in semi-shade. Tall, upright and bushy. (Hill, UK, 1982) (RIV)

Brenda Moss
Single H2 Bush
Tube and *sepals* of this delightful flower white. *Corolla* petals garnet red. The natural growth is as an upright self-branching plant. Named after a delightful lady and very keen ambassador for fuchsias in East Anglia. (Stiff, UK, 1998) (BAK)(PER) (*See* photograph on page 59.)

Brentwood
Semi-Double H2 Bush
Tube and *sepals* waxy white, the latter being tipped with green. *Corolla* petals are near white also edged with pale green. The medium-sized flowers are very charming but the plant has the disadvantage of flowering in flushes. Growth is as a low bush, compact but not vigorous. Has been used extensively in hydridizing programmes as it was probably the first of the near whites. ('Rolla' × 'Duchess of Albany') (Evans and Reeves, USA, 1936) (BAK)

BORDE HILL

BOSOM PALS

BORNEMANN'S BESTE

BOY MARC

Brian A. McDonald

Brian A. McDonald
Double H2 Semi-Trailer
Tubes and fully recurving sepals
light tangerine. *Corolla* petals in
the centre rich salmon, the outer
petals marbled with tangerine.
Spreading habit. Ideal for
sheltered baskets. Could be useful
in other containers as a bush
provided that supports were in
position.
(Goulding, UK, 1996)
(GOU)(WV)(HYDE)

Brian Ellis
Single H2 Trailer
Tube and *sepals* very pale pink.
Corolla petals dark pink. A good
trailing basket variety that carries
its medium to large-sized flowers
over a long period.
(ARC)

Brian G. Soanes
Single H2 Bush
Tube and *sepals* of this upright
and strong growing plant red.
Corolla petals rich lilac. *Foliage*
mid-green. The strong growth
makes it an excellent plant for
use in large pots or on the patio.
(Stiff, UK, 1992)
(BAK)(FEN)(RIV)(CLI)

Brian Kimberley
Single H1 Bush
A terminal-type flowering fuchsia.
Tubes long and thin. *Sepals* short
and *corolla* petals quite small.
The flower is a complete orange
'self'. Very floriferous and has the
attribute of holding its flowers for
a long time. Growth is strongly
upright and, as with most
triphylla-types, is very heat-
tolerant. Would be ideal as a
show plant or in large tubs.
(Goulding, UK, 1999)
(GOU)

Brian Stannard
Single H2 Bush
Tube medium-sized, flesh-
coloured. *Sepals* are flesh-
coloured, recurved and upswept.
Corolla petals have an attractive
lavender hue with a hint of rosy
red. The base of the petals shades

to white. Medium-sized flowers
are freely produced. Growth is
very strong and upright with
plenty of side shoots on spreading
branches.
(Goulding, UK, 1988)
(GOU)(FEN)(CL)(WV)(RIV)

Briarlee
Single H2 Bush
Tube and *sepals* of this delicate
single flower pale pink. The
sepals turn back onto the tube.
Corolla petals also pale pink. An
excellent bushy plant with its
upright growth and delicacy of
flower and will also make a good
Standard.
(Strawson, UK, 1998) (WAL)

Brigadoon
Double H2 Bush
Tube pink. *Sepals* long, broad,
recurved and pink. *Corolla* violet
blue overlaid and marbled near
the base with fuchsia pink.
Blooms are large and free.
Growth upright and bushy
although could also be described
as a willowy grower.
(Erickson, USA, 1957)
(LOK)(FEN)(BRI)(WV)
(RIV)(BAK)

Brixham Orpheus
Single H2 Bush
Tube medium-length venetian
pink. The long *sepals*, that are
held out to just below the
horizontal, venetian pink on the
outer surface and azalea pink on
the inner. *Corolla* petals blood
red. Medium-sized flowers with
long pistil and large yellow
stigma. Growth upright and
bushy.
(R. Holmes, UK, 1981)
(BRI)(WV)(ROO)(BRY)

Broadbent
Double H2 Bush
Tube and *sepals* of this medium-
sized flower light pink. *Corolla*
petals lilac. A very attractive
colour combination. *Foliage* is
mid-green. Growth is upright and
bushy.
(RIV)

Brodsworth
Single H2 Bush
Tube and *sepals* cherry red to
scarlet. *Corolla* petals deep
purple. Medium-sizes flowers very
freely produced. Growth is as an
upright bush. Extremely useful
grown in the hardy border.
(B. Nuttall, UK, 1977)
(SIL)(FEN)(RKY)(ASK)(SMI)

Brookwood Dale
Single H2 Bush
Flowers are held erect from the
plant. *Sepals* pale pink. *Corolla*
petals a deeper pink and semi-
flared. Very free-flowering. Good,
strong, upright-growing plant.
(Gilbert, UK, 1997)
(BLA)(CLI)(WHE)

Brookwood Gem
Single H2 Bush
Sepals and *tube* rose-coloured.
Corolla petals mauve. The
blooms that are freely produced
are held horizontally.
(Gilbert, UK, 1996)
(BLA)

Brookwood Lady
Single H2 Bush
Tube and *sepals* white. *Corolla*
petals blue. Very floriferous.
Flowers are held horizontally. The
hydridizer produced just a few
cultivars bearing the Brookwood
prefix but all are well worth
growing. Careful selection
produced plants that were all of
show bench quality.
(Gilbert, UK, 1995)
(BLA)(WHE)

Brookwood Petite
Single H2 Bush
Tube and *sepals* pink. *Corolla*
petals violet. Upward-looking,
medium-sized flowers. Very
floriferous.
(Gilbert, UK, 1996)
(BLA)

58

BREACH LANE LADY

BRENDA MOSS

BRIAN STANNARD

BRODSWORTH

Bryan Breary
Single H2 Bush
Encliandra-type of fuchsia. The thin willowy or wiry stems carry very small *foliage* and very small flowers. Close examination is necessary to convince oneself that this is a fuchsia. Devotees of the Encliandra-type fuchsias can make very good collections. Very bushy with small pink flowers that darken with age.
(Breary, UK, 1995)
(KM)(GOU)(ROO)

Bubba Jack
Single H2 Bush
Tube and *sepals* crimson. *Corolla* petals a delightful shade of lavender. Good, strong and upright growth.
(Waving, UK, 1998) (SIM)

Bud Stubbs
Double H2 Trailer
Tube short, stubby and scarlet. *Sepals* that are fully reflexed also scarlet. *Corolla* petals white veined with red and with smooth edges. The flowers are of medium size. *Foliage* medium green. Self-branching fairly stiff trailer, very short on the internodes. May require the assistance of weights to make a good basket.
(Garrett, USA, 1986) (EX)

Bugle Boy
Single H1 Bush
This triphylla-type fuchsia carries its flowers in terminal bunches. *Tube* long, dark rose. *Sepals* also dark rose. *Corolla* petals small and orange. Very attractive and well worth trying.
(*F. vulcanica* × 'Fanfare')
(Jones, USA, 1991)
(GOU)(ISL)

Burma Star
Double H2 Bush
Sepals cerise. *Corolla* petals imperial purple with a touch of orange at the base. Petals age to ruby red. The blooms are medium-sized and fully double. The natural growth is upright,

short-jointed and compact.
(W.E. Wilson, UK, 1989)
(FEN)(ASK)

Burnside
Single H2 Bush
Tube thin, short and pale cerise. *Sepals* recurved half up, pale cerise on top and slightly paler underneath. *Corolla* opens mauve-purple veined cerise and matures slightly paler with smooth turned-under petal edges. *Foliage* yellow and green variegation, best colour in bright light. 'Sport' of 'Pixie'.
(Downs, UK, 1986) (BUR)

Burton Brew
Single H2 Bush
Tube and *sepals* rose red, turning up with underside deep rose. *Corolla* white with deep rose veining. Very free-flowering medium-sized blooms. *Foliage* dark green and glossy. Upright growth.
(Plant, UK, 1996) (JAK)(FEN)

Buttercup
Single H2 Bush
Tube and *sepals* pale pink. *Corolla* orange. *Foliage* medium green. Medium-sized flowers freely produced. The medium upright growth makes it ideal for bush or Standard training. Colours show best in the shade.
(Paskesen, USA, 1976)
(SIL)(FEN)(ROU)(RKY)(EX)
(ARC)(CHA)(WV)(BAK)(ROO)
(BRY)(RIV)(CLI)(ASK)(FUC)
(GLE)(ISL)(OLD)(OLI)(LOK)

Butterfly
Single H2 Trailer
Tube and recurved *sepals* bengal rose. *Corolla* bengal rose and crimson at the base. Almost a self-coloured flower. Flowers are large and free. Trailing style of growth.
(Reiter, USA, 1942) (ASK)

Buttons and Bows
Double H2 Bush
Tube and *sepals* red. The very full *corolla* has white petals that open

into a cup-shape. *Foliage* small and stiff. Growth is upright and bushy.
(Machedo, USA, 1962) (WV)

Byron Rees
Double H2 Lax Bush
Tubes ivory white. *Sepals* a delightful pale salmon. *Corolla* petals rather darker salmon with orange marbling. In spite of the large size of the flowers, the plants are muti-flowered. Growth is strong, upright and arching. Excellent when used in large tubs or in hanging containers.
(Goulding, UK, 1998)
(GOU)

C

Caesar
Double H2 Lax Bush or Trailer
Tube and *sepals* red. *Corolla* purple fading to burgundy. The large flowers are produced fairly freely. Petals curl to a rose-shaped bloom. *Foliage* medium green. Will need some supports to make a good bush. Can be trained as a basket with weights.
(Fuchsia Forest, USA, 1967)
(BAK)(FOX)(FEN)(BRE)(WAY)
(EX)(ARC)(CHA)(WV)(RIV)(BRY)
(CLI)(ASK)(FUC)(GLE)(ISL)

California
Single H2 Bush
Tube and *sepals* orange pink. *Corolla* petals bright orange. *Foliage* light green. The flowers are of medium size and are freely produced. Growth is naturally upright and bushy. Well worth trying as a Standard with its strong upward growth.
('Fireflush' × unnamed seedling)
(Evans and Reeves, USA, 1936)
(ROU)

Camarade
Single H2 Bush
Has medium-sized flowers. *Sepals* deep red. *Corolla* petals blackish purple. Good, strong, upright growth.
(Masse, France, 1985) (BAK)

BRYAN BREARY

BUBBA JACK

BUTTERCUP

CAESAR

F. campii (Green)

F. campii (Green)
Single H1 Species
Tubes long, gently tapering and pink. *Sepals* short and pink. *Corolla* petals also pink. Axillary flowering near the branch ends. *Foliage* green and growth spreading unless supported. Easy to grow.
(GOU)

F. campii var. rubra
Single H1 Species
Tubes long and gently tapering. *Sepals* short and red. *Corolla* also red. Leaf veins and young branches are tinged with red. Growth requires some support unless plants are grown in baskets.
(GOU)

Cancun
Double H2 Bush
Tube and *sepals* pink orange. *Corolla* petals red-purple. The flowers are large and fully double. Good, strong, upright growth.
(Redfern, UK, 1994)
(JAK)(FEN)(EX)

Candy Kisses
Double H2 Bush
Sepals of the large flowers creamy white splashed with pink. *Corolla* petals also creamy white and splashed with pink.
('String of Pearls' ×)
(Laburnum, UK, 1986)
(STM)(RIV)(FUC)

Candy Stripe
Single H2 Bush
Tube and *sepals* pink, deeper on the underside. *Tube* shortish with *sepals* curling attractively upwards. *Corolla* starting pink and changing to pale violet. Excellent fuchsia for the show bench.
(Endicott, UK, 1965)(LOK)(WV)

Cannenburch Floriant
Single H2 Trailer
Tubes long and dark pink. *Sepals* are also long but paler pink with green tips. *Corolla* petals salmon to orange. Growth is long-jointed

and pendant. Best growing in mixed baskets.
(Stoel, Holland, 1991) (RKY)

Canny Bob
Single H2 Bush
Tubes and *sepals* white. *Corolla* petals fluorescent pink. The flowers are held clear and erect from the foliage.
('Bon Accord' × 'Lyes Unique')
(Hewitson, UK, 1997)
(JAK)(ARC)(PER)

Canopy
Double H2 Trailer
Tube and *sepals* pink. *Corolla* large, petals magenta and pink. The large blooms are carried very freely and a very lovely basket can be grown.
('Cheers' × 'Ruby Wedding')
(Forward, UK, 1993)
(BRI)(WV)

Capt. Al Sutton
Semi-Double H2 Trailer
Tube and fully reflexed *sepals* bright red. *Corolla* petals rose red with white insertions. The natural habit is strongly spreading. Best if grown in full or wall baskets. An excellent and attractive flower.
(Goulding, UK, 1999)
(GOU)

Captivating Kelly
Double H2 Trailer
Tube long and pink. *Sepals* pale pink darker near the tube. *Corolla* petals pink splashed with red, mauve, orange and lilac. A very free-flowering trailer and will make an excellent basket. The blooms are very attractive.
(Allsop, UK, 1996) (ROO)

Caradella
Single H2 Trailer
Sepals bright pink. *Corolla* petals violet pink with deeper picotee edging. A very free-flowering trailer with little fading of the blooms. Excellent for all hanging containers.
(Delaney, UK, 1992)
(BLA)(LB)(BRE)(ALD)

Cardinal
Single H2 Bush
Tube and *sepals* dark red. *Corolla* petals rich dark red. An extremely vigorous and upright-growing fuchsia. Will make an excellent Standard in a very short time.
(Evans and Reeves, USA, 1938)
(FOX)(ARC)(BRI)(CHA)(FUC)
(GLE)

Carefree
Double H2 Bush
Medium-sized flowers. *Tubes* white. *Sepals* very broad and tipped with green. *Corolla* petals pale pink, flushed with rose bengal. Very rich colouring. Floriferous.
(Pacey, UK, 1984) (BRI)(WV)

Carillon van Amsterdam
Single H2 Lax Bush
Medium-sized flowers. *Tubes* long, slender and red. *Sepals*, also slender, are red with green tips and stand out at the horizontal. *Corolla* petals dark red. Growth is as a lax bush or as a trailer.
(van Wieringen, Holland, 1970)
(FEN)(WAY)(ROO)(RIV)(WHE)
(FUC)

Carioka
Single H2 Lax Bush
Tube and *sepals* rose cerise with green tips. *Corolla* petals purple changing to rosy carmine. The medium-sized flowers open spreading flat. Very floriferous. The lax bushy growth needs supports if grown as a bush but will make an excellent subject for a hanging pot.
(Schmidt, USA, 1951)
(BAK)(RIV)

Carisbrook Castle
Double H2 Trailer
Tube and *sepals* white. *Corolla* petals marbled in pale lilac and white. The flowers are freely produced and naturally trailing. Will make an excellent basket.
(Porter, UK, 1993) (KM)

CANCUN

CANNY BOB

CAPTIVATING KELLY

CARADELLA

Carleton Blue
Single H2 Trailer
Small to medium-sized flowers. *Tubes* white. *Sepals* white flushed with pink. *Corolla* petals vivid blue. The lax habit and an abundance of flowers make it an excellent plant for hanging containers. Well worth using as a weeping Standard.
(('Harry Lye' × 'Coquet Dale') × 'Midwinter')
(George Evans, UK, 1998) (BUR)

Carmen
Semi-Double H3 Bush
Sepals glossy cerise. *Corolla* petals purple with red veins and small petaloids purple splashed with pink. Small flowers but profuse. Mid-green *foliage*. Height of growth in open garden no more than 15in (39cm). Excellent for the hardy border. (Acceptable on the show bench.)
(Lemoine, France, 1893)
(SIL)(FEN)(BAK)

Carmen Maria
Single H2 Trailer
Tube pink. *Sepals* which are long and narrow standing straight up, are real pink. The four petals in the *corolla* overlap and are baby pink with deeper pink veins. The blooms are of medium size. A very prolific bloomer of perfect shape. The growth is lax bush or trailer so can be used as a bush if given supports or in a hanging container.
('Sport' of 'Leonora')
(Breitner, USA, 1970) (CL)(WAY)(STM)(ARC)(JAK)(RIV)(BRY)

Carnea
Single H2/3 Bush
Sepals red. *Corolla* petals purple. Small flowers. *Sepals* open about 25 per cent with flared corolla just showing. *Foliage* small and pale green. Excellent for the front of a hardy border with H: 12in (30cm).
(Smith, UK, 1861) (SIL)(BRY)

Carole Scott
Double H2 Trailer
Large blooms. *Tubes* and *sepals* magenta. *Corolla* petals dark

reddish purple. *Foliage* medium green on the upper surface and slightly lighter on the lower. Excellent for basket work.
('Hula Girl' × 'Seventh Heaven')
(Brough/Laburnum, UK, 1989)
(FOX)(CHA)

Carol Nash
Double H2 Bush
Tube medium-length and white. *Sepals* white, tipped with green, crêpy on the underside, medium and broad. *Corolla* a full white, slightly flushed with pink. Petals are short and the blooms medium-large in size. Upright, strong grower.
(Dyos, UK, 1992) (LOK)

Catharina
Single H1 Bush
Triphylla-type flower. A dark red self with a thin *Tube* and small *sepals* and *corolla* petals. Growth strongly upright. *Foliage* darkly stained with red. Taller than most triphyllas so will do best at the back of a border.
(Smits, Holland, 1995) (ISL)

Cecile
Double H2 Trailer
Tube thick and pink. *Sepals* deep pink curling back from the lavender blue *corolla*. Fairly large flowers and plentiful for a double. *Foliage* medium green.
(Whitfield, USA, 1981) (SIL)(FOX)(FEN)(RKY)(KM)(WAR)(LB)(BRE)(WAY)(VER)(EX)(ARC)(JAK)(BRI)(CHA) (WV)(PER) (BEL)(GOU)(BLA)(ALD)(RID)(RIV)(HYDE)(POT)(BRY)(CLI)(ASK)(WHE)(FUC)(GLE)(ISL)(SMI)(OLI)

Celia Smedley
Single H2 Bush
Tube and *sepals* neyron rose. *Corolla* vivid currant red. *Foliage* largish leaves of medium green. Growth is extremely strong and vigorous and with careful pinching produces an excellent bush or Standard in just one season. One of the very best.
(Chance seedling from 'Pepi')

(Bellamy, UK, 1970) (SIL)(FOX)(FEN)(ROU)(RKY)(KM)(WAR)(CL)(LB)(BRE)(MO)(BUR)(WAY)(VER)(STM)(EX)(ARC)(JAK)(BRI)(CHA)(WV)(WAL)(PER)(BEL)(BAK)(GOU)(ROO)(BLA)(RID)(ALD)(RIV)(HYDE)(POT)(BRY)(CLI)(ASK)(WHE)(FUC)(GLE)(ISL)(OLD)(OLI)(SIM)(LOK)

Central Scotland
Single H2 Trailer
Medium-sized flowers very freely produced. *Sepals* red. *Corolla* petals light purple or bright violet. Excellent trailing cultivar for basket work.
(Reynolds, UK, 1992)
(PER)(HYDE)(CLI)
(*See* photograph on page 67.)

Chalk 'n' Cheese
Double H2 Bush
Medium-sized flowers. *Tube* and *sepals* pale pink. *Corolla* petals lavender. Growth is strong, self-branching and upright. Makes a very balanced plant suitable for the show bench quite easily.
(Coupland, UK, 1995) (BUR)

Chameleon
Single H2 Bush
Sepals red. *Corolla* pink edged with purple. *Foliage* beautiful – yellowish green leaves overlaid with red/bronze with red veining. Smaller than 'Autumnale' with much softer growth.
(Dowson, UK, 1991) (SIL)(FEN)(ROU)(WAY)(STM)(EX)(ARC)(BRI)(CHA)(CLI)(FUC)(GLE)(OLI)

Champagne Celebration
Single H2 Bush
Tube very pale pink. *Sepals* also very pale pink at base blending to deeper pink with green tips. The sepals are well reflexed when fully open. *Corolla* shades from palest pink to imperial purple edged with salmon, maturing to pale magenta. The stamens are long with spiraea-red anthers. An excellent grower.
(S.M. Jones, UK, 1988)
(RKY)(EX)(ISL)(LOK)

CARMEN

CAROLE SCOTT

CARNEA

CECILE

CELIA SMEDLEY

Champagne Gold
Single H2 Bush
Tube long and white. *Sepals*
orange. *Corolla* petals bright red.
The medium-sized blooms are
freely produced. Good, strong,
upright and bushy growth.
(F. Holmes, UK, 1989) (RIV)

Chancellor
Double H2 Bush
Tube and *sepals* pink. *Corolla*
opens dark red purple streaked
rose and matures to magenta
streaked with rose. Good,
upright, bushy plant.
(Forward, UK, 1993)
(WV)(FUC)(GLE)(ISL)

Charles Edward Forward
Double H2/3 Bush
Tube pale orange. *Sepals* rose.
Corolla petals purple with a
white base and veined with red.
Upright bush that is probably
very hardy. H: 24in (60cm).
(Rolt, UK, 1992)
(KM)(EX)(ROO)(SIL)

Charles Lester
Single H2 Bush
Tube and *sepals* cardinal red.
Corolla petals bishop's violet red.
A very vigorous upright grower
that is self-branching and makes a
good balanced bush.
(R. Holmes, UK, 1999) (OLD)

Charles A. Remnant
Double H2 Bush
Sepals cardinal red. *Corolla* petals
aster violet veined with red, and
fading to violet purple giving a
lovely two-tone effect. Upright,
self-branching growth.
(R. Holmes, UK, 1998)
(OLD)

Charlot Reane
Single H2 Bush
Tube and *sepals* of the medium-
sized flowers light pink. *Corolla*
petals a darker shade of pink.
The good, strong, upward and
bushy growth makes this an ideal
type of plant to use when
growing Standards.
(W. Smith, UK, 19??) (CLI)

Charlotte Clyne
Single H2 Bush
Small single flower. An all-white
flower that stays white. *Tube*,
sepals and *corolla* are a perfect
white, although there is a faint
touch of pink at the base of the
reflexing sepals. The flowers are
beautifully bell-shaped and are
produced over a long period.
Foliage light green. Growth can
be described as small to medium
upright with a good self-
branching habit. A nice cultivar
well worth growing.
(Clyne, UK, 1990)
(JAK)(ISL)

Charlotte Paige
Single H2 Bush
Large flowers. *Tube* and *sepals*
pale pink and quite long.
Corolla petals pinkish violet,
streaked with whitish pink.
Upright and self-branching
growth.
(Brigadoon Fuchsias, UK, 1995)
(BRI)

Charlotte Summers
Double H2 Bush
Tube and *sepals* of this
delightful flower are of the
palest pink. *Corolla* petals
creamy white. The natural
growth is as an upright, self-
branching and bushy plant.
(Summers, UK, 1994)
(BLA)

Chase Delight
Single H2 Bush
This variegated *leaved* 'sport'
from 'Lady Kathleen Spence' has
its parents' whitish rose *sepals*
and delicate lavender petals in
the *corolla*. Retains the
floriferousness of its parent. The
variegation is very attractive and
gives an added dimension to a
patio tub or even a hanging
basket.
(Chase Fuchsias, UK, 1992)
(ISL)(STM)(EX)(CHA)(CLI)
(FUC)(GLE)

Chase Gold
Single H2/3 Bush
This plant, being a 'sport' of
'White Pixie' has the same
characteristics and flower colour.
Will make an ideal addition to
the hardy border although
perhaps a little more care will
need to be given to its winter
protection. *Tube* and *sepals* red.
Corolla petals white. *Foliage* has
delightful variegation.
(Chase Fuchsias, UK, 1996)
(STM)(EX)(CHA)(GLE)

Chase Joy
Single H2 Bush
Tube and *sepals* rose. *Corolla*
petals purple. The flowers are of
medium size and are produced
very freely. *Foliage* is a delightful
yellow that is best in full sun.
(Chase Fuchsias, UK, 1996)
(EX)(CHA)(GLE)(ISL)

Chase Royal
Double H2 Bush
This large-flowered fuchsia is well
worth growing as it carries the
attributes of both its parents.
Tube and *sepals* red. *Corolla*
petals a delightful deep purple.
Growth is rather lax for a bush
so this will be ideal both as a
bush with supports or in hanging
containers.
('Royal Velvet' × 'Pink Galore')
(Chase Fuchsias, UK, 1996)
(FOX)(CHA)(CLI)(GLE)

Chase Surprise
Double H2 Trailer
Tube and *sepals* of these medium-
sized flowers white. *Corolla*
petals deep violet blue. The
natural growth is rather lax so
will make an excellent plant for
use in hanging baskets or
containers.
(Chase Fuchsias, UK, 1998)
(FOX)(CHA)

CENTRAL SCOTLAND

CHARLES EDWARD FORWARD

Checkerboard
Single H2 Bush
Tube long, red. *Sepals* recurve slightly, start red and change abruptly to white. *Corolla* a deeper red than the tube and white at the base of the petals. The flowers are fairly long but are produced in profusion. Flowers early in the season and is never out of bloom. *Foliage* medium green, finely serrated. An excellent cultivar for the beginner and can be trained to virtually any shape other than for a basket.
(Walker and Jones, USA, 1948)
(SIL)(FOX)(FEN)(ROU)(RKY)
(KM)(WAR)(CL)(LB)(BRE)(MO)
(BUR)(WAY)(VER)(STM)(EX)
(ARC)(JAK)(CHA)(WV)(WAL)
(PER)(BAK)(GOU)(ROO)(BLA)
(RID)(ALD)(OAK)(RIV)(BRI)
(CLI)(ASK)(WHE)(FUC)(GLE)
(ISL)(SMI)(OLD)(OLI)(SIM)
(LOK)

Cheeky Chantelle
Double H2 Lax Bush
Tube pink striped with red. *Sepals* a deep waxy red on top and deep red on the underside. *Corolla* petals burgundy marbled with red. The medium-sized blooms produced in profusion are carried on rather lax but upright growth. Supports will be necessary for bush training but this is an excellent plant for use in hanging containers.
(Allsop, UK, 1998)
(LB)(ROO)

Cheeky Charlie
Double H2 Bush
Large-flowered fuchsia. *Sepals* rosy pink salmon. *Corolla* petals deep rose salmon. A delightful fuchsia.
(Brigadoon Fuchsias, UK, 1989)
(BRI)

Chelsea Girl
Single H2 Bush
Medium-sized flower. *Tubes* and *sepals* bright carmine. *Corolla* petals pink veined with red.

Growth is stiffly upright. Very floriferous. Excellent for patio work.
(Sinton, UK, 1987) (BUR)

Cherry Pie
Single H2/3 Bush
Sepals cherry red on small flowers. *Corolla* petals mauve to pink. The flowers are carried in great profusion. *Foliage* dark green. Dwarf growing variety with H: approx. 9in (22cm). Useful for the hardy border or rockery.
(Tabraham, UK, 1982)
(BRI)(ROO)

Cherry Ripe
Single H2 Bush
Tube and *sepals* on the medium-sized blooms cherry red. *Corolla* petals dark cherry. The flowers are freely produced. Strong, upright, self-branching growth.
(Travis, UK, 1961) (SIM)

Cheryl
Single H2 Lax Bush
Medium-sized flowers. *Tubes* and *sepals* white. *Corolla* petals salmon rose. Growth is rather spreading and upright. Will be very useful for pot work, with supports, and for growing in hanging containers.
(Kirby, UK, 1998)
(JAK)(EX)(CLI)

Cheryl Ann
Double H2 Trailer
Tube and *sepals* reddish-orange. *Corolla* blue violet. A natural trailer that will make a good basket. *Foliage* medium green on the upper surfaces and yellowish green on the lower surfaces. The stems and branches are bright red. Does best in filtered light.
('Ann's Beauty' × 'Deep Purple')
(Garrett, USA, 1991)
(EX)

Cheviot Princess
Single H2 Bush
Tube and *sepals* white. *Corolla* ruby red maturing to spiraea red. Very free-flowering cultivar with

the flowers hanging in trusses. A good self-branching bushy plant. There is an aura of luminosity surrounding the flowers that make it a very attractive proposition for the show bench.
(Ryle, UK, 1977)
(WV)(CLI)

Chips
Single H2 Bush
Tube and *sepals* orange red. *Corolla* petals pink. The flowers are of a medium size and are freely produced. Growth is upright and bushy.
(Markham Grange, UK, 1992)
(FEN)

Choir Boy
Single H2 Bush
Small flowers. *Tubes* and *sepals* white. *Corolla* petals red. A natural bush-shape of medium size is easily formed.
(BEL)

Christine Bamford
Single H2/3 Bush
Tube and *sepals* pale red with a hint of aubergine. *Corollas* pink, veins darker. Multi-flowering. Different. Worth trying as a hardy fuchsia with upright self-branching growth. H: approx. 24in (60cm).
(Carless, UK, 1996)
(GOU)(FOX)(CHA)(WV)(PER)
(ROO)(RIV)(ISL)

Christine Becker
Single H2 Lax Bush
Tube and partially recurving *sepals* rosy red. *Corolla* petals rose-coloured with a porcelain blue cast. The medium-sized flowers are cup-shaped and are very freely produced. *Foliage* medium green. Growth is rather lax so a plant grown as a bush will need some supports. Could be very useful in hanging pots and containers.
(K. Strumper, Germany, 1987)
(RIV)

CHECKERBOARD

CHEEKY CHANTELLE

Christine Truman
Double H2 Lax Bush
Tube greenish white. *Sepals* white
striped with pink on the upper
surface and rose on the lower
surface and green-tipped. *Corolla*
petals violet with rose at the base.
The flowers are bell-shaped.
Foliage dark green. Growth is
rather lax so will make a bush
with supports but is a good
subject for use in hanging pots
and containers.
('Perky Pink' × 'Tutti Frutti')
(Welch, UK, 1991) (RIV)

Christmas Elf
Single H2 Bush
Tube and *sepals* bright red. *Sepals*
fully reflexed and encircle the
ovary. *Corolla* near white with
red veining. *Foliage* small and
dark. Small flowers. Growth
upright, compact and bushy.
(Gentry, USA, 1972)
(FOX)(BRE)CHA)(GLE)

Cicely Ann
Single H2 Trailer
Tube long, thin and crimson.
Sepals upswept, crimson with
yellow-green tips. *Corolla* petals
mallow purple with crimson at
the base. They are veined with
crimson and have an extremely
fine crimson edging. The medium-
sized flowers have a very neat
bell-shape. Growth is naturally
trailing and self-branching.
(R. Holmes, UK, 1975)
(RIV)

Cindy Robyn
Tube and *sepals* flesh pink.
Corolla petals rose red. The large
flowers are produced very freely
throughout the season.
(Stubbs, USA, 1982) (BRE)

F. cinerea
Single H1 Species
Tube long, narrow, funnel-shaped
widening at the base of the
sepals. *Tube* and *sepals* dull
orange. *Corolla* orange to
crimson. Flowers rather sparsely.
Foliage medium-sized and light
green turning to purplish red. In

the wild, grows to approx. 10ft
(3m).
(Colombia and Equador)
(Berry, USA, 1978)

Circus
Single H2 Bush
Tube and *sepals* pinkish coral.
Corolla petals coral pink to
magenta orange. The flowers are
of medium size and are produced
very freely. Strong upright
grower.
(Fuchsia Forest, America, 1967)
(BAK)(RKY)(BRY)(CLI)(OLI)

City of Carlisle
Single/Semi-Double H2 Bush
Tube and *sepals* very pale
rhodamine with deep pink stripes.
Corolla petals open dark violet
fading somewhat as they mature.
Very prolific flowering on strong,
upright-growing bushes.
(Coupland, UK, 1998)
(BUR)(BLA)

C.J. Howlett
Single H2/3 Bush
Sepals reddish pink. *Corolla*
bluish carmine. The flowers,
though small, are freely produced
and appear early in the season.
Good bushy hardy fuchsia.
(Howlett, UK, 1911)
(SIL)(RKY)(RIV)(HYDE)(BRY)

Claire
Single H2 Bush
Tube and *sepals* creamy white.
Corolla petals pale blue. The
growth is naturally upright and
bushy.
(ROU)

Claire Bell
Double H2 Trailer
Tube and *sepals* waxy pink.
Corolla shades of rose. The large
flowers are freely produced. The
naturally trailing branches will
help to make a very good basket.
(Head, UK, 1996) (LB)

Claire Evans
Double H2 Bush
Tube and *sepals* white to shell
pink. *Corolla* mauvish blue.

Medium to large flowers are
produced early in the season.
Easy growing plant that breaks
naturally and will make a good
show specimen. Best grown with
protection.
(Evans and Reeves, USA, 1951)
(BRI)(WV)(LOK)

Claire Oram
Single H2 Bush
Tube white. *Sepals* white with
faint pink on the underside.
Corolla magenta edged with
crimson and white at the base.
Medium-sized blooms are freely
produced on a very vigorous
upright growth.
(J. Day, UK, 1995) (LOK)

Claudine Sandford
Double H2 Stiff Trailer
Tube short, thick, flesh-coloured
and streaked with green. The
sepals coral pink. *Corolla* mottled
coral and pink maturing to
lavender rose. Large clean-
coloured blooms. *Foliage* dark
green. Rather lax for an upright
bush but is rather stiff for a
trailer so will need the assistance
of weights to fully cover the
basket.
(Sandford, USA, 1986)
(ISL)

F. coccinea (Berry)
Single H1 Species
Tube and *sepals* deep pink.
Corolla light purple with the
stamens extended well beneath.
Foliage light green. This
example found by Berry differs
from the original specimen
found in 1789 both in flower
and leaf colour.
(Berry, Brazil, 1996) (CL)

F. coccinea var. solander
Single H1 Species
Tube short and red. *Sepals*
drooping and waxy red. *Corolla*
petals dark violet. Flowering
occurs near the ends of the
branches. Upright habit. Unlike
some species will tolerate early
'pinching'. Useful in large pots.
(Location not known) (GOU)

CINDY ROBYN

C.J. HOWLETT

CIRCUS

F. COCCINEA ('BERRY')

Colin Chambers
Double H2 Lax Bush
Large and heavy flowers. *Tubes* and recurving *sepals* red. *Corolla* petals dusky red with lighter marbling. Best grown in light shade. Growth strong and versatile. Looks best in tubs and half baskets.
(Goulding, UK, 1995)
(GOU)(WV)(RIV)

Colne White Pat
Single H2 Bush
Tube, *sepals* and *corolla* the palest pink and white. This is a 'sport' from 'Lady Patricia Mountbatten' found in 1994.
(Percival Fuchsias, UK, 1994)
(PER)

Conchilla
Semi-Double H2 Bush
Tube and *sepals* shell pink. *Corolla* petals amethyst violet. The medium-sized flowers are freely produced on upright and bushy growth.
('Margarita' × 'Rolla')
(Niederholzer, USA, 1941)
(BAK)(RIV)

Coniston Water
Single H2 Bush
Tube soft rosy pink. *Sepals*, very long and recurving, soft rose. *Corolla* deep lavender blue. Large pagoda-shaped blooms. *Foliage* dark green. Good, strong, upright growth.
(Travis, UK, 1959) (BRY)

Constance Comer
Single H2 Bush
Small single flower. *Tube* orange pink. *Sepals* salmon orange. *Corolla* bright orange red. Strong, upright and short-jointed. Good exhibition variety.
(Kirby, UK, 1995)
(JAK)(FEN)(RKY)(WAY)(EX)
(ROO)(RIV)(LB)

Coombe Park
Single H2 Bush
Tube cream. *Sepals* pink with rose on the undersurface. *Corolla* petals open light purple marbled

with pink and white, and deepen with age. *Foliage* pale green. Best described as a lax upright-growing fuchsia that may need some supporting to make a good bush plant. Worth trying in a hanging container. Introduced at Coombe Park to celebrate the British Fuchsia Society Diamond Anniversary.
(Rowell, UK, 1998)
(BRE)(JAK)(HYDE)

Coral Baby
Single H2 Encliandra Bush
Very small perfect flowers. *Tubes* and *sepals* light red. *Corolla* reddish orange. A different and interesting combination of colour in the flower. *Foliage* soft green. Produces lots of seedpods that enhance the appearance of the plant. The growth is naturally very willowy although rather slow for an Encliandra but could be used for all types of topiary.
(Drapkin, USA, 1989)
(BRE)(BRI)(GOU)(ISL)

Coral Rose
Double H2 Bush
Tube and *sepals* coral pink. *Corolla* rose pink. The flowers are small but freely produced. An excellent plant for the small pot classes as it is a natural miniature. Very suitable for rockeries or window-boxes as it only achieves a height of 6–9in (15–22cm).
(Tabraham, UK, 1982)

Coralina Variegata
Single H2 Bush
Tube and non-reflexing *sepals* scarlet. *Corolla* rich purple, pink at the base. Identical to 'Coralina' except for the variegated *foliage*. Leaves are green with a distinct pink centre and edge, extremely attractive.
(Verdeur, Belgium, 1979)
(ISL)

Cornelia Smith
Single H2 Bush
Tube broad and bright red. *Sepals* spreading, also bright red.

Corolla petals even brighter red and slightly deeper. Growth is spreading upright, highly versatile and heat-tolerant. Ideal in patio tubs or as a Standard.
(Smits, Holland, 1995) (GOU)

Cornwall Calls
Semi-Double H2 Bush
Tube and *sepals* white. *Corolla* petals lavender. Excellent bushy growth.
(Stiff, UK, 1994)
(BAK)(PER)

Corryn Gilchrist
Single H2 Trailer
Sepals a mixture of light and dark pink. *Corolla* opens a reddish purple maturing to light purple. The semi-lax, self-branching and compact growth is vigorous. Ideal for hanging pots or baskets.
(Jackson, UK, 1997)
(BRE)

Corsair
Double H2 Trailer
Sepals white and *corolla* petals sky blue, marbled with white and purple. The flowers are extra large and the colour combination is very striking. Excellent for basket work as it has a natural trailing habit.
(Kennett, USA, 1965)
(SIL)(FOX)(ROU)(KM)(WAY)
(STM)(EX)(ARC)(BRI)
(CHA)(WV)(BAK)(RIV)(BRY)
(GLE)(SMI)(OLI)

Cottinghamii (Enc)
Single H2 Bush
Single pink, green-tipped, small encliandra-type flowers. Rather larger than those normally seen with encliandras and produced solitarily in leaf axils. This cultivar always seems to be in bloom. *Foliage* small, mid-green. Strong upright growth to about 24in (60cm). Seems to be prone to botrytis so will need careful watering. Could be hardy in milder areas. An old cultivar but one about which little information is known.
(SIL)(EX)(ASK)

COLIN CHAMBERS

CORNELIA SMITH

COLNE WHITE PAT

COTTINGHAMII

Countdown Carol
Double H2 Bush
Tube and *sepals* creamy white.
Corolla petals aster violet.
Good, upright-growing plant.
(Potash Nurseries, UK, 1994)
(POT)

Cove Bay
Single H2/3 Bush
Tube short and greenish pink.
Sepals white deepening to pink.
Corolla petals violet with white
bases maturing to imperial
purple. The buds are long and
banana-shaped. *Foliage* mid-
green on top and slightly lighter
on the undersides. A bushy plant
that will do well in the hardy
border.
('Norman Mitchinson' ×)
(Dunnett, UK, 1984) (FEN)
(RKY)

Cracker
Double H2 Bush
Tube and *sepals* very light pink.
Corolla petals creamy white.
Foliage medium green. Very
floriferous plant carried on
strong, upward-growing stems.
(RIV)

Cracklin Rose
Double H2 Bush
Medium-sized flowers. *Tubes* and
sepals carmine rose. *Corolla*
petals Tyrian purple and rose
with white at the base. *Foliage*
mid-green. Good, bushy, upright
plants.
(BRI)

Crescendo
Double H2 Bush
Tube and *sepals* turkey red.
Corolla – outer third peony-
purple, margin and two-thirds
turkey red. Medium-sized blooms
that flower early and freely.
Upright and shrubby growth.
(Reiter, USA, 1942) (LOK)(WV)

Crinkley Bottom
Double H2 Bush
Tube white. *Sepals* pink. *Corolla*
petals rose with a pink flush at
the base. The flowers are fairly

large and the bottom edges of
the petals have a distinctly
crinkled appearance.
(Welch, UK, 1993) (FOX)(FEN)
(ROU)(RKY)(KM)(CLI)(LB)
(MO)(VER)(EX)(JAK)(BRI)
(CHA)(ROO)(RID)(POT)(ISL)

Crystal Anniversary
Double H2 Bush
Tube and *sepals* light pink.
Corolla a pastel lavender blue.
Tidy, upright-growth habit.
Medium to large flowers.
Named to commemorate the
Bournemouth and District
Fuchsia Society's 15th
Anniversary.
(Forward, UK, 1996)
(BRI)(WV)(FUC)(GLE)(ISL)

Cutie Karen
Double H2 Trailer
Tube long and deep pink. *Sepals*
red and reflex right back to the
tube. *Corolla* petals deep purple
maturing to purple. The natural
trailing habit makes it ideal for
all types of hanging containers.
Ideal in both sun and shade.
(Allsop, UK, 1997) (LB)(ROO)

Cylindracea (Male)
Single H2 Bush
Single without seedpods. *Tubes*
cylindrical and orange. *Sepals*
held downwards, orange with
green tips. *Corollas* orange.
Growth thin, wiry and
spreading. Versatile and suitable
for growing in large pots. A
member of the encliandra group
with the very small flowers.
(Lindley, Mexico, 1838)
(CL)(GOU)

Cyndy Robyn
Double H2 Trailer
Tube and *sepals* flesh pink.
Corolla coral red. Large flaring
blooms that make a truly
wonderful basket. *Foliage* large
and dark green with a central
red vein. A self-branching
natural trailer.
(Stubbs, USA, 1982)
(FOX)(CHA)(ISL)(WV)
(PER)(RIV)(HYDE)

F. cyrtandroides
Species H1 Bush
One of the New Zealand
species. *Tubes* small and amber-
coloured. *Sepals* recurved, amber
to brown. *Petals* chocolate-
coloured. Growth is slow and
scandent.
(New Zealand, date unknown)
(GOU)

D

Daddy Long Legs
Single H2 Trailer
Tube and *sepals* rose red.
Corolla petals pink/orange. A
natural trailer, will make a good
basket with its medium-sized
flowers.
(FEN)

Daffodil Dolly
Double H2 Trailer
Tube and *sepals* dark pink on
the upper surface and lighter on
the lower. *Corolla* petals light
violet/light pink maturing to
pale purple/light pink. *Foliage* is
light yellowish green. Good
trailer so will make an excellent
basket.
(Johnson/Laburnum, UK, 1987)
(ARC)(BLA)

Dainty
Single H2 Bush
Tube and *sepals* cerise. *Corolla*
petals bluish mauve. The flowers
are medium-sized, open and
flared. Growth is upright and
bushy.
(UK) (FEN)(RKY)(BAK)

Dainty Lady
Semi-Double H2 Bush
Tube and *sepals* cerise. *Corolla*
white veined cerise at the base.
The flowers are medium-sized
and the natural growth of the
plant is as a bush.
(Lowe, UK, 1878)
(FEN)(WV)(BAK)(BRY)

CRINKLEY BOTTOM

CUTIE KAREN

DAINTY LADY

Daisy Bell
Single H2 Trailer
Tube long, white with orange cast, shading to green at base. *Sepals* pale orange shading to apple green at tips. *Corolla* vermilion shading to pale orange at base of petals. Small but very numerous flowers, petals forming a narrow cone. *Foliage* small, medium green with a lighter shade underneath. Growth naturally trailing, self-branching and vigorous. Makes an excellent basket or half basket. Best colour in full sun.
(Mieke, USA, 1977) (SIL)(FOX) (FEN)(ROU)(RKY)(KM)(CLI) (BRE)(BUR)(WAY)(BAL)(EX) (ARC)(JAK)(BRI)(CHA)(WV) (WAL)(PER)(BAK)(ROO)(RIV) (WHE)(BRY)(CLI)(ASK)(FUC) (GLE)(OLI)(SIM)(LOK)

Dal's Conquest
Double H2 Bush
Medium-sized blooms. *Tubes* and *sepals* of cream to pink. *Corolla* petals mauve. Fairly strong upright growth.
(Gubler, UK, 1988) (BRI)

Dancing Bloom
Single H2 Bush
Tubes and *sepals* white. *Corolla* petals cerise-pink. Strong upright growth. Will make a good Standard.
(Fix, UK, 1995) (ROU)(PER)(HYDE)(POT)(CLI)

Daniel
Double H2 Bush
Tube and *sepals* pink. *Corolla* petals also pink. Growth is naturally upright and bushy. A very attractive plant.
(Stiff, UK, 1998)

Daniel Austin
Double H2 Bush
Tube thin and pink. *Sepals* held upwards, light pink and slightly darker underneath. *Corolla* petals dark mauve maturing to pale purple. The flower is small to medium in size. Very free-flowering. *Foliage* dark green.
(Rowell, UK, 1998) (JAK)

Dark Lady
Single H2 Bush
A very floriferous small-flowered single. The *tube* and *sepals* are red and the petals in the *corolla* are purple. Good upright self-branching plant which makes an excellent show specimen. Well worth trying as one of the smaller Standards.
(Raiser and date unknown) (WHE)

Danielle
Single H2 Trailer
A trailing cultivar that is excellent for all types of hanging containers. *Tube* and *sepals* pink striped with dark rose. *Corolla* petals white. *Foliage* greyish-green. Very free growing.
('Harry Gray' × 'Harry Gray') (Dunnett, UK, 1989) (FEN)(ROO)

Danson Belle
Semi-Double H2 Bush
Tube and *sepals* rose. *Corolla* petals pale violet. Upright and bushy growth.
(Raiser and date unknown) (RIV)

Dark Mystery
Double H2 Trailer
Large-flowered beauty. *Tube* and *sepals* light orange. *Corolla* petals orange magenta. The natural trailing habit makes this an ideal plant for use in all types of hanging containers.
(LB)(HYDE)

Darling Danielle
Double H2 Trailer
Tube pink striped with red. *Sepals* pink on top, crêped pink underneath and recurve right over. *Corolla* petals deep purple, slightly lighter at the base, veined with red and maturing to deep rose red. A compact and self-branching trailer that will make an excellent hanging pot.
(M. Allsop, UK, 1996) (ROO)

David Alston
Double H2 Bush
Tube and *sepals* carmine. *Corolla* petals white, tinged with pink and veined with carmine. The flowers

are large and very full. The size and weight of the flowers means that some support will be needed for the arching stems.
(Forbes, UK, 1906) (BAK)(WV) (LOK)

David Jason
Double H2 Bush
Tube and *sepals* white. *Corolla* petals lilac. An upright-growing self-branching plant.
(EX)

David Smith
Single H2 Bush
Tube white. *Sepals* white with green tips. *Corolla* petals reddish purple with a white stripe. An upright bushy plant that is self-branching.
(FEN)

Dawning
Single H2 Bush
Tubes pink. *Sepals* pink with green tips, recurving. *Corolla* petals pink with a suggestion of grey in their colouring. A very strong upright and self-branching plant that will make an excellent display plant in a large container.
(Shaffery, UK, 1994) (RKY)(ROO)(HYDE)

Dawn Mist
Double H2 Trailer
Corolla opens light blue and pink with darker veins. *Sepals* pink. The young *foliage* is pale gold darkening with maturity. Excellent basket variety.
('Snowfire' × ('Party Frock' × 'So Big'))
(Sharpe/Proffit, New Zealand, 1988) (EX)(RID)

Dawn Sky
Double H2 Bush
Tube and *sepals* neyron rose. *Corolla* heliotrope with neyron rose at the base, all fading to petunia purple. Large flowers freely produced. The spreading bush is vigorous and will need some supporting to make a well-shaped bushy plant.
(Crockett, UK, 1967) (BAK)(BRI)

DAISY BELL

DANCING BLOOM

DANIELLE

DARK MYSTERY

DARLING DANIELLE

DAWNING

Day Star
Single H2 Bush
Sepals pale rose to opal. *Corolla* petals magenta rose. Good, strong, upright growth. Deserves to be grown more widely.
(Baker, UK, 1970)
(BAK)(BRY)(OLI)

Daytime Live
Single H2 Bush
Tube and *sepals* cerise. *Corolla* petals deep purple with pink and red veining at the base of the petals. The medium-sized flowers are very freely produced. Good, strong, bushy growth.
(Rolt, UK, 1989)
(RKY)(KM)(RIV)

D Day 44
Double H2 Bush
Tube cream. *Sepals* white with pink outer edges, are fairly large, wide and waxy. *Corolla* petals white-veined with pink on the edges. The flowers are of medium size and are freely produced. *Foliage* medium green with finely toothed serration on the edges. The upright growth makes it an ideal plant for patio tubs or for growing as Standards.
('Bobby Shaftoe' × 'Stanley Cash')
(Redfern, UK, 1985)
(FOX)(CHA)(RIV)(HYDE)

Deal Marine
Semi-Double H2 Bush
Tube and *sepals* rose-coloured. *Corolla* petals lavender. A delightful colour combination. A naturally self-branching plant, this will make an ideal subject for use in patio tubs.
(RIV)

Deben Petite
Single H2 Bush
This inter-specific hybrid of the encliandra type has very small flowers that are borne in upright clusters. *Sepals* dark cerise. *Corolla* petals cerise pink. The flowers can be both perfect and pistillate. Very vigorous upright bush. *Foliage* glossy, dark green. Another of the ideal subjects for

use in fuchsia 'topiary'.
('*F. parviflora*' × '*F. arborescens*')
(Dunnett, UK, 1975)
(SIL)

Deborah
Double H2 Trailer
Tube and *sepals* rosy-white. *Corolla* petals orangey red. Natural trailer so makes a good basket. Medium-sized flowers produced in profusion throughout the season.
(Tiret, USA, 1970)
(BRI)(SMI)

Deborah Street
Semi-Double H2 Bush
Tube white and long. *Sepals* white with a pink underside. *Corolla* neyron rose to strawberry pink with good-sized blooms. Strong upright grower suitable for making columns and other large structures. Strongly recommended.
(J. Day, UK, 1993)
(LOK)

Dedham Vale
Single H2 Bush
Tubes short and orient pink. *Sepals* horizontally held, rosy pink. *Corolla* mauve. Extremely floriferous. Neat, self-branching bushy growth. *Foliage* small, matt green. Makes a superb small Standard.
(Goulding, UK, 1984)
(WV)

Dee Star
Double H2 Trailer
Tube greenish-white. *Sepals* horizontally held, white on the outside and rose white underneath. *Corolla* opens violet maturing to violet purple. Many pink, white and purple petaloids. Very large blooms freely produced over a long season. *Foliage* medium-green. Natural trailer.
('Pink Marshmallow' × 'Midnight Sun')
(Richardson, Australia, 1986)
(CLI)(FOX)(BRE)(WAY)(STM)
(ARC)(CHA)(FUC)(HYDE)(GLE)

De Groot's Dreumes
Single H2 Trailer
Tubes and *sepals* of this small-flowered trailer aubergine. *Corolla* petals also aubergine. A naturally trailing plant that will do well in all types of hanging containers.
(De Groot, Holland, 1997)
(HYDE)

De Groot's Moonlight
Single H2 Trailer
Tubes, longer than average, and the spreading *sepals* aubergine. *Corolla* petals a much darker aubergine. The spreading growth makes this a suitable plant for a hanging container.
(De Groot, Holland, 1997)
(GOU)(ROO)(HYDE)

De Groot's Parel
Single H2 Bush
Tube and *sepals* red. *Corolla* petals aubergine. A very attractive colour combination carried on self-branching and upright stems.
(De Groot, Holland, 1997)
(HYDE)

Delicata
Single H2 Bush
Large flower. *Tubes* and *sepals* white with a crimson flush. *Corolla* petals Imperial purple.
(Newberry, UK, 1847) (EX)

Delta's Angelique
Single H2 Bush
Tube white. *Sepals* white with green tips. *Corolla* a very attractive lilac rose. A fairly strong upright-growing shrub that carries its numerous small flowers to perfection.
(Vreeke/van't Westeinde, Holland, 1991) (HYDE)

Delta's Bambi
Single H2 Bush
Tube and *sepals* pale pink. *Corolla* pink with magenta shading. *Foliage* medium green. The bush-shaped plants produce numerous medium-sized flowers.
(Vreeke/van't Westeinde, Holland, 1997) (BRY)

DEBORAH

DEE STAR

DAY STAR

DELTA'S ANGELIQUE

DELTA'S BAMBI

Delta's Bride
Single H2 Bush
Tube and *sepals* pale pink.
Corolla petals white. The flower
flares to a saucer-shape.
(Vreeke/van't Westeinde, Holland,
1992) (LB)(GOU)(ROO)(ALD)

Delta's Dream
Single H2 Bush
Tube and *sepals* white with grey-
green flush. *Corolla* pale shell-pink
with darker veining and with
purple rose edges. Fairly small
flower. Good, strong, upright
grower. The flower colour
combination is delightfully delicate.
(Vreeke/van't Westeinde, Holland,
1991) (GOU)(MO)(EX)(ARC)
(BRI)(CHA)(ROO)(RIV)(HYDE)
(BRY)(GLE)

Delta's Drop
Single H2 Bush
Tube crimson with darker
stripes. *Sepals* also crimson.
Corolla petals dull purple fading to
beetroot red and with a crimson
splash at the base. Medium-sized
flower. Growth upright and bushy
although it does require some early
pinching. For best colouring it
needs a sheltered spot.
(Vreeke/van't Westeinde, Holland,
1992) (GOU)(BAL)(ROO)(HYDE)

Delta's Fellow
Single H2 Trailer
Tube longish, thin and soft rosy
red. *Sepals*, held horizontally, are
white with green tips. *Corolla*
petals soft lilac. *Foliage* rather
long and small, medium green
with a faint red hue. A self-
branching natural trailer.
('Longfellow' × 'Iceberg')
(Vreeke/van't Westeinde, Holland,
1991) (ROO)

Delta's Groom
Single H2 Lax Bush
Tubes and flyaway *sepals* dark
aubergine red. The petals in the
square bell-shaped *corolla* are
darker. Vigorously self-branching
in habit. Looks well in show pots
and window-boxes.
(Vreeke/van't Westeinde, Holland,

1993)
(MO)(GOU)(ROO)(HYDE)

Delta's Midnight
Double H2 Bush
Tube and *sepals* deep purple.
Corolla petals aubergine. Growth
is naturally upright and bushy.
(Vreeke/van't Westeinde, Holland,
1994) (RIV)

Delta's Night
Single H2 Trailer
Tube and *sepals* very dark glossy
red. *Corolla* petals dark red
almost black. A very floriferous
plant with the flowers carried on
strong and trailing branches. Will
be at its best in large hanging
baskets.
(Vreeke/van't Westeinde, Holland,
1994)
(GOU)(RKY)(STM)(ROO)
(HYDE)

Delta's Nursery
Double H2 Trailer
Tube and *sepals* rose red. *Corolla*
petals brownish red. The
numerous medium-sized flowers
are carried on strong but trailing
stems. Excellent in hanging pots
or containers.
(Vreeke/van't Westeinde, Holland,
1994) (HYDE)

Delta's Parlais
Single H2 Trailer
Tube and *sepals* are apple-
blossom rose. *Corolla* petals
fuchsia purple to robin red. The
medium-sized flowers are quite
profuse and are carried on good
trailing stems.
(Vreeke/van't Westeinde, Holland,
1994) (HYDE)

Delta's Prelude
Single H2 Trailer
Tube dull carmine-pink. *Sepals*
rose red with green tips. *Corolla*
petals bright robin red, all with
small stems. The medium-sized
flowers are quite freely produced
and are carried on strong trailing
stems. Enjoys being in full sun.
(Vreeke/van't Westeinde, Holland,
1994) (HYDE)

Delta's Star
Single H2 Bush
Smallish flowers. *Tubes* and
sepals red. *Corolla* petals also
red. Growth is naturally upright
and bushy. Will make a good
plant for a patio container.
(Vreeke/van't Westeinde, Holland,
1994) (HYDE)

Delta' Symphonie
Double H2 Lax Bush
Tubes short and ivory white.
Sepals long, pale purple-pink,
recurved and flushed with
aubergine. *Corolla* petals
aubergine. Growth is strong and
arching. At its best in hanging
pots.
(Vreeke/van't Westeinde, Holland,
1992) (WV)(ROO)(HYDE)

Delta's Trick
Single H2 Bush
Tubes and swept-back *sepals*
bright red. *Corollas* large and
bell-shaped variably marbled
with pink, red and violet.
Growth is upright and strong.
Makes a good bush or
Standard.
(Vreeke/van't Westeinde, Holland,
1993) (ROO)(HYDE)

Desperate Daniel
Single H2 Bush
Tube and *sepals* cerise. *Corolla*
petals purple. Good, compact
bush with flowers held out
horizontally.
(Blythe, UK, 1994)
(CL)(ISL)

Deutsche Perle
Single H2 Bush
Tube and *sepals* white.
Corolla petals crimson. The
flowers are of medium size.
Growth is upright and self-
branching. Will make an
excellent large plant in a large
container on the patio. This
plant appears to be synonymous
with 'Water Nymph' and is
often so named on the
Continent.
(Twrdy, Germany, 1874)
(RIV)

DELTA'S DROP

DELTA'S GROOM

DELTA'S NIGHT

DELTA'S PARLAIS

DELTA'S SYMPHONIE

DESPERATE DANIEL

Diamond Celebration
Double H2 Lax Bush
Tube white. *Sepals* white flushed
with pink and with a pink
stripe. *Corolla* petals in this
medium-sized double flower
creamy white. The lax growth
enables it to be used as a bush
plant with some supporting and
also as a hanging container.
Released in time to celebrate the
Diamond Anniversary of the
formation of the British Fuchsia
Society.
(Johns, UK, 1997)
(KM)(WAR)(CL)

Diana
Double H2 Trailer
Tube and *sepals* white. *Corolla*
light marbled lavender that fades
to bright old rose. The large
flowers are freely produced for
their size. *Foliage* light green.
Good trailer so will make an
excellent basket.
(Kennett, USA, 1967)
(BAK)(FOX)(RKY)(EX)(CHA)
(RIV)

Diana Wright
Single H3 Bush
Tubes pink. *Sepals* pink tipped
with green. *Corolla* petals phlox
pink. The small flowers are very
freely produced. Upright and
bushy growth. *Foliage* medium-
sized, dark green. A good plant
for the hardy border. H: approx.
2ft (60cm).
('*F. magellanica alba*' × '*F.
fulgens*')
J.O. Wright, UK, 1984)
(SIL)(BRE)(HYDE)

Dilly Dilly
Double H2 Trailer
Tube white. *Sepals* pale pink on
top, deeper underneath with
green tips. *Corolla* lilac, pink at
petal base. The largish flowers
are freely produced. *Foliage*
medium green, large with slight
serration.
Although this plant can only
really be described as a semi-
trailer, it will make a nice basket.
(Tiret, USA, 1963)

Dirk van Deelan
Single H2 Bush
Tube and *sepals* pink. *Corolla*
petals dark pink. The flowers are
of medium size. *Foliage* dark
green. Growth is strong and
upright – a very easy plant to
grow.
(Steevens, Holland, 1971)
(PER)(ROO)(ISL)

Doctor
Single H2 Bush
Tube longish and flesh pink.
Sepals also flesh pink. *Corolla*
petals rosy salmon. The largish
flowers are freely produced.
Growth is rather lax and will
make a good bush with some
supports as also an excellent
weeping Standard. Will also make
a good hanging basket.
(Castle Nurseries, UK, date
unknown) (BAK)

Doctor Brendan Freeman
Single H3 Bush
Tube pale pink. *Sepals* rhodamine
pink shading to phlox pink.
Corolla petals white. The
medium-sized flowers are freely
produced. Growth is as a medium
upright and bushy plant. Makes a
good hardy.
('Cloverdale Pearl' × 'Grace
Darling')
(Gadsby, UK, 1977) (BRE)(STM)
(JAK)(CHA)(CLI)(GLE)

Doctor (Dr) Foster
Single H3 Bush
Tube and *sepals* scarlet. *Corolla*
petals violet. The large flowers are
freely produced. Growth is upright
and very bushy being self-
branching. Probably one of the
largest flowers for a 'hardy'.
(Lemoine, France, 1899) (LOK)

Doctor Judith
Double H2 Trailer
Tube and *sepals* rose. *Corolla* red
purple streaked with rose. The
large flower is appropriate when
considering the parentage. A
superb and attractive flower that
will make an excellent hanging
basket.

('Ruby Wedding' × 'Pink
Marshmallow')
(Forward, UK, 1993)
(WV)(HYDE)(FUC)(GLE)(ISL)

Doctor (Dr) Olson
Double H2 Trailer
Tube and upturned *sepals* bright
red. *Corolla* is the palest orchid
pink with large central petals
surrounded by shorter spreading
petals, heavily overlaid mallow
purple with a salmon flush. The
large blooms are produced very
freely. The natural growth is as
a strong trailer.
(Mrs D. Lyon, USA, 1959)
(BAK)(LOK)(SMI)

Doctor (Dr) Robert
Single H2 Bush
Tube short, thick, fluted and
creamy pale pink. *Sepals* have a
similar colouring. *Corolla* rose
red with four neatly folded over
petals. The smallish flowers are
very freely produced. *Foliage* is
dark green. Growth is medium
upright and short-jointed. Not
the easiest to train but very
worthwhile when success is
achieved.
('Bobby Shaftoe' × 'Santa
Barbara')
(G. Roe, UK, 1987) (POT)

Doctor (Dr) Topinard
Single H2/3 Bush
Tube and *sepals* rose. *Corolla*
petals white, veined with rose.
The medium-sized flowers are
very freely produced. *Corolla*
flared and open is not dissimilar
to 'Display'. Growth is upright
and bushy.
(Lemoine, France, 1890) (LOK)

Dolly Roach
Double H2 Trailer
Tube and *sepals* rose. *Corolla*
petals white. Very free-flowering
trailing variety. Makes an
excellent basket.
(Roach, UK, 1992)
(BUR)(EX)(OLI)

DIANA WRIGHT

DILLY DILLY

DOCTOR FOSTER

DOCTOR JUDITH

Dominique
Double H2 Bush
Tube short and pink and the fully up *sepals* also pink. *Corolla* petals white with a pale pink flush. A compact and bushy plant that comes into flower quite early. Can be described as a small double that holds its flowers above the foliage.
(Johns, UK, 1998) (KM)

Don Peralta
Single to Semi-Double H2 Bush
Tube and *sepals* carmine. *Corolla* strongest magenta. Large long blooms on strong arching growth. Growth is vigorous. Makes heavy wood.
(Tiret, USA, 1950) (BAK)(ISL)

Doodie Dane
Double H2 Trailer
Tube yellowish white. *Sepals* waxy white on top and white blushed pink on the underside. *Corolla* petals violet purple splashed with white and pink. Makes a good basket as it is fast growing and self-branching.
(M. Allsop, UK, 1996) (ROO)

Doreen Gladwin
Single H2 Bush
Tube and *sepals* rose flushed with salmon. *Corolla* petals magenta. Fairly small, upward-looking flowers.
(Humphries, UK, 1995) (LB)

Doris Deaves
Single H2 Bush
Tube and *sepals* dark rose pink. *Corolla* dark lilac-lavender. Short-jointed variety, smothered in blooms. Good show bench variety.
(UK, 1994) (CLI)(BEL)

Doris Joan
Single H2 Bush
Tube and *sepals* creamy white and carmine. *Corolla* petals pink and lavender with carmine veining. Extremely floriferous with medium-sized blooms. *Foliage* small and dark green. The petals are triangular, each having a double saw-toothed edge – the

apex of each indentation having a deep carmine edging. The plant is self-branching and short-jointed with good upright growth.
(Sheppard, UK, 1997)
(SIL)(BRE)(CHA)(RIV)(ISL)

Dorothea Flowers
Single H2 Bush
Tube and *sepals* white. *Corolla* petals smoky blue. Small dainty single flowers with delicate colouring. Blooms profusely on compact growth.
(Thornley, UK, 1969)
(SIL)(RKY)(BRE)(WV)(BAK)(RIV)(LOK)

Dorothy Cheal
Single H2 Bush
Tube and *sepals* red. *Corolla* petals purple. An upright-growing, self-branching bush.
(Forward, UK, 1996) (WV)

Dorothy Day
Double H2 Bush
Tube and *sepals* bright red and reflexing. *Corolla* a rich purple flecked with pink; quite frilly, creating a larger appearance. Strong upright bush. Early blooms are sometimes single.
(Day, UK, 1987) (LOK)(BRI)

Dorothy Hanley
Semi-Double H2/3 Bush
Tubes and *sepals* dark red with a flush of aubergine. *Corollas* dark aubergine. A vigorously self-branching upright habit is here combined with hardy parentage. H and S: 2ft 6in (76cm)
(Carless, UK, 1997)
(MO)(PER)(GOU)(ROO)(HYDE)

Dorrian Brogdale
Triphylla-Type H1 Bush
Sepals and *Tubes* pink. *Corolla* pink with orange shading. The flowers are carried in profusion over a long period.

Dorset Abigail
Double H2 Bush
Tube and *sepals* white flushed with pink. *Corolla* petals white. An excellent large-flowered

cultivar that will train into a perfect bush-shape with its self-branching habit.
(Forward, UK, 199?)
(FUC)(GLE)(ISL)

Dorset Delight
Double H2 Trailer
Tube and *sepals* pink. *Corolla* magenta streaked pink. Petals are half flared. Distinguished by the colour and profusion of the blooms. A natural trailer, the cascading effect is accentuated by the weight of the large fully double blooms.
(Forward, UK, 1993)
(BRI)(WV)(FUC)(GLE)(ISL)

Double Dribble
Single H2 Trailer
Tube and *sepals* rose white. *Corolla* petals have the same very delicate pastel shade. A natural trailer, the small flowers are carried in profusion.
(Smits, Holland, 1997) (HYDE)

Double Otto
Double H2 Bush
Large double blooms. *Tubes* and *sepals* red. *Corolla* petals purple. Growth is strongly upright and self-branching.
(FOX)(CHA)

Douglas Boath
Double H2 Bush
Sepals pink and white with green tips. *Corolla* rich cerise splashed with pink. Large double flowers. Growth is vigorous, bushy and upright.
(Boath, UK, 1994)

Dove House
Single H2 Bush
Tube whitish to pale pink. *Sepals* whitish rose on top and amaranth rose underneath. *Corolla* a very delicate lavender fading to light lilac. The medium to larger sized flowers are freely produced and are enhanced by the variegated leaves.
(Variegated leaf 'sport' of 'Lady Patricia Mountbatten')
(Crawshay, UK, 1993)
(FEN)(KM)(WAL)

DORIS JOAN

DOROTHY HANLEY

DORRIAN BROGDALE

DORSET DELIGHT

DOUBLE DRIBBLE

DOUGLAS BOATH

Dr Manson
Single H2 Bush
Tube tapering and carmine rose.
Sepals that are completely
upswept, carmine rose, tipped
with green. The very open *corolla*
is violet shading to pale pink at
the base with veining. The
medium-sized flowers are freely
produced. Growth is strongly
upright and self-branching.
('Cloverdale Pearl' × 'Glyn Jones')
(Roe, UK, 1983) (WV)

Duchess of Cornwall
Double H2/3 Bush
Tube and *sepals* bright red.
Corolla petals white splashed
with red. Large flowers on an
upright bush. Dark green *foliage*.
Considered to be hardy in the
South. H and S: 1ft 6in–2ft
(45–60cm).
(Tabraham, UK, 1986) (SIL)

Duet
Double H2 Trailer
Tube red. *Sepals* that recurve to
cover the *Tube* are bright pink.
Corolla pale raspberry pink.
Large flowers with some of the
petals forming a bell-shape.
Foliage large, spring green. The
natural trailing habit will produce
a good basket. Needs light
conditions for best results.
(Hall, UK, 1982) (SIL)(WAY)
(STM)(BRI)(CHA)(RIV)(CLI)
(FUC)(GLE)(SIM)

Duke of Wellington
Double H2 Bush
Tube and *sepals* carmine red.
Corolla petals violet purple, pink
at the base and veined with
cerise. Flowers are very large.
Excellent upright grower.
(Haag, USA, 1956)
(BAK)(BRI)(LOK)

Dusky Blue
Double H2 Trailer
Tube is medium green. *Sepals*
rose with twisted light
yellow/green recurved tips.
Corolla petals open violet blue
shaded with light reddish purple
and mature to light purple edged

with blue. Large flowers produced
in profusion. *Foliage* dark green.
('Dusky Rose' × 'Drama Girl')
(Riley, USA, 1991)
(BRE)(EX)(BRI)(ISL)(HYDE)

Dusted Pink
Single H2 Trailer
Tube and *sepals* white flushed rose.
Corolla white. Large attractive
blooms. A 'Devonshire Dumpling'
seedling.
(Forward, UK, 1993)
(WV)(FUC)(ISL)

Dutch Flamingo
Single H2 Lax Bush
Tube rhodonite red. *Sepals*
crimson-carmine on top, crimson
underneath. *Corolla* crimson with
smooth green petal edges. The
flowers are of small to medium
size. *Foliage* dark green and is
quite large in comparison to the
size of the flowers. Growth is
medium upright and could be
useful as a semi-weeping Standard.
(de Graaff, Holland, 1985)
(CL)(ROO)

Dutch Geesji
Single H2 Bush
Tube rose. *Sepals* pink on top and
dark rose on the underside.
Corolla petals dark rose. *Foliage*
dark green on the upper surfaces
and lighter on the lower. Self-
branching, small, upright. The
best colour of bloom comes when
grown in full sun.
('Leverkusen' × ('Solitaire' ×))
(Veen, Holland, 1991) (ROO)

Dutch King Size
Single H2 Bush
Almost terminal-flowering. *Tubes*
very long, thin and salmon-
coloured. *Sepals*, short, drooping
and green. *Corollas* small and
bright orange. *Foliage* large.
Growth is strong and upright. A
bit of a novelty and may be rather
difficult at first.
(de Graaff, Holland, 1992) (GOU)

Dutch Perle
Single H2 Bush
Tube and *sepals* pale pink. *Corolla*

petals coral. Early and free-
flowering. Growth upright and
bushy.

Dutch Shoes
Double H2 Trailer
Tube and *sepals* rose pink with
pink tips in the form of little Dutch
shoes. *Corolla* petals rose pink.
The trailing style of growth makes
this an ideal hanging container
plant.
(Pennisi, USA, 1970)
(RIV)

E

Earre Barre
Single H2 Bush
Medium-sized flowers. *Tube* and
sepals reddish purple. *Corolla*
white with reddish purple veins
and base. *Foliage* medium green.
The flowers flare open unusually
and very attractively.
(de Graaff, Holland, 1989)
(GOU)(RKY)(EX)(ROO)(ALD)

Easter Bonnet
Double H2 Bush
Tube short and flushed rose. *Sepals*
broad, frosty and upturned,
shading from deep pink at base of
petals to pale pink tipped with
green. *Corolla* dusky rose pink
with a deeper shade at the base of
the petals. The beautiful buds open
out into a wide-spreading, ruffled,
cup-shaped bloom that matures to
a deeper shade of rose. *Foliage*
dark green.
(Waltz, USA, 1955)
(CLI)(FEN)(WV)(BRY)(LOK)

Ebb 'n' Flow
Single H2 Lax Bush
Tube and *sepals* pink. *Corolla*
petals purple. Lax-growing fuchsia
suitable for basket work. Will also
make a good plant for pot work
provided the necessary supports
are used. (Also written as
'Ebbanflo').
(Stiff, UK, 1995)
(RKY)(BAK)(ROO)
(*See* photograph on page 89.)

DR MANSON

DUCHESS OF CORNWALL

DUET

DUTCH GEESJI

EARRE BARRE

EASTER BONNET

Ebb Tide
Double H2 Trailer
Tube and *sepals* white. *Corolla* petals phlox pink, fading to lavender blue and pink. The flowers are large and freely produced. This naturally cascading plant makes an excellent basket.
(Erickson-Lewis, USA, 1959)
(LOK)(RKY)(RIV)

Echo
Single H2 Bush
Tube and *sepals* pink. *Corolla* petals mauve. Upward-growing fuchsia with flowers that are semi-upward looking.
(GLE)(OLI)

Ecstasy
Double H2 Trailer
Tubes and *sepals* neyron rose. *Corolla* petals hyacinth blue splashed with phlox pink. Naturally trailing, this will make a good basket.
(Tiret, USA, 1948) (BRI)

Eden's Delight
Single H2 Bush
Tube and reflexing *sepals* pale pink. *Corolla* small, saucer-shaped and pale lavender. A bright-looking fuchsia.
(Beige, Holland, 1994) (MO)

Eileen Norman
Single H2 Bush
Tube and *sepals* greenish white. *Corolla* petals neyron rose. Good, strong, upright growth with flowering continuing over a long season.
(Ron Holmes, UK, 1996)
(CLI)(OLD)

Eira Goulding
Semi-Double/Double H2 Lax Bush
Tubes ivory. *Sepals* recurving, pale pink. *Corolla* petals lavender at first, maturing to magenta. The arching branches carry a heavy supply of flowers. Very versatile – can be used in hanging pots or in tubs.
(Goulding, UK, 1996)
(GOU)(FEN)(RKY)(ROO)

Elfin Glade
Single H2/3 Bush
Tube and *sepals* pink with a rosy tint. *Corolla* purplish mauve, paling at the base and veined with pink. The medium-sized blooms are freely produced. Growth is upright and bushy (like a darker-coloured 'Margaret Brown').
(Colville, UK, 1963) (SIL)(WAY) (WV)(BAK)(RIV)(HYDE)(LOK)

Elizabeth Travis
Double H2 Bush
Fairly large blooms. *Tubes* and *sepals* pale pink edged with deep rose. *Corolla* petals white. A very attractive upward-growing bush fuchsia.
(J. Travis, UK, 1956)
(BAK)(BRI)(BRY)

Elly
Double H2 Trailer
Tube and *sepals* of these large flowers white. *Corolla* petals lilac. A very attractive colouring that, with the natural trailing of the stems carrying heavy flowers, will make a superb basket.
(Krom, Holland, 1997) (HYDE)

Elma
Single H3 Bush
Tube, *sepals* and *corolla* petals of this bushy fuchsia all aubergine. Fairly strong upright growth.
(Van den Bergh, Holland, 1990) (RKY)

El Matador
Semi-Double/Double H2 Trailer
Tube and *sepals* pink to salmon. *Corolla* petals dark shades of purple and burgundy with streaks of salmon. The flowers, on which the petals flare out, are very large. The buds are also distinctive by their length. The natural growth is as a self-branching trailer so will make an excellent basket.
(Kennett, USA, 1965) (RIV)

Elsa
Single/Semi-Double H2 Trailer
Tube and recurving *sepals* frosty pink. *Corolla* petals purple. The medium-sized single flowers are very freely produced. The pendulous and bushy growth makes this plant ideal for basket work. Often confused with 'Lena' and 'Eva Boerg'.
(Bull, UK, 1901)
(WV)

Elsie Maud
Double H2 Bush
Tube and *sepals* rosy purple. *Corolla* petals deep lilac. The flowers are medium to large in size and are carried on strong, upright-growing bushes.
(WV)

Elysee
Single H3 Bush
This small-flowered hardy fuchsia carries the main characteristics of its parent 'Ricartonii'. *Tube* and *sepals* red and *corolla* petals purple. Nothing particularly distinguishes it from other similar hardy 'hedge type' fuchsias.
(Lemoine, France, 1886)
(RKY)

Emily Salisbury
Single H2 Lax Bush
Tube and recurving *sepals* claret rose. *Corolla* petals purple and rose bengal. Blooms are medium-sized. *Foliage* mid-green. Growth is rather lax upright and self-branching. The flowers are very striking in their appearance.
('Tolling Bell' × 'Border Queen')
(Reynolds, UK, 1986)
(BUR)

Emma Alice
Double H2 Trailer
Tube and *sepals* magenta. *Corolla* petals violet. The flowers are fairly large. Their size and weight give the plant a natural trailing habit and it will therefore make a superb basket quite quickly.
('Ruby Wedding' × 'Pink Marshmallow')
(Forward, UK, 1993)
(WV)(FUC)(GLE)(ISL)

EBB 'N' FLOW

EDEN'S DELIGHT

ELLY

F. ENCLIANDRA

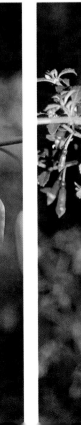

F. encliandra
Single H3 Bush
Fuchsia species previously known as *Breviflora*. There are a number of plants within this section all of which are well worth growing. They are all distinguishable by their small flowers, usually carried singly within the leaf axils, and that can either be staminate or pistillate.
(Steudal, Mexico, 1840)
(ROU)(RKY)
(*See* photograph on page 89.)

Enid Joyce
Single H2 Trailer
Tube and *sepals* pink. *Corolla* petals white with a tinge of pink. Medium-sized flowers that are produced continuously. An excellent cultivar for a hanging pot.
(Lorimer, UK, 1984) (SIM)

Enstone
Single H3 Bush
Tube small, long and narrow, white tinged with the palest green. *Sepals* that are held at the horizontal are narrow, pointed and white tinged with the palest pink. *Corolla* petals also white but tinged with the palest lilac. The small flowers are freely produced. *Foliage* is variegated with green and gold.
(D. Dawson, UK, 1986)
(FOX)(CHA)(PER)(RIV)(OLI)

Erica Frohmann
Double H2 Bush
Tube and *sepals* white. *Corolla* petals blue purple. Good, strong, upright and self-branching growth.
(Strumper, Germany, 1990) (SIM)

Eric's Hardy
Semi-Double H3 Lax Bush
Tube thickish and striped pinkish red. *Sepals* white on top and crêped pink on the underside. *Corolla* opens blue-pink and white maturing to mauve pink and white with turned-up petal edges. Medium-sized flowers. Lax upright or stiff trailer. Will

require supports if grown as an upright plant.
(Weeks, UK, 1986) (SIL)(ISL)

Eric's Majestic
Double H2 Bush
The medium-sized blooms are very full. *Tube* and upswept *sepals* pale pink. *Corolla* petals a slightly darker soft pink. Responds well to pinching and will make a nicely shaped plant with many flowers. Similar to, but more floriferous than, 'Flirtation Waltz'.
(Eric Johns, UK, 1996)
(KM)(BRE)(JAK)(RO)(RIV)

Ernestine
Double H2 Trailer
Tubes flesh-coloured. *Sepals* flesh-coloured but slightly more orange. *Corolla* scarlet with a hint of orange. Growth very strong and spreading. *Foliage* medium-green. Will make a large basket very quickly.
(Stubbs, USA, 1981)
(ROU)(RKY)(STM)(ARC)(BLA)
(RIV)(HYDE)(CLI)(ISL)(OLD)
(SIM)

Errol
Double H2 Bush
Tube and *sepals* scarlet. *Corolla* petals pink. Large flowers fairly freely produced and heat-resistant. Growth is fairly strong, upright.
(Brand, USA, 1967) (WV)

Eschott Elf
Single H2 Trailer
Tube thin, white and flushed with pale pink. *Sepals* of this superb variety are white flushed with pink as are also the *corolla* petals. The small flowers are very freely produced. The trailing growth will make a very attractive bush but will need some supporting. It will make a superb basket.
(Ryle, UK, 1976) (WV)

Esther
Double H2 Bush
Tube short, thick, white, globular and ribbed. *Sepals* semi-recurving

white with green tips. *Corolla* petals purple violet. Blooms are of medium size and are freely produced. The best colour is achieved in the shade. Upright and bushy growth.
(Pugh, UK, 1974) (RIV)

Ethel
Semi-Double/Double H2 Bush
Tube white. *Sepals* white with green tips on the top side and pale pink on the underside. *Corolla* lavender-centred with pink petaloids on the outside. The large blooms are fairly freely produced. Growth is upright and bushy.
(Martin, USA, 1967)
(CLI)(FOX)(CHA)(EX)(WV)

Eureka Red
Double H2 Trailer
Tube and *sepals* white and dark rose. *Corolla* rose and red-purple. The fully flared and fairly large blooms have smooth waxy edges. Very popular basket variety.
(Stubbs, USA, 1991)
(WAL)(FOX)(FEN)(EX)(BRI)
(CHA)(PER)(BEL)(RIV)(HYDE)
(CLI)(ASK)(FUC)(ISL)

Eurydice
Double H2 Bush
Tube and *sepals* red. *Corolla* petals white. No other details are available.
(LOK)

Eva Dayes
Single/Semi-Double H2 Bush
This plant is a 'sport' from 'Loeky'. *Foliage* small bright-green. Good vigorous growth and fairly self-branching. The flower, generally single but occasionally semi-double, is cup-shaped to saucer-shaped with the sepals arching back almost to the flower stalk and is very freely produced. *Tube* light pink. *Sepals* almost white at the tips. *Corolla* petals white with a pink lacing.
(Bielby/Oxtoby, UK, 1999)
(MO)(KM)

ERIC'S MAJESTIC

ERNESTINE

EUREKA RED

EVA DAYES

Evanson's Choice
Single H2 Bush
Tube and *sepals* crimson, the
latter being held horizontally.
Corolla venetian pink. The
medium-sized slender flowers are
produced on a tall and vigorously
upward-growing plant.
('Snowcap' × 'Cloverdale Pearl')
(Roe, UK, 1980)
(CLI)(STM)(EX)(CHA)(WV)
(GLE)

Eva Thwaites
Single H1 Bush
Paniculate-type fuchsia with
'perfect' blooms. The long *tubes*,
the slightly drooping *sepals* and
the petals in the *corolla* are all
pink. The blooms are rather
unusual in their shape. Growth is
rather long-jointed but wiry. Will
make a large plant with care.
Very versatile.
(Breary, Britain, 1994)
(CL)(GOU)

Evelyn S. Little
Single H2 Trailer
Tube and *sepals* rosy red. *Corolla*
petals lavender pink flecked with
magenta. The medium-sized
flowers are freely produced
although the plant has the habit
of dropping its flowers before
they reach maturity. Growth is
naturally cascading so will make
a good basket.
(Greene, USA, 1930) (RIV)

Evelyn Stanley
Double H2 Bush
Tube and upward-swept *sepals*
pink. *Corolla* petals marbled in
light and dark pink. Growth is
sturdily upright and self-
branching. Best in large tubs.
(Goulding, UK, 1995)
(WV)

Exeter
Single H2 Trailer
Tube white. *Sepals*, fully
recurving also white. *Corolla*
petals rosy red with white veining
at the base. The flowers are
medium-sized. Growth is
spreading and free-branching.

Excellent for hanging containers.
(Goulding, UK, 1989) (CLI)

Exton Beauty
Double H2 Trailer
Tube and *sepals* white. *Corolla*
very full and exotic-looking also
white. Excellent for basket work.
The flowers are medium-sized.
(Laburnum, UK, 1994)
(ARC)

Eynsford
Semi-Double H2 Bush
Tube and *sepals* of this upright-
growing plant rose. *Corolla* petals
lavender.
(RIV)

F

Fairy Bell
Double H2 Bush
Tube short and pink. *Sepals*
candy pink with recurving tips.
Corolla white. Medium-sized
blooms slightly bell-shaped.
Foliage medium-green. Upright
growth will make a good bush or
Standard.
(Howarth, UK, 1983)
(BRY)

Fairy Floss
Single H2 Lax Bush
An encliandra-type fuchsia with
'perfect' flowers. *Foliage* small
and neat with spreading habit.
Tubes pale pink. *Sepals* spreading,
darken with age. *Corolla* petals
white flushed with pink. Short-
jointed. Excellent for use in
hanging containers.
(Robson, UK, ?)
(BLA)

Falmouth (Beauty?)
Double H2 Lax Bush
Fairly large flowers. *Tube*
greenish white. *Sepals* long,
pinkish white on top and light
pink underneath. *Corolla* petals
white with candy pink veining at
the base. The long, pinkish white
buds are tipped with green.
Upright but lax growth. Will

make a good plant for pot work
if given supports or could be
useful in hanging containers.
('Annabel' × 'Dark Eyes')
(E. Weeks, UK, 1987)
(BRI)

Fancy Free
Double H2 Trailer
Medium to large-sized flowers.
Tube and *sepals* rose. *Corolla*
petals light purple maturing to
pale purple. Early-flowering
trailing growth. Excellent for
basket work. The flowers are
freely produced.
(Sinton, UK, 1995) (ISL)(FEN)
(WAY)(STM)(BRI)(RIV)(FUC)
(OLI)

Fancy Sockeye
Double H2 Stiff Trailer
Tube long, thin and medium
pink. *Sepals* salmon red with pink
on top and crêped salmon red
underneath. *Corolla* opens dark
pink shaded to salmon pink at
base and maturing darker.
Smooth-edged petals give a
skirted appearance. Largish
blooms fairly freely produced.
Foliage medium green. A self-
branching rather stiff trailer.
(J. Brough, UK, 1986)
(BRY)

Fan Dancer
Semi-Double H2 Lax Bush
Tube and *sepals* reddish
carmine. *Corolla* light orchid blue
with a mixture of pink and red.
Medium-sized blooms freely
produced. Lax bush or trailer
type of growth. Will make a good
plant for a pot with some
supports and may well need
weights to secure a good weeping
habit in a basket.
(Castro, USA, 1962)
(BAK)(STM)(BRI)(CLI)

Farningham
Single H2 Bush
Tube and *sepals* rose. *Corolla*
petals light mauve. Growth is
sturdily upright and self-
branching.
(RIV)

FEATHER DUSTER

FANCY FREE   FANCY SOCKEYE

Fashion
Semi-Double H2 Bush
Tube white. *Sepals* rose-coloured, upturned, flushed, with pink on the outside. *Corolla* petals a deep methyl-violet marbled with mauve and an extra thin overlayer of rose petals. Medium-sized flowers freely produced. Growth upright and bushy.
(Niederholzer-Waltz, USA, 1951) (BAK)(BRI)

Favourite
Single H2 Bush
Tube long and creamy pink. *Sepals* of same colour. *Corolla* petals rosy red. *Foliage* has a delightful velvety texture. Good, strong, upright growth.
(Bland, UK, 1868) (BAK)(RIV)

Feather Duster
Double H2 Bush
Sepals of this large-flowered American plant white. *Corolla* petals pure white with a faint tinge of pink. Extremely profuse in its flowering.
(McLaughlin, USA, 1994) (SMI) (*See* photograph on page 93.)

Felthams Pride
Single H2 Lax Bush
Tube and *sepals* red. *Corolla* petals purple with red veins form a beautiful bell-shape. An upright bushy growth. *Foliage* dark green on the upper surface and medium green on the lower. Prefers overhead filtered light.
(Feltham/Longleat Enterprises, UK, 1988) (WV)

Feepie
Single H2 Bush
Tubes and *sepals* rose. *Corolla* rose – the petals are quite small. *Foliage* small and medium green. The plant makes a very attractive small bush. Ideal for growing in smaller pots.
(Franck, Holland, 1988) (LB)

Fenrother Fairy
Single H2 Bush
Tube and horizontally held *sepals* are white with a pink flush and green tips. *Corolla* petals pale pink. Good, strong, bushy growth although small and dainty and of 'dwarf' height.
('Blue Satin' × 'Royal Velvet') (Ryle, UK, 1979) (CLI)

Festival
Semi-Double H2 Bush
Tube and *sepals* pale pink. *Corolla* petals claret rose. Medium-size flowers – fairly free. Upright bushy growth.
(Schnabel, USA, 1948) (CLI)(FEN)(ASK)(WHE)

Festoon
Single H2 Bush
Tubes pale pink. *Sepals* pink with green tips. *Corolla* petals china rose at the base darkening to magenta rose. The flowers are small and produced prolifically. Growth is strong and upright.
(Baker, UK, 1970) (BAK)

Figaro
Double H2 Trailer
Tube and *sepals* very deep red. *Corolla* petals magenta with deep red splashes at the base. Strong trailing variety with large flowers.
(Franklin, UK, 1994) (ISL)(BRI)

Finn
Single H2 Bush
Tubes ivory. *Sepals* white and gracefully upturned. *Corolla* an unusual shade of rusty red. *Foliage* medium green. Flowers are produced in profusion from an early start. Strong, upright growth and a good bushy habit. The distinctive colouring of the flowers is an eye-catcher. A very attractive fuchsia.
(Goulding, UK, 1988) (GOU) (FOX)(RKY)(CHA)(WV)(PER) (RIV)(HYDE)(POT)(CLI)(SIM)

Fiona Pitts
Single H2 Bush
(Encliandra type) 'perfect' flowers. *Tubes* and recurving *sepals* pink. The flared petals in the *corolla* are paler pink. Growth is self-branching and spreading. Makes a good foil to other plants in mixed baskets.
(Saunders, UK, 1989) (CLI)(PER)(ROO) (RIV)(HYDE)

Firecracker
Single H1 Bush
Triphylla-type fuchsia with rich orange-scarlet flowers. Extremely floriferous. *Foliage* very attractive, olive green. Fresh growth is tinged with pink. A superb variegated form of 'Thalia' that really needs no description. Important note from the finder – 'Grow it dry or it will die'.
(Protected Breeders Rights applied for, EU APP No. 98/0638) Propagation for onward sale prohibited.
(Fuchsiavale, UK, 1998) (RID) (BRE)(JAK)(PER)(FUC)(ISL)

Firefox
Single H2 Trailer
Tube crimson. *Sepals* crimson but are slightly darker on the lower surface. *Corolla* petals are red with smooth edges. *Foliage* light green. A good trailing cultivar that will make a good basket.
(Laburnum, UK, 1987) (ARC)

First Kiss
Semi-Double H2 Bush
Tube and *sepals* light neyron rose. *Sepals* reflex and have green tips. *Corolla* petals French rose. *Foliage* dark green. The growth is as a small upright bush. Prefers cool conditions.
('La Campanella' ×) (de Graaff, Holland, 1985) (CLI)(BRI)(WV)(RIV)

First Lord
Double H2 Bush
Tube and *sepals* a deep magenta. *Corolla* petals magenta. Strong upright grower excellent for patio containers. Lovely, rich-coloured, large blooms.
(Forward, UK, 1993) (WV)(FUC)(GLE)(ISL)

FEEPIE

FINN

FIONA PITTS

FIRECRACKER

First Love
Double H2 Trailer
Tube and *sepals* white. The long
sepals have lower surfaces that
are crêpe textured and flushed
with pink. *Corolla* clear orchid,
the outer petals spreading with
marbling of pink and white.
Large blooms of loose form.
Freely produced. *Foliage* lightish
green. A natural trailer.
(Ross, USA, 1957)
(FEN)(BRI)(HYDE)

First of the Day
Single H2 Bush
Medium-sized blooms. *Sepals* red.
Corolla petals purple. The petals
are held in a delightful saucer-
shape. A good, upright, short-
jointed plant that will make a
good specimen for the patio.
(Banks, UK, 1872) (RIV)

Flamenco Dancer
Double H2 Trailer
Tube and *sepals* white. *Corolla*
red-mottled lavender peach. A
truly outstanding colour
combination. Excellent trailer for
basket work.
(Riley, USA, 1990) (FOX)(FEN)
(LB)(WAY)(EX)(WV)(PER)(BEL)
(ROO)(RID)(OAK)(HYDE)(CLI)
(FUC)(GLE)(SMI)(OLI)(LOK)

Flarepath
Single H2 Bush
Tube and *sepals* deep pink.
Corolla rose madder. Medium-
sized flowers. Growth upright
and bushy.
(Hobson, UK, 1976) (BRY)

Flirtation
Double H2 Bush
Tube and *sepals* pale rose-madder.
Corolla very pale petunia purple.
The petals are picotee edged. Large
flowers fairly freely produced.
Growth is as an upright bush.
'Sport' of 'Lucky Strike'.
(Leitner, USA, 1946) (OLI)

Flora
Semi-Double H2 Bush
Tube and long, thin turned back
sepals bright cerise. *Corolla* petals

pale violet with pink veining.
Large blooms – fairly floriferous.
Foliage yellowish-green with red
veining. Strong upright growth.
(Tolley, UK, 1971) (ROO)

Florabelle
Single H2 Trailer
Tube and *sepals* red. *Corolla*
petals dark mauve. An extremely
floriferous plant that, with its
trailing habit, makes an ideal
subject for use in hanging
containers.
(Sold initially as seeds) (BRE)

Floral City
Double H2 Bush
Tube and *sepals* very pale pink.
Corolla petals pale lilac. The
medium-sized blooms and the
delightful delicate pastel
colouring put this well within the
showclass category. Growth is
upright and bushy.
(Holmes, UK, 1974) (BAK)(RKY)
(EX)(ARC)(BRI)(RIV)(LOK)

Florence Taylor
Double H2 Trailer
A large-flowered fuchsia with
ruffled blooms. *Sepals* blood red.
Corolla petals purple. The flowers
are very freely produced for a
large-flowered double. The
natural trailing habit makes it an
ideal subject for use in hanging
containers.
(Harris, UK, 1978)
(OAK)(OLD)

Florida
Double H2 Trailer
Tube and *sepals* of this large-
flowered double deep rose.
Corolla petals in shades of white,
pink and violet. The natural
trailing habit makes it an ideal
plant for use in hanging baskets.
(Strumper, Germany, 1986) (BRI)

Florrie Lester
Double H2 Bush
Sepals rich red. *Corolla* petals
dark red-purple. *Foliage* light
green. Upright and bushy growth.
(Ron Holmes, UK, 1996)
(CLI)(RIV)(OLD)

Fluffy Ruffles
Double H2 Trailer
Tube and *sepals* rosy red. *Corolla*
petals white. The large and fluffy
blooms are very freely produced.
A natural trailer that will make a
very good basket.
(Copley, USA, 1966)
(RIV)

Forest '78
Single H2 Lax Bush
Tube magenta. *Sepals* flat, broad
and green-tipped also magenta.
Corolla petals are white with red
veining. The medium-sized
flowers are freely produced. The
lax growth makes it suitable for
training as a bush if some support
is given or as a plant in a hanging
container.
('Cloverdale Pearl' × 'Icecap')
(Roe, UK, 1980) (WV)

Formossima
Single H2 Bush
Tube and *sepals* creamy white.
Corolla purplish violet.
Medium-sized flowers and free-
flowering. Upright and bushy
growth.
(Girling, UK, 1846)
(STM)(CHA)(RIV)(CLI)(GLE)

Foxgrove Wood
Single H2/3 Bush
Has delightful flowers. *Tubes* and
sepals pink. *Corolla* blue. *Foliage*
medium green. Growth upright,
short-jointed and bushy. Well
worth trying in the hardy border.
H and S: 24–30in (60–75cm)
(Stiff, UK, 1993)
(SIL)(FEN)(RKY)(CL)(LB)(BRE)
(CHA)(PER)(BAK)(ALD)(RIV)
(POT)(CLI)(GLE)(ISL)
(OLI)

Foxy Lady
Double H2 Trailer
Tube and *sepals* rose and pale
pink. *Corolla* opens light purple
and matures to rose. Large
flowers with a delightful colour
combination. Trailing type
growth excellent for basket work.
(Forward, UK, 1993)
(WV)(RIV)(FUC)(GLE)(ISL)

FLAMENCO DANCER

FLORABELLE

FIRST LOVE

FLAREPATH

FLORRIE LESTER

Frances Haskins
Single H2 Bush
The very small flowers are typical of the Encliandra-type fuchsias. The minute flowers are white. *Foliage* light green and feathery. Grows well in all conditions and appears to be very heat-tolerant. Natural branching bushy plants that can be used for training into all sorts of 'topiary' shapes.
(Boor, UK, 1997) (BRE)(ISL)

Frankie's Magnificent Seven
Double H2 Trailer
Tube and *sepals* red. *Corolla* petals lavender blue. A natural trailing habit makes it useful for basket work.
(UK, 1997) (POT)

Frauke
Single H2 Bush
Tube crimson. *Sepals*, horizontally held, crimson on the upper surface but light pink on the lower. *Corolla* petals orange with smooth edges. *Foliage* medium green. The veins are reddish with greyish brown stems.
('Speciosa' × 'Ting-a-ling')
(Bogemann, Germany, 1987) (ARC)(ROO)

Fred Farmer
Single H2 Bush
Tube and *sepals* pale lavender. *Corolla* petals also pale lavender and slightly lighter at the base. Upright, self-branching growth.
(Pacey, UK, 1990) (FEN)

Freefall
Single H2 Trailer
Tube long and pale rose opal. *Sepals* of the same colours. *Corolla* petals china rose. Naturally cascading in its growth so that, with its large flowers continuously produced, it will make an excellent basket plant.
(Baker, UK, 1970) (BAK)(RIV)

Frenchi
Double H2 Bush
Tube flushed white. *Sepals* wide, recurving and salmon pink. *Corolla* petals silvery blue and pale mauve with splashes of pink. Large flowers are freely produced. Growth upright, self-branching and bushy.
(Waltz, USA, 1953)

Friendship
Double H2 Bush
Tube cream. *Sepals* cream blushed with pink. *Corolla* petals open pale purple and mature to violet. Good, strong, upright growth.
(CLI)

Frome in Bloom
Single H2 Stiff Trailer
Tube bright red. *Sepals* horizontally held, also bright red. *Corolla* petals white veined with red. The medium-sized flowers are freely produced. *Foliage* dark green on the upper surface and much lighter on the lower. The growth is rather lax for a bush but is somewhat stiff for a trailer. The plant will need assistance to fulfil either of these functions.
('Ballet Girl' × 'Meditation')
(M. Robertson, UK, 1985) (CHA)

Frozen Tears
Semi-Double H2 Bush
Tube and *sepals* red with a blue glow. *Corolla* petals red purple with a red base. Large flowers. Very attractive.
(de Cooker, Holland, 1992)
(FOX)(FEN)(EX)(CHA)(RIV)
(HYDE)

Fuchsia
Single H1 Bush
Single of the terminal-flowering type. *Tubes* long trumpet-shaped and dark orange. *Sepals* short and dark orange. *Corolla* petals red. *Foliage* dark green and felt-like. Growth is upright. Needs extra care for good growth.
(GOU)

Fuchsia Fanfare
Semi-Double H2 Bush
This prolific flowering plant with its medium-sized flowers was introduced to celebrate the 60th anniversary of the formation of the British Fuchsia Society at the Fuchsia Festival held at Borde Hill, Haywards Heath, Sussex. *Tube* and *sepals* cerise. *Corolla* petals lilac blue. Good for all types of work but will make an excellent standard.
(Waving, UK, 1998) (LB)(SIM)

Fuchsiarama '91
Single (Triphylla-Type) H1 Bush
Flowers long and borne at the end of each branch so are fully terminal-flowering. *Tube* and *sepals* pink. *Corolla* petals short and also pink. Growth is vigorous and upright. *Foliage* medium to darker green. Responds well to 'pinching' so will make a good balanced shape for the show bench.
(Stannard, UK, 1991) (FEN)(ROU) (RKY)(WV)(CLI)(ASK)(OLI)(SIM)

Fuchsia Raspberry
Double H2 Trailer
Tube and *sepals* of this medium to large-flowered fuchsia pink and white. *Corolla* petals raspberry rose. The natural trailing habit makes it ideal for hanging containers.
(RKY)

Fudzi San
Single H2 Bush
Tube and *sepals* light green. *Corolla* petals bright orange. A very attractive colour combination with the flowers being carried on strong, self-branching, upright stems.
(Bogemann, Germany, 1990) (ALD)

F. fulgens
Single H1 Bush
Tube long and pale red. *Sepals* pale red and yellowish green towards the tips. *Corolla* petals bright red. Very attractive flowers are up to 5in (13cm) in length. *Foliage* very large and pale green, tinged with red. Growth is very strongly upright. One of the easiest of the species to grow although it does need some extra warmth and plenty of space for its tuberous roots.
(Sesse and Mocino, Mexico, 1888)
(KM)(CL)(PER)(BLA)

FRANCES HASKINS

FRAUKE

FUCHSIA FANFARE

FUCHSIARAMA '91

FUDZI SAN

F. FULGENS

fulgens machoacans
Single H1 Species hybrid
Typical '*fulgens*' having long,
bright vermilion flowers borne in
racemes. *Foliage* dark red – a
distinguishing feature of this
variety.
(Raiser and date unknown)
(KM)(CL)

fulgens var. michocan
Single H1 Species hybrid
Flowering in small terminal
racemes. *Tubes* long, thin and
deep orange. *Sepals* short,
pendant and green-tipped.
Corolla petals short and dark
orange. *Foliage* and stems stained
very darkly with red.
(Raiser and date unknown)
(GOU)(HYDE)

fulgens var. minuata
Single H1 Species hybrid
Typical '*fulgens*' flowers carried
in terminal racemes. The major
difference is the very thin base to
the *tube*.
(Raiser and date unknown)
(KM)(CL)

fulgens variegata
Single H1 Species hybrid
Description as with *F. fulgens* but
variegated *foliage* of cream, pink
and green. Lovely and showy
plant.
(Raiser and date unknown)
(SIL)(FEN)(RKY)(KM)(CL)(BRE)
(GOU)(BLA)(LOK)

Fulofun
Double H2 Bush
Tube and *sepals* pale pink flushed
white. *Corolla* petals white
flushed with pink with wavy
edges. *Foliage* medium green.
Upright bushy growth.
(Hall, UK, 1992) (CLI)

Fulpila
Single H1 Species hybrid
Terminal-flowering fuchsia. *Tubes*
long, thin and pale tangerine.
Sepals short and a paler shade
with green tips. *Corolla* petals a
darker orange. Good, strong,
upright growth. Not the easiest to

grow and may be considered a
collector's item.
('*F. fulgens*' × '*F. pialoensis*')
(Betje, Holland, 1998)
(GOU)(ROO)(HYDE)

Fur Elise
Double H2 Lax Bush
Tube pink. *Sepals* white with pink
underneath. *Corolla* petals pale
lavender blue ageing to pale
purple. *Foliage* light green.
Growth is rather lax upright and
needs support if grown as a bush.
(Blackwell, UK, 1968) (BAK)
(BRI)(CHA)(CLI)(GLE)(SIM)

G

Gateshead Festival
Single H2 Bush
Tube and *sepals* dark rose.
Corolla petals open dark violet
maturing to violet. They have
smooth edges and the flower is
quarter-flared and bell-shaped.
Foliage medium green on the
upper surface and yellowish green
on the lower. Prefers full sun in a
cool climate with best bloom
colour in bright light.
(Mrs M. Hall, UK, 1990) (CLI)

Gay Melanie
Single H2/3 Bush
Tube short and carmine rose.
Sepals horizontally held, also
carmine rose. *Corolla* petals rose
pink edged with carmine rose.
The medium-sized flowers are
flared and have carmine rose
veining. *Foliage* light green. Good
upright growth that will develop
into a good bush. As a 'sport'
from 'Constance' it is likely to be
hardy.
(Russell, UK, 1982) (RIV)

Gay Spinner
Semi-Double H2 Bush
Tube and very large *sepals* pink.
Corolla pink at the top changing
to imperial purple. Medium-sized
flowers nicely formed. Growth
tall upright.
(Lockyer, UK, 1978) (LOK)(EX)

Gazebo
Semi-Double H2 Trailer
Tube and *sepals* rose. *Corolla*
petals red. The medium to large-
sized flowers are produced
continuously on naturally trailing
branches. A good basket can be
produced.
(Tiret, USA, 1969) (CLI)(FOX)
(STM)(CHA)(HYDE)(SMI)

Gelre
Double H2 Lax Bush
Medium-sized flowers. *Tubes*
cream flushed with orange.
Sepals carmine. *Corolla* carmine
red. *Foliage* medium green.
Growth rather lax so will make a
good basket although weights
might be required, and will make
a good bush if supports are
provided.
(Beiji, Holland, 1990) (HYDE)

Gemma Fisher
Double H2 Bush
Tube and *sepals* of these medium-
sized flowers white flushed with
pink. *Corolla* petals powder blue.
Good, strong, upright and self-
branching growth. Excellent for
pot or patio work.
(1995) (POT)

General Voyron
Single H3 Bush
Tube and *sepals* cerise. *Corolla*
petals violet magenta. The
medium-sized flowers are very
freely produced from early in the
season. Growth upright and
bushy. Excellent as a permanent
bedding plant (very similar to
'Empress of Prussia').
(Lemoine, France, 1901)
(SIL)

General Wavell
Double H2 Bush
Tube and *sepals* pale cerise.
Corolla petals salmon magenta.
The medium-sized blooms are
freely produced. Growth is
upright and bushy.
('Blands New Striped' × 'Beauty
of Exeter')
(Whiteman, UK, 1942)
(BRI)(CHA)(GLE)(CLI)

FULGENS VARIEGATA

FULPILA

GAZEBO

GELRE

Geoff Amos
Double H2 Bush
Sepals pink. *Corolla* petals pure white. Large blooms fairly freely produced. The most important feature of this plant is its very striking variegated *foliage*. Should be included in all collections. Strong, upward-growing bush.
(CLI)(SMI)

Gerharda's Kiekeboe
Single H2 Bush
The small flowers are held erect. *Tubes* and *sepals* red. *Corolla* petals red-purple. Growth is rather unusual and can be described as 'Lycioides type'.
(de Graaff, Holland, 1989) (KM)

Gerharda's Sofie
Double H2 Bush
Medium-sized double flowers. *Tube* and *sepals* white. *Corolla* petals deep purple. Strong, upright and bushy growth.
(de Graaff, Holland, 1988) (ISL)

Ghislaine
Double H2 Trailer
Tube unusually long and pale coral. *Sepals* pale coral. *Corolla* petals rose to orange. The natural growth is as a trailer and will make a good basket.
(Claes, Holland, 1993) (FOX)(EX)(CHA)

Giant Falls
Double H2 Trailer
Tube and broad, upcurved *sepals* on this large-flowered trailing variety pink. *Corolla* petals creamy white with slight pink veining at the base. The large globular flowers are freely produced. The natural trailing habit makes it an ideal plant for any hanging container. *Foliage* deep green.
(Erickson, USA, 1957) (FEN)

Gina's Gold
Double H2 Lax Bush
Tube carmine rose streaked with white. *Sepals* carmine rose streaked with white on the top side and carmine underneath. *Corolla* petals imperial purple splashed with pink and white, maturing to slightly lighter. Blooms are fairly large and broad. *Foliage* citron green on the topside shading to red underneath. The leaves are quite large with serrated edges. Lax upright grower suitable for all types of training.
(Dunnett, UK, 1985) (ASK)

Gingham Girl
Double H2 Trailer
Tube and *sepals* white with pale yellow/green recurved tips. *Corolla* petals open pale purple variegated white maturing to light purple with the same variegation. *Foliage* is medium green on the upper surface and light olive green on the lower. Naturally trailing plant but is strong enough to make a good Standard. Best bloom colour in filtered light.
('Hula Girl' × 'Marcus Graham') (Riley, USA, 1991) (FOX)(MO) (EX)(JAK)(BRI)(CHA)(BLA) (RID)(RIV)(HYDE)(FUC)(GLE)

Giovanna and Wesley
Double H2 Bush
Tubes and recurved *sepals* ivory flushed with pink. *Corolla* petals rich plum red. Growth is strong and upright. Best used as a bush on the patio or as a Standard.
(Goulding, UK, 1999) (GOU)

Gipsy Princess
Double H2 Bush
A little known fuchsia with scarlet *tube* and *sepals*. *Corolla* petals white. Good, strong, upright grower.
(Introduced by Abermule Nursery, UK, 1969) (LOK)

Gladys Godfrey
Double H2 Bush
Tube and *sepals* creamy white. *Corolla* petals mauve. The strong upright growth of this superb flower will provide an excellent plant for patio tubs.
(Stiff, UK, 1995) (BAK)

Gladys Hadaway
Single H2 Bush
Tube and *sepals* deep rose. *Corolla* petals violet. Good, upright, bushy growth.
(Wilson, UK, 1994) (SIM)

Gladys Miller
Single H2 Bush
Short narrow *tube* and *sepals* cream, flushed with pink and tipped green. *Corolla* white at the base shading to pale amethyst-violet. Flowers are large for a single. Growth upright and bushy.
(V. Miller, UK, 1970) (LOK)

F. glazioviana
Single H1 Species
Tube and *sepals* deep pink. *Corolla* petals violet. Short-jointed and strong, spreading growth.
(Berry, Mexico, 199?) (SIL)(FOX) (KM)(CL)(LB)(BRE)(EX)(CHA) (WV)(PER)(GOU)(HYDE)(ISL)

Glendale
Single H2 Bush
Tube, sepals and *corolla* petals all coral pink. The flowers are small to medium in size and bell-shaped. Very freely produced and carried in clusters. Growth is as a tall, vigorous bush.
(Evans and Reeves, USA, 1936) (BRY)(WV)(CLI)

Globosa
Single H3 Bush
Tube and *sepals* greenish cream. *Corolla* rich plum purple. Medium-sized flowers freely produced. Growth upright and bushy.
(Raiser and date unknown as there are many forms of Globosa) (FEN)(RIV)(OLI)

Glow
Single H2/3 Bush
Tube and *sepals* cerise. *Corolla* wine purple suffused with scarlet at base of petals. Small flowers freely produced. Growth as a low bush. An excellent plant for the hardy border.
('Seedling' × 'Mrs Rundle') (Wood, UK, 1946) (SIL)(RKY)(BAK)(RIV)(BRY)(ISL)

102

GEOFF AMOS

GINGHAM GIRL

F. GLAZIOVIANA

GLENDALE

Goena-Goena
Single H2 Trailer
Tube and *sepals* vivid purplish red shading to deep purplish red. *Corolla* petals deep purplish red ageing to dark red. The flowers are of medium size. *Foliage* is mid-green. The natural habit is as a trailer so will make a good basket.
(de Graaff, Holland, 1996) (SIL)

Golden Amethyst
Double H2 Bush
Tube and *sepals* crimson. *Corolla* petals cyclamen purple. *Foliage* yellow. An upright bush.
(Ron Holmes, UK, 1995) (OLD)

Golden Border Queen
Single H2/3 Bush
The short thin *tube* and the *sepals* are rhodamine pink. The sepals flare out and are upturned with neyron rose colouring underneath. *Corolla* petals amethyst purple flushed pale pink with dark pink veining. *Foliage* is bright golden yellow without any variegation.
(Penhall, UK, 1980) (ROU)(BRE)(EX)(CHA)(BRY)(CLI)(GLE)(OLI)(LOK)

Golden Cloverdale Pearl
Single H2 Bush
Foliage variegated form of 'Cloverdale Pearl'. *Tube* and *sepals* rhodamine pink. *Corolla* petals amethyst violet. Good, strong, upright growth makes this a superb plant for pot or garden work.
(Fuchsiavale Nurseries, UK, 1983) (STM)(EX)(CHA)(GLE)(ISL)(OLI)

Golden Crest (Gold Crest?)
Single H2/3 Bush
Free-flowering plant. *Sepals* red. *Corolla* petals pale mauve and pink. The flowers are very small but are produced in great quantities. *Foliage* a delightful golden colour. Very dwarf growing so will be ideal in window-boxes or the front of a hardy border.

(Tabraham, UK, 1982)
(WAY)(STM)

Golden Lady Kathleen Spence
Single H2 Lax Bush
Tube and *sepals* amaranth rose. *Corolla* petals lavender. The blooms are identical in size (medium) with 'Lady Kathleen Spence' but the *foliage* is a beautiful cream/green.
(RKY)(GLE)

Golden Margaret Roe
Single H2/3 Bush
Medium-sized flowers. *Tubes* and *sepals* rosy red. *Corolla* petals pale violet purple. Strong, upright growth with the flowers held outward. *Foliage* has a delightful cream/green variegation.
(Coupland, UK, 199?) (BUR)

Golden Penny Askew
Single H2 Bush
Tube scarlet. *Sepals* recurved, scarlet. *Corolla* petals magenta. The medium-sized flowers are exactly the same as its parent 'Brilliant' except for golden coloured ovary. *Foliage* olive green and variegated with gold. Growth is medium upright, self-branching and good for bushes or Standards.
(Askew, UK, 1983) (CLI)(ASK)

Golden Runner
Single H2 Bush
Sepals pale pink. *Corolla* petals pink. An easy to grow, short-jointed bush. *Foliage* with delightful golden variegation.
(Tolley, UK, 1984) (OLI)(STM)(FUC)(PER)(ASK)(CLI)

Golden Swingtime Variegata
Double H2 Trailer
The flowers are identical with 'Swingtime' (red *sepals* with white veined red petals). *Foliage* golden with some variegation.
(Found in several parts of the UK in 1981)
(OLI)

Golden Tolling Bell
Single H2 Bush
'Sport' from 'Tolling Bell'. *Tube*

white. *Sepals* horizontally held, red. *Corolla* petals open white maturing to cream with smooth petal edges. *Foliage* light to dark green with yellow to gold edging. Some leaves have mottled gold pattern in addition to the variegated edging.
(Pacy, UK, 1985) (CLI)(SIM)

Golden Vergeer
Single H2 Bush
Tube and *sepals* flesh pink with green tips. *Corolla* petals matt red. *Foliage* has yellow margins. Growth upright and self-branching. Perfect for growing in pots.
(De Jong, Holland, 1992) (GOU)(RKY)(LB)(ROO)(RIV)(ISL)

Gold Leaf
Single H2 Lax Bush
Tube china rose. *Sepals* china rose tipped with green and held well back. *Corolla* a clear creamy white. Medium-sized blooms of uniform shape and freely produced. *Foliage* citron-green on fresh growth in cool conditions giving a golden effect. Growth is as a lax bush and self-branching.
(Gadsby, UK, 1974)
(CLI)(STM)(WV)(RIV)

Golondrina
Single H2 Lax Bush
Tube and *sepals* rose madder. *Corolla* petals magenta streaked with light pink. There are dark edges that are emphasized by crimson blotches. Large flowers fairly freely produced. Rather lax bushy growth with a spreading habit.
(Niederholzer, USA, 1941) (SIL)(WV)(BAK)(RIV)(HYDE)(BRY)(WHE)(ISL)

Goody Goody
Single H2 Bush
Tube and *sepals* white. *Corolla* a deep purple fading to orchid. The medium-sized flowers are freely produced. Very showy. Good upright and bushy growth.
(Castro, USA, 1969) (BAK)(FOX)(RKY)(EX)(CHA)(RIV)

GOLDEN BORDER QUEEN

GOLONDRINA

Gooseberry Belle
Single H2 Trailer
Tube and *sepals* light purple.
Corolla petals dark pink. The
natural growth is as a trailer so
will make a good basket. Very
floriferous.
(Hutchins, UK, 1998)
(FEN)(RKY)(HYDE)

Gooseberry Hill
Single H2 Bush
Has small flowers that are
produced in abundance. *Tubes*
and *sepals* pinky white. *Corolla*
petals a dark purple. The
compact and bushy growth gives
this plant show bench potential.
(Hutchins, UK, 1998) (RKY)

Gordon's China Rose
Single H2 Bush
Tube and *sepals* white flushed
china rose. *Corolla* petals
magenta rose. The medium-sized
blooms are freely produced.
Upright growth.
(Gordon, UK, 1953)
(FOX)(CL)(CHA)(OLI)

Gorgeous Gemma
Double H2 Trailer
Tube pure white. *Sepals* white but
tipped and tinged with pink.
Corolla petals purple marbled
with pink and with pink petaloids
that are marbled red and purple.
A natural trailer that, with its
large flowers continuously
produced, makes an excellent
subject for hanging containers.
(Allsop, UK, 1997) (LB)(ROO)

Goteborgskan
Semi-Double H2 Bush
Tube and *sepals* light red. *Corolla*
petals white with pink veining.
The blooms are of medium-size
and have stamens that are deep
pink. *Foliage* medium green and
the leaves are rather small.
Upright, bushy and self-branching
growth.
(Sweden(?), 1920) (EX)

Gothenburg
Double H2 Bush
The *sepals* are red and the petals

in the *corolla* are white. Growth
is upright and self-branching.
(OLI)

Grace Durham
Single H2 Bush
Tube short and rhodamine-red.
Sepals fully up, neyron rose.
Corolla petals start purple
maturing to cyclamen purple.
Medium-sized, wide, bell-shaped
flowers. *Foliage* dark green.
Upright, bushy, self-branching
growth. Needs little pinching or
shaping to produce a superb plant
in a pot or patio tub.
(Goulding, UK, 1984)
(ROO)(RIV)

Gracilis
Single H3 Bush
Sepals bright red. *Corolla* petals
violet. Upright strong-growing
very hardy bush.
('Magellanica Gracilis'). (OLI)

Graf Christian
Single H2 Bush
Tubes ivory white. *Sepals* swept
back, white tinged with pink.
Corolla petals marbled in pink
and mauve with picotee edges.
Growth is sturdily upright. Will
make an excellent Standard.
(Strumper, Germany, 1993)
(GOU)

Graham Summers
Single H2 Bush
Tube and *sepals* scarlet. *Corolla*
petals white. Good bushy growth.
(Summers, UK, 1993)
(FOX)(CHA)(BLA)

Granada
Double H2 Bush
Tube and *sepals* deep carmine.
Corolla petals rich purple. Very
large blooms and free. *Foliage*
dark green and leathery. Growth
upright bush.
(Schnabel, USA, 1957) (FOX)
(FEN)(BRI)(CHA)(FUC)(GLE)

Grand Duke
Single H1 Bush
A terminal-flowering triphylla-
type fuchsia. *Tubes*, *sepals* and

petals all orange. A miniature
upright. Excellent for use in small
pots. An unusual novelty but not
easy to grow.
(Goulding, UK, 1987)
(GOU)(WV)

Grandiflora
Synonymous with *F. denticulata*.
(Ruiz ex Dahigren, 1940)
(ROU)

Grandad Fred
Double H2 Trailer
Tube and *sepals* creamy white,
tipped with pink. *Corolla* petals
carmine. The colouring is very
distinctive and attractive. Will
make an excellent basket with its
lax form of growth.
(J. Allsop, UK, 1998)
(LB)(ROO)

Grandma Flo
Double H2 Trailer
Tube white. *Sepals* pale pink on
top and orange pink on the
undersides, tipped with green.
Corolla pink, tinged with blue
with a dark pink edge, maturing
to deep rose pink splashed with
pale pink. A natural trailer with
large fully double blooms.
(Allsop, UK, 1996) (ROO)

Grandpa Bill
Double H2 Trailer
Tube pure white. *Sepals* white,
tipped with green. *Corolla* petals
a deep purple blue pink at the
base and maturing to bishop's
purple splashed with pink. As a
self-branching trailer with large
flared blooms, this makes an ideal
plant for hanging baskets. A
delightful overall colour
combination.
(Allsop, UK, 1996) (ROO)

Grandpa Jack
Double H2 Bush
Tube pink. *Sepals* red. *Corolla*
petals purple splashed with red.
Good, strong, upright-growing
plant with large fully double
flowers.
(Allsop, UK, 1998)
(LB)(MO)(ROO)

GORGEOUS GEMMA

GRANDPA BILL

GOOSEBERRY BELLE

GRANDAD FRED

GRANDPA JACK

Great Ouse
Double H2 Bush
Tube and *sepals* pinkish red.
Corolla petals red streaked with
white. The medium to large
flowers are carried on strong,
upright-growing plants.
(1993) (POT)(HYDE)

Greenpeace
Single H2 Bush
Tube and *sepals* light green,
flushed with rose. *Corolla* ivory.
Medium-sized flowers produced
very freely and hanging in
clusters. *Foliage* large, fuchsia
green and lighter underneath,
very serrated, light green veins.
Very rampant grower so will
require regular 'stopping' to
produce a manageable bush.
('Speciosa' × 'Ting-a-Ling')
(de Graaff, Holland, 1985)
(FOX)(KM)(CL)(LB)(EX)(CHA)
(RIV)(BRY)(CLI)(ASK)

Greeta
Single H1 Bush
Triphylla-type single flower. *Tube*
and *sepals* pale pink. *Corolla*
petals very pale. The flowers have
long tubes but are not really
borne in terminal clusters. *Foliage*
bronze green with a light green
tint and red vein. Excellent in a
hanging pot.
(Knoppert, Holland, 1992)
(HYDE)(SIL)(FOX)(LB)(BRE)
(MO)(CHA)(PER)(GOU)

Grietja
Single H2 Bush
Encliandra type that carries both
perfect and pistillate flowers.
Long thin *tube* and *sepals* pink
slightly tipped with green. The
wide oblong petals in the *corolla*
are bright pink. Upright and very
vigorous. Needs a lot of space.
(Boremann, Germany, 1984)
(BRY)(GOU)(RIV)(ISL)

Groovy
Single H2 Lax Bush
Tube and *sepals* coral. *Corolla*
petals fuchsia pink to magenta.
The medium-sized blooms are
bell-shaped and freely produced.

Growth is rather lax for a bush
and will make a pot plant with
some supports. Could be useful in
hanging containers.
(Castro, USA, 1969) (RIV)

Guinevere
Single H2 Trailer
Tube and long, spreading *sepals*
white. *Corolla* petals blue-violet,
ageing to pale purple. The large
flowers are freely produced.
Rather lax growth that will make
a good basket or a bush if
pinched frequently and
supported.
(Dale, USA, 1950)
(BAK)(FEN)(WV)

Gwen Burralls
Double H2 Lax Bush
Tube pale pink. *Sepals* pink with
green tips, the undersides having
a definite crêpy texture. *Corolla*
petals purple-violet heavily
veined. Growth is a lax bush or
stiff trailer. *Foliage* light green
maturing to green with red veins.
(J. Burralls, UK, 1998) (ROO)
(*See* photograph on page 111.)

Gwend-a-Ling
Single H2 Bush
Tube and *sepals* white. *Corolla*
petals deep lilac with a pink base.
Small to medium-sized flowers.
Upright and bushy growth of
medium height.
('Ting-a-Ling' seedling)
(Mrs G. Rolt, UK, 1988) (RIV)

Gwen Dodge
Single H2 Bush
Tube the palest waxy pink. *Sepals*
pale pink with a faint flush of
rose. *Corolla* purple fading to
white towards the centre of the
flower. The medium-sized flowers
are fully flared and upward-
looking. Very prolific in its
flowering. *Foliage* medium green.
(Dyos, UK, 1988)
(CL)(EX)(GOU)(ISL)(SMI)(OLI)

Gwendoline
Double to Semi-Double H2 Stiff
Trailer
Tubes and spreading *sepals* light

pink. *Corollas* pale lavender
centred, ruffled pink on the
outside. Spreading habit. Best
when growing in sheltered
hanging pots.
(Goulding, UK, 1996)
(GOU)(HYDE)

Gwen Wakeling
Double H2 Trailer
Tube and *sepals* light pink.
Corolla petals purple. Large
flowers fairly freely produced.
Excellent for baskets as the
natural desire is to trail.
(Johnson, UK, 1993)
(ARC)

Gwen Wallis
Double H2 Trailer
Tube and flyaway *sepals* white,
tinged with pink. *Corollas* pale
lilac. Growth spreading and self-
branching. Will make a good
basket or hanging pot.
(Goulding, UK, 1997)
(GOU)(CHA)(HYDE)

Gypsy Queen
Double H2 Bush
Tube reddish scarlet. *Sepals* broad
and upsweeping, also reddish
scarlet. *Corolla* petals a delightful
colour of lilac and mauvish pink.
The large, well-shaped blooms
are very freely produced for a
double. Upright, vigorous and
bushy plant.
(Bull, UK, 1865)
(FOX)(CHA)

H

Halsall Belle
Double H2 Trailer
Tube and *sepals* white. *Corolla*
petals mid-purple. The natural
self-branching growth is as a
trailer and will make a good
basket.
(Sinton, UK, 1995)
(FOX)(RKY)(BRE)(WAY)
(RIV)
(*See* photograph on page 111.)

GREENPEACE

GRIETJA

GREAT OUSE

GUINEVERE

GWEN DODGE

Halsall Pride
Double H2 Bush
Tube and *sepals* red. *Corolla* petals white. Vigorous and upright, short-jointed and self-branching, bush type of growth. (Sinton, UK, 1996) (BRE)(BUR)(WAY)(GLE) (ISL)

Hampshire Leonora
Double H2 Bush
Medium to large flowers. *Tubes* cream. *Sepals* cream, tinged with pink and very distinctive green tips. The petals in the fully double *corolla* pale pink with a broad lilac pink basal patch that extends halfway up each petal. Growth is strongly upright and self-branching. (Clark [Oakleigh], UK, 1991) (OAK)

Hannah Gwen
Double H2 Bush
Medium-sized double flower. *Tube* short and bright rose. *Sepals* half up and slightly twisted, also bright rose. *Corolla* petals pure white with slight rose veining. Very bushy and upright plant. (Jones, UK, 1998) (KM)

Hannah Louise
Semi-Double H2 Bush
Medium-sized flowers. *Tubes* and *sepals* white flushed with pink. *Corolla* petals white. Fairly strong upright and self-branching growth. (Potash Nursery) (POT)(BRE)

Hannah Smith
Single H2 Bush
Medium-sized flowers. *Tube* and *sepals* white. *Corolla* petals reddish purple. Upright-growing plant excellent for patio work. (FEN)

Hannah Williams
Double H2 Bush
Tube and *sepals* carmine rose. *Corolla* petals pale lavender striped with rose and with smooth edges. The bud is pear-shaped. *Foliage* light green on the upper side and grey green on the lower. Self-

branching, upright-growing shrub. (Johnson/Laburnum, UK, 1987) (ASK)

Hanser's Flight
Single H2/3 Bush
Sepals full and recurving and medium-sized *tube* ivory white. *Corolla* petals pale lavender. The strong growth and long-jointedness make it an ideal plant for the back of a border. (Goulding, UK, 1990) (SIL)(RKY)

Harmony 1
Single H2/3 Bush
Tube and *sepals* pale pink. *Corolla* petals deep purple. The medium-sized flowers are freely produced. Growth is upright and bushy. (Tabraham, UK, 1978) (BRI)

Harmony 2
Single H2 Trailer
Tube and *sepals* light geranium lake. *Corolla* petals rose. The medium-sized flowers are produced on naturally trailing stems. A good basket can be grown quite quickly and easily. (Niederholzer, USA, 1946) (BAK)

Harold
Double H2 Bush
Tube and *sepals* pink. *Corolla* petals violet maturing to light purple. *Foliage* yellowish green. Fairly large blooms are plentifully produced. (Mrs M. Hall, UK, 1989) (CLI)

Harold Coals
Semi-Double H2 Lax Bush
Tube and *sepals* white, tipped with green. *Corolla* petals pure lilac. The large flowers are supported by rather lax upright growth. *Foliage* medium green. Supports will be needed to develop a good bush or it can be used, although rather stiffly trailing, as a hanging container plant. (Coals, UK, 1983) (OLI)

Harriet
Double H2 Trailer
Tube white. *Sepals* also white but have light pink on the undersides.

Sepals stand straight up when in full bloom. *Corolla* petals blue with centre swirls. The large flowers are freely produced on naturally trailing branches. (Soo Yun, USA, 1971) (BRY)(RKY)(WAY)(EX)(BRI) (RIV)(CLI)(ASK)

Harry Dunnett
Single H1 Bush
A triphylla-type fuchsia. *Tube* longish and spinel red. *Sepals* neyron rose, pointed and tend to close over the *corolla*. *Corolla* petals shrimp red. The tapering flowers hang in clusters. *Foliage* mid-green with a velvety sheen. (Dunnett, UK, 1974) (BAK)

Harry Hotspur
Single H2 Bush
Tube pink. *Sepals* short, thick and white flushed with pink. *Corolla* petals violet. The medium-sized flowers are freely produced. *Foliage* mid-green with red stalks. Medium upright bush. (Ryle, UK, 1975) (CLI)

Harry Moss
Double H2 Trailer
Tube waxy white. *Sepals* very deep pink on top and pale red on the undersides. *Corolla* petals purple splashed with salmon pink. The flowers are produced in great profusion. A natural trailing plant, this one will make a superb basket. (Allsop, UK, 1998) (ROO)

Harry Pullen
Single H2 Bush
Tube and *sepals* orange. *Corolla* petals deep orange. Growth is naturally strong, upright and self-branching. Will make an excellent plant for the patio tub. (Stiff, UK, 1992) (BAK)

Hawaii
Double H2 Trailer
Tube and *sepals* of this large-flowered fuchsia white. *Corolla* petals white. The natural trailing habit makes it an excellent plant for baskets. (BRI)

HALSALL PRIDE

HARRIET

GWEN BURRALLS

HARRY MOSS

HALSALL BELLE

Hayley Marie
Single H2 Bush
Tube and *sepals* creamy white.
Corolla petals lilac speckled and
edged with purple. Extremely
floriferous. Upright, bushy
growth.
(Smith, UK, 1998) (LB)(BRE)

Haywain
Single to Semi-Double H2 Lax
Bush
Tube empire rose. *Sepals* held out
horizontally, pink with a shade of
blue on the top. *Corolla* opens
bishop's violet maturing to
cyclamen-purple. The medium-
sized flowers are freely produced
on self-branching rather lax
growths. *Foliage* matt green.
(Goulding, UK, 1984)
(BRI)(RIV)

Heather Rose
Double H2 Bush
Tube and *sepals* pink. *Corolla*
petals lilac. The flowers are fairly
large and quite freely produced. A
very nice and attractive plant.
(BRI)

Heathfield
Double H2 Bush
Tube and *sepals* pink. *Corolla*
petals mauve purple splashed with
pink. The medium-sized blooms
are full and tightly furled. *Foliage*
largish, shiny bright green. Appears
to be synonymous with
'Constance'.
(St Agnes Garden, UK, 1970)
(FOX)(ROU)(BRE)(GLE)(SMI)

Heavenly Hayley
Double H2 Trailer
Tube white flushed with pink.
Sepals white, flushed with pink on
top and pink on the underside. In
the *corolla* the outer petals are
pink marbled and veined purple
whilst the inner petals are violet
with red. A natural trailer, this will
make an excellent basket and the
unusual ruffled appearance to the
flowers will draw admiring
attention.
(Allsop, UK, 1997)
(LB)(ROO)

Hebe
Single H2 Lax Bush
Medium-sized flowers. *Tubes* and
sepals white. *Corolla* petals violet
at first then rich reddish crimson.
A very profuse bloomer. The
rather willowy growth requires
some supporting when grown as
a bush or could be useful in
hanging containers.
(Stokes, UK, 1848)
(BAK)(WHE)

Helena Rose
Double H2 Bush
Tube pink. *Sepals* pale rose.
Corolla petals creamy white
slightly veined with pink. Very
free-flowering. Strong, upright,
self-branching type of growth.
(ROO)

Helen Elizabeth
Double H2 Trailer
Medium-sized flowers. *Tube* pale
pink. *Sepals* that curl and twist
cerise. *Corolla* petals are light
purple flushed pink and veined
with red. A super variety for the
baskets as the growth is naturally
trailing.
(Rowell, UK, 1993)
(KM)(RKY)

Helen Gair
Double H2 Bush
Tube and *sepals* of these large-
flowered plants are rose. The
petals in the very full *corollas*
purple streaked with rose. This
has a naturally trailing growth so
a good basket will quickly be
formed.
(Forward, UK, 1995)
(FOX)(CHA)(FUC)(GLE)(ISL)

Helen Spence
Double H2 Lax Bush
Tube light pink. *Sepals* coral on
the upper surface and rose on the
lower. *Corolla* petals red orange
and splashed with dark rose.
Foliage medium green. Self-
branching and lax in growth so
will make a rather stiff basket.
The flowers are fairly large.
(Johnson, UK, 1991)
(KM)(FEN)(ARC)(BRI)(ROO)

Hello Dolly
Single H2 Bush
Tube and *sepals* pink with a
deeper pink on the undersides.
Corolla petals white and slightly
veined light pink. The flowers are
long budded and give a very
'pointed' effect. The large flowers
are freely produced early in the
season. Growth is upright and
bushy.
(E. Holmes, UK, 1969) (LOK)

Henkelly's Dikbuk
Single H2 Trailer
Tube and *sepals* rose. *Corolla*
petals orange. The medium-sized
flowers are freely produced.
(Spierings, Holland, 1997)
(HYDE)

Henkelly's Stippelke
Single H2 Trailer
Tube and *sepals* aubergine. *Corolla*
petals also aubergine. The natural
trailing habit of this plant makes it
a good choice for hanging baskets.
(Spierings, Holland, 1997)
(HYDE)

Henning Becker
Single H2 Bush
Tube and *sepals* which reflex back
to the *tube*, both red. *Corolla* plum
purple. The flowers are quite small.
Foliage medium green. Growth is
upright and bushy.
(Strumper, Holland, 1991)
(HYDE)

Henrietta Prins
Single H2 Bush
Perfect blooms. *Tubes*, *sepals* and
corolla petals lilac to rose pink.
The flowers are held in small semi-
paniculate clusters. Its habit is
sturdy and bushy. Best grown as an
upright pillar.
(Prins, Holland, 1992) (RKY)

Henry Hoefsloot
Double H2 Trailer
Tube and *sepals* of these large-
flowered plants white with lilac
rose. *Corolla* petals old rose and
violet. The natural trailing habit
makes this ideal for baskets.
(Giesen, Holland, 1996) (HYDE)

HEAVENLY HAYLEY

HELEN GAIR

HENKELLY'S DIKBUK

HENNING BECKER

HELEN SPENCE

Herman de Graaff
Semi-Double H2 Trailer
The glossy *tubes* and swept-back *sepals* red tinged with aubergine. *Corolla* petals pink touched with aubergine and darkly veined. The spreading and self-branching habit makes this a good plant for hanging pots.
(Bas Weeda, Holland, 1991) (GOU)(ROO)(HYDE)

Hidden Treasure
Single H2 Bush
Tube long and orange. *Sepals* that are usually held together lantern-like at their tips, also orange. *Corolla* petals have a similar colouring. Growth is strongly upward and the flowers are produced in profusion. A novelty that attracted quite a lot of attention when displayed in the 'Catch All' Class at the BFS London Show (1999).
(de Graaff, Holland, 1997) (GOU)

High Peak
Double H2 Lax Bush
Tube and *sepals* white. *Corolla* petals also white. Could almost be described as a pure white self except for a slight tinge of pink. Medium-sized blooms very free for a double. Growth lax bush or semi-trailer. Short-jointed.
(Brough, UK, 1977) (BRI)

Hi Jinks
Double H2 Lax Bush
Tube and *sepals* pale pink on the underside and white on top. *Corolla* petals are dianthus blue with streaks of white marbling. The large blooms are freely produced. As the growth is rather lax this will make a good bush if supported but excels when grown in a hanging container.
(J. Kennett, USA, 1968) (RKY)(RIV)(SMI)

Hilda May
Semi-Double H2 Bush
Tube and long *sepals* very deep salmon pink. *Corolla* petals royal purple with streaks of deep

salmon pink fading to magenta. Strong upright growth arches with the weight of the large flowers that are freely produced.
(Drinkwater, UK, 1995) (JAK)

Hiroshige (Tri)
Single H1 Bush
Tube long, broad and dark red. *Sepals* short and dark red. *Corolla* petals magenta. This terminal-flowering fuchsia is rather too shy to open fully in flower. Growth is extremely vigorous and huge plants can be grown.
(Bogemann, Germany, 1992) (CL)(ISL)

His Excellency
Double H2 Bush
Tube and long *sepals* pale pink. *Corolla* petals violet changing to orchid purple with rosy white base, outer petals being streaked with pink. *Foliage* mid-green enhances the large flowers. Strong upright and bushy growth.
(Reiter, USA, 1952) (SIL)(FOX)(RKY)(BRI)(CHA)(BAK)(RIV)(GLE)(OLI)

Hobo
Semi-Double H2/3 Bush
Tubes and upswept *sepals* dark red. The whiskery petals in the *corolla* very dark aubergine maturing to ruby red. Growth is upright, bushy and self-branching. Another unusual hardy.
(Carless, UK, 1997) (GOU)

Holly's Beauty
Double H2 Trailer
Tube white. *Sepals* white flushed with pale rose. *Corolla* pale orange. *Foliage* light to medium green. The natural growth habit is trailing so will make a good basket.
(Garrett, UK, 1989) (FOX)(FEN)(ROU)(WAR)(BRE)(WAY)(EX)(CHA)(WAL)(BLA)(RID)(ALD)(RIV)(HYDE)(ASK)(FUC)(GLE)(ISL)(SMI)

Hollywood Park
Semi-Double H2 Bush
Tube and *sepals* cerise. *Corolla* petals white with faint pink blendings. Flowers of medium size are very freely produced. Upright, bushy and self-branching growth.
(Fairclo, USA, 1953) (BAK)

Holy Mackerel
Double H2 Bush
Tube and *sepals* rose madder. *Corolla* petals a lovely shade of lavender with white marbling. Large flowers are held well on strong laterals. *Foliage* is a golden yellowy colour with red veining.
(Antonelli, USA, 1997) (ISL)

Honnepon
Single H2 Trailer
Tube and *sepals* of this medium-sized flower white. *Corolla* petals are lilac. As the growth is naturally trailing it will make a superb basket.
('La Campanella' × 'Florentine') (Brouwer, Holland, 1988) (WV)

Houpeland
Single H2 Trailer
Tube and *sepals* of this small-flowered cultivar magenta to rose. *Corolla* petals red purple. The growth is naturally trailing so this will make a good basket.
(de Graaff, Holland, 1997) (HYDE)

Howard's Own
Semi-Double H2 Bush
Tube and *sepals* are violet edged with violet blue. *Corolla* petals red. A natural self-branching and upward grower, this plant will make a good specimen in a patio tub.
(Hutchins, UK, 1998) (FEN)(RKY)

Howden Minster
Double H2 Bush
Tube and *sepals* creamy white. *Corolla* petals also creamy white. The flowers are fairly large and freely produced. A 'sport' from 'Blue Veil' and the flowers are produced over a long period.
(Belcross Nursery, UK, 1995) (BEL)

HERMAN DE GRAAFF

HOLLY'S BEAUTY

HIDDEN TREASURE

Hugh Morgan
Semi-Double H2/3 Bush
Tube short and crimson. *Sepals*
crêpe neyron rose on the inside
and crimson neyron rose flushed
and veined crimson on the
outside. *Corolla* petals white
veined with neyron rose with
added petaloids that are heavily
flushed with neyron rose. The
flowers are long, loose and bell-
shaped. They are very freely
produced. Growth is upright,
bushy and probably hardy.
('Fascination' × 'Flamingo')
(R. Holmes, UK, 1974) (RIV)

Hummeltje (Enc)
Single H2 Bush
Encliandra-type. Female plant
with pistillate flowers. *Tube* rose
red. *Sepals* white ageing to rose.
Corolla petals have similar
colouring. The flowers are very
small. *Foliage* dark green and very
fern-like. Rather rampant, wiry
growth. This is a short-day plant
that resents higher temperatures.
(van der Grijp, Holland, 1977)
(LB)

Humpty Dumpty
Single H2/3 Dwarf Bush
Tube pink. *Sepals* reflexing, deep
pink. *Corolla* petals bright blue.
The small flowers are borne in
profusion. *Foliage* pale green.
Strong yet spreading habit
achieving a height of no more
than 6in (15cm). Another for the
front of the hardy border or the
rockery.
(Tabraham, UK, 1987)
(BEL)(BLA)(HYDE)

Huntsman
Double H2 Bush
Tube and *sepals* dark rose.
Corolla petals open violet
maturing to dark purple.
Attractive large blooms as befit
the issue of parents 'Royal Velvet'
and 'Pink Galore'.
(Francis, UK, 1993)
(KM)(FOX)(FEN)(ROU)(BRE)
(STM)(EX)(BRI)(CHA)
(BLA)(RID)(RIV)(HYDE)(ASK)
(WHE)(FUC)(GLE)(ISL)(OLI)

I

Ian Botham
Double H2 Bush
Tube and *sepals* pale pink.
Corolla petals deep lilac. With its
good, strong, upright and self-
branching growth, this makes a
good plant for the patio.
(EX)

Ian Brazewell
Double H2 Bush
Tube and *sepals* claret rose.
Corolla petals plum purple. The
early-flowering, medium-sized
blooms are plentiful. Upright,
bushy and vigorous growth. Will
make excellent bush or Standard.
(J. Day, UK, 1986)
(LOK)(BRI)

Ice Festival
Single H2 Trailer
Tube white. *Sepals* also white
fading to pale pink. *Corolla*
petals also white with the faintest
hint of pink. The medium-sized
flowers are bell-shaped and are
freely produced.
('Coquet Bell' × 'Cloverdale
Pearl')
(Clitheroe, UK, 1986)
(RIV)

Ida
Double H2 Bush
Tube and *sepals* red. *Corolla*
petals purple splashed with pink
and layered. Good, strong,
upright growth.
(EX)

Impala
Double H1 Trailer
Tube very long, thin and ivory
white. *Sepals* pale pink and swept
back. *Corolla* pink. *Foliage*
medium green. The growth is
very slender and spreading.
Excellent for hanging pots or
baskets, but one that benefits
from protection from adverse
weather.
(Moerman, Holland, 1990)
(GOU)(FEN)(RKY)(EX)(WV)
(RID)(HYDE)

Ina 1
Double H2 Bush
Tube and *sepals* pale cerise.
Corolla petals powder blue
streaked with pink. The medium-
sized blooms are produced in
profusion. Growth is strong and
upright.
(Akers, UK, 1976) (ASK)

Ina 2
Single H2 Bush
Medium-sized fully erect flowers.
Tube short, thick and greenish
white. The *sepals*, held
horizontally, greenish white with
a pink flush. The curved tips are
green. *Corolla* petals light old
rose colour with purple edging.
(Flowers are very similar to 'Bon
Accord'.)
('Bon Accord' × 'Venus')
(de Groot, Holland, 1973)

Ina Jo Marker
Double H2 Lax Bush
Tube and *sepals* pinkish red.
Corolla petals deep fluorescent
violet. The large flowers are
produced quite freely. *Foliage*, a
beautiful lime green, enhances the
flowers.
(McLaughlin, USA, 1995)
(CLI)(FOX)(CHA)(PER)(GLE)
(ISL)(SMI)

Ingram Maid
Single H2 Bush
Tube white. *Sepals* held
horizontally, white, flushed with
neyron rose. *Corolla* creamy white
and tube-like. The flowers are of
medium size. Very free-flowering.
The best colour is produced when
grown in full sunshine. Growth
tall, upright and bushy.
(Ryle, UK, 1976)
(ROU)(ASK)(OLI)

Insa
Single H2 Lax Bush
Tube and *sepals* reddish purple.
Corolla petals have the same
colouring. Growth is rather lax
upright. Will need supporting to
form a good bush but will also be
useful in hanging containers.
(Strumper, Germany, 1985) (ARC)

HUMPTY DUMPTY

IMPALA

INSULINDE

Insulinde
Triphylla-Type H1 Bush
A true terminal-flowering triphylla-type and one that stands out like a beacon on the show bench. *Tube* long and orange. *Sepals* short, orange. *Corolla* also orange. *Foliage* bronze green. Growth is bushy and self-branching. Excellent for big bedding schemes but must be taken under cover during the winter months.
(de Graaff, Holland, 1991)
(SIL)(FOX)(FEN)(ROU)(KM)
(WAR)(CL)(LB)(BRE)(MO)
(WAY)(ARC)(BRI)(CHA)
(PER)(GOU)(ROO)(BLA)
(ALD)(CLI)(FUC)(GLE)(ISL)
(OLI)(SIM)
(*See* photograph on page 117.)

Interlude
Double H2 Trailer
Tube slender, waxy white. *Sepals* also waxy white with a pink flush. *Corolla* petals violet purple, the outer petals a delicate orchid pink. Medium-sized blooms. Fairly freely produced flowers. A natural trailer so will, with its self-branching habit, make a superb hanging container.
(Kennett, USA, 1960) (BAK)(RIV)

Irene Lamont
Semi-Double H2 Lax Bush
Tube light pink. *Sepals* light pink underneath with a darker pink on the upper surfaces and tipped with green. *Corolla* petals bright purple. The medium-sized blooms have red stamens. Growth is rather lax and will need support if trained as a bush.
(Robinson, UK, 1986) (ROO)

Irene van Zoeren
Double H2 Bush
Medium-sized flowers. *Tube* light orange. *Sepals* light rose red. *Corolla* lilac rose with a reddish purple border. *Foliage* medium green. The growth is very strong and upright.
(Beije, Holland, 1989)
(ARC)(ALD)(BRY)

Ivy Grace
Single H2 Lax Bush
Tube short and white, tinged with green. The half-down *sepals* open white flushed with palest pink and edged finely with rose red. *Corolla* petals are spiraea red. *Foliage* rather small and mid-green. Growth is rather lax so will make a bush with some supports but will also make a good hanging pot.
('Carla Johnson' ×)
(Gilbert, UK, 1995) (SIL)

Ivy Lisney
Double H2 Lax Bush
Sepals pink. *Corolla* petals white. This is a 'sport' from 'Texas Longhorn' and has a similar manner of growth and size to its parent. It is however rather easier to grow.
(Hooper, UK, 1996) (BRE)

Ivy Swales
Double H2 Lax Bush
Tube short and pale pink. *Sepals* creamy white on the upper surface and white on the underside. *Corolla* petals pale mauve maturing to rosy pink. *Foliage* dark green. The medium to large flowers are carried on rather lax but upright-growing bushes.
(Swales, UK, 1983) (BEL)

J

Jackie Bow
Double H2 Lax Bush
Tube and *sepals* rose. *Corolla* petals orange rose and tipped with lilac. Good but rather lax bushy growth.
(Redfern, UK, 1985) (BAK)

Jackie Bull
Double H2 Stiff Trailer
Tube long, shell-pink. *Sepals* rose-coloured, veined deeper rose on top and orange rose underneath. *Corolla* petals lilac mauve. The medium-sized, fluffy-looking blooms are freely produced. The growth is rather lax so this plant will make a good bush with supports and also a good basket. Try it as a weeping Standard where the weight of the medium-sized blooms will create a cascading effect.
('Bicentennial' × 'Papa Bleus')
(Redfern, UK, 1985)
(WV)(RIV)

Jack King
Double H2 Bush
Tube and *sepals* crimson – inside of sepals rose red and nicely crêped. *Corolla* petals lilac and veined with rose red. Some petals are overlaid very pale pink at the base and fade to rose purple. Blooms are of medium size. Strong, upright and bushy growth.
('sport' from 'General Monk')
(R. Holmes, UK, 198?)
(FEN)(RIV)

Jack Rowlands
Double H2 Trailer
Tubes ivory white. *Sepals* swept-back, flesh pink. *Corolla* petals lavender blue maturing to pale salmon, slightly marbled. Growth is strong and spreading. Ideal for hanging baskets and containers.
(Goulding, UK, 1998)
(GOU)(HYDE)

Jack Stanway
Single H2 Bush
Tube and *sepals* rhodamine pink. *Sepals* have recurving tips. *Corolla* white with pink veining that appears with maturity. The petal edges turn under. The flowers are small to medium-sized and quarter flared. *Foliage* sage green edged with cream – perhaps the most redeeming feature of this plant. The growth upright and self-branching – a good decorative foliage plant can be produced.
(Rowell, UK, 1985)
(SIL)(ROU)(RKY)(WAR)(WAY)
(CHA)(WV)(GOU)(ROO)(RIV)
(HYDE)(CLI)(ASK)(ISL)(SMI)
(OLI)(SIM)

IRENE LAMONT

IRENE VAN ZOEREN

JACK ROWLANDS

JACK STANWAY

Jack Wilson
Single H2/3 Bush
Tube medium to long, white.
Sepals white with pale pink
underneath. *Corolla* petals violet
cerise shading to blue. *Foliage*
mid-green. The medium-sized
flowers are very freely produced.
The upright bushy growth will
make it very useful in the hardy
border.
('Brutus' × 'Swingtime')
(J.W. Wilson, UK, 1979) (HYDE)

Jade's Gem
Double H2 Trailer
Tube pink striped with darker
pink. *Sepals* pale pink but are
darker near the tube and have
white tips. *Corolla* petals pale
pink veined with red and
maturing to very pale pink.
Growth is naturally very lax and
this will therefore make an
excellent plant for hanging
containers.
(J. Allsop, UK, 1998) (ROO)

James Lye
Double H2 Bush
Tube and *sepals* cerise. *Corolla*
petals bluish mauve flushing to
pale mauve at the base. The
medium-sized flowers are freely
produced. Growth upright and
bushy. Often confused with
'Constance' but the flower is
somewhat darker.
(Lye, UK, 1883) (BAK)(FEN)
(RKY)(RIV)(ASK)

James Shurvell
Single H2 Bush
Tube and *sepals* glossy crimson.
Corolla petals are also crimson.
The medium-sized flowers are
freely produced. *Foliage* mid-
green. An upright bushy plant.
(Story, UK, 1862) (SIL)

Jandel
Double H2 Lax Bush
Tube white. *Sepals* white, reflexed
and tipped with pink. *Corolla*
petals orchid. The medium-sized
blooms are fairly freely produced.
Growth is as a lax bush but this
will make a good basket with the

right type of encouragement.
(Walker, Fuchsia-La, USA, 1975)
(EX)(BRI)(CHA)(WV)(GLE)

Jane Lye
Single H2 Lax Bush
Tube and *sepals* pink. *Corolla*
petals mauve pink. This plant is
often confused with 'Lady
Patricia Mountbatten' but the
flowers of the latter are rather
smaller. The natural growth is as
a lax bush.
(Lye, UK, 1870) (BRE)(BAK)(OLI)

Janessa
Double H2 Bush
Tube and *sepals* white. *Corolla*
petals bright red mottled with
orange. Strong upright grower
with large blooms. Ideal for
Standards and large tubs.
(Stubbs, USA, 1996) (BEL)(GLE)

Janet Goodwin
Double H2 Stiff Trailer
Naturally trailing cultivar with
light pink *tube* and *sepals*.
Corolla petals are pink with
deeper colouring at the base of
each petal. *Foliage* medium
green. Growth is rather stiff but
self-branching so will need some
assistance to make a good
basket.
(Laburnum, UK, 1988) (ARC)

Janet Williams
Double H2/3 Bush
Tube and *sepals* red. *Corolla*
petals amethyst blue. Medium-
sized blooms that are very
striking. *Foliage* is deep golden-
green slowly changing to pale
green with maturity. May be
hardy in southern areas.
H: 1ft 6in–2ft (45–60cm).
(Tabraham, UK, 1976)
(SIL)(BRY)

Jan Houtsma
Single H2 Bush
Tube and *sepals* white. *Corolla*
petals dark purple. An extremely
attractive colour combination on
medium-sized flowers. Fairly
strong upright and bushy growth.
(Giessen, Holland, 1986) (HYDE)

Janice Ann
Single H2 Lax Bush
Tube and *sepals* turkey red. The
medium-sized flowers have a
corolla of violet blue. *Foliage*
medium green. Growth being
rather lax makes it useful as a
basket or as a bush with some
supports.
(R. Holmes, UK, 1994)

Janice Perry's Gold
Single H2 Bush
Tube creamy white. *Sepals*
creamy white blushed with pink
on the underside, and very well
reflexed. *Corolla* pale
lavender/pink, cerise-edged and
white at the base. A stunning
bloom freely produced and
enhanced by the spectacular
bright yellow goldy green
variegated *foliage*. Exceedingly
strong versatile grower suitable
for bush or Standard growing. An
exotic cultivar combining both
excellent blooms and brilliant
foliage.
(Perry, UK, 1999) (LOK)

Janie
Double H2 Trailer
Tube and *sepals* white. *Corolla*
petals lavender blue. The natural
growth is as a trailer so it will
make a good basket with its
medium-sized flowers.
(Araujo, USA, 1970) (BRY)

Janneke
Double H2 Trailer
Tube and *sepals* of these large
flowers rosy red. *Corolla* petals
dark red purple. Although large,
the flowers are freely produced on
naturally trailing stems.
(Giessen, Holland, 1987) (HYDE)

Janneke Brinkman Salentijn
Single H2 Bush
Tubes and *sepals* very dark red.
Corollas cup-like and dark
aubergine, almost black. Very
floriferous. The habit of growth is
slow, small but bushy. An unusual
cultivar and a bit of a novelty.
(Betje, Holland, 1992)
(GOU)(LB)

JANICE ANN

JANICE PERRY'S GOLD

JAMES LYE

JANESSA

JANNEKE BRINKMAN SALENTIJN

Jan S Kamphuis
Single or Semi-Double H2 Bush
Tubes and spreading *sepals* pink
with pale green. *Corolla* mauve
with pale pink marbling, the
petals being somewhat irregular
in outline. The flowers are
produced very freely. As the
growth is stiffly upright, this
plant will do best in large tubs on
the patio.
(Betje, Holland, 1999) (GOU)

Jan Veen's Memorial
Single H2 Bush
Tube and *sepals* of these medium-
sized flowered. *Corolla* petals
lilac. Good, strong, upright and
self-branching growth.
(Veen, Holland, 1997) (HYDE)

Jap Van't Veer (Tri)
Single H1 Bush
Terminal-flowering fuchsia. *Tubes*,
sepals and *corolla* bright glossy
orange red. Growth is sturdily
upright and requires some early
pinching. Looks attractive in the
garden or on the show bench.
(Smits, Holland, 1994)
(CL)(ISL)(LB)

Jayess Helen
Double H2 Trailer
Tube and *sepals* red. *Corolla* petals
blue. The natural growth is as a
trailer so it will make an excellent
hanging pot or basket.
(Sumner, UK, 1994)
(STM)(EX)(CHA)(PER)(RIV)
(GLE)

Jayess Wendy
Single H2 Bush
Tube and *sepals* pink. *Corolla*
petals tinted blue. This self-
branching plant forms a good
medium-sized bush. The flowers
are prolifically produced
throughout a long season.
(Sumner, UK, 1994)
(PER)(ROO)(RIV)

Jayne Louise Mills
Single H2 Bush
Tube and *sepals* red. *Corolla* petals
lavender. The flowers are of
medium size and are freely

produced. Growth is as an
upright bush.
('sport' of 'Dutch Mill')
(Roe, UK, 1970) (ARC)

Jean
Single H2 Trailer
Tube and *sepals* white, touched
with palest pink. *Corolla* petals
deepest Tyrian rose. The medium-
sized blooms are freely produced.
The rather lax growth makes it
ideal as a trailing plant.
(Reiter, USA, 1953) (CLI)

Jean Baker
Single H2 Bush
Tube carmine. *Sepals* also
carmine but tipped with light
green. *Corolla* petals dark lilac
and bluish pink. Rather small
Magellanica-type flowers that are
carried on strong upright-growing
bushes. *Foliage* dark green.
(Weeks, UK, 1984) (SIL)

Jean Campbell
Single H2 Bush
Tube and *sepals* rose pink and
suffused pink underneath. *Corolla*
petals rose red with purple at the
base. The largish blooms are freely
produced. Similar in appearance to
'Queen Mary'. Growth is upright,
bushy and self-branching.
(Raffill, UK, ?) (BAK)

Jeanne (Genii)
There is some debate as to
whether 'Jeanne' or 'Genii' is the
correct name for this delightful
hardy cultivar. A full description
has previously appeared under
the more widely accepted name of
'Genii'.
(KM)(MO)(BAL)(OAK)

Jean Pidcock
Double H2 Bush
Tube and *sepals* light pink.
Corolla petals wisteria blue. The
medium-sized flowers are carried
on strong arching branches.
(ARC)

Jean Smith
Double H2 Bush
Tube and *sepals* red and reflex.

Corolla petals red purple. A very
attractive plant that is self-
branching and floriferous.
Medium-sized blooms.
(Smith, UK, 1998) (SMI)

Jenessa
Double H2 Bush
Tube and *sepals* cream and pink.
Corolla petals bright red, mottled
orange. The large blooms are
carried on strong, upward-
growing stems. Will be an ideal
plant for growing as a Standard
or in large patio tubs.
(Stubbs, USA, 1996) (ISL)(SMI)

Jennifer Lister
Semi-Double H2/3 Bush
The medium-sized flowers have
short *tubes* and upswept *sepals*
that are white flushed with pink
and with green tips. *Corolla*
petals are a deep red shading to
white at the base. Sub petals have
an orange flush. A very attractive
plant on a good strong bush
found to be hardy in the vicinity
of Harrogate.
(Johns, UK, 1998) (KM)(WAL)

Jenny May
Single H2 Bush
Tube and *sepals* creamy pink.
Corolla petals violet pink. Very
floriferous. This naturally bushy
plant should make an excellent
addition to the show bench.
(Bush, UK, 1998) (LB)

Jennie Rachael
Double H2 Bush
Tube and *sepals* white flushed
with pink. *Corolla* petals rose-red
veined with rose-bengal. The
large blooms are freely produced.
Foliage large, dark green.
(Cheetham, UK, 1979)
(PER)(RID)(ISL)

Jessica's Dream
Double H2 Trailer
Tube and *sepals* of this medium-
sized flower sparkling white.
Corolla petals cerise streaked with
white. The growth is rather lax so
it will make an excellent basket.
(Allsop, UK, 1998) (LB)(ROO)

JAYESS HELEN

JAN VEEN'S MEMORIAL

JEAN BAKER

JENNY MAY

JESSICA'S DREAM

Jezebel
Semi-Double H2 Bush
Tubes short, cherry red. *Sepals*
cherry red, tipped with green.
Corolla petals peony pink
streaked with cherry red. Large
blooms are produced on upright-
growing plants.
(Walker, USA, 1979)
(BRE)(EX)(BRY)(RIV)

Jiddles
Single H2 Bush
Encliandra-type fuchsia with
small flowers that have *tubes*,
sepals and *corolla* all of sparkling
white. *Foliage* light-coloured and
small but the upright growth of
the plant is very wiry and sturdy.
(Iddles, UK, 1996)
(LB)(PER)(ROO)(HYDE)

Jill Storey
Single H2 Bush
Tube and horizontally held *sepals*
white. *Corolla* white shading to
rose purple at the edges. The
medium-sized blooms are saucer-
shaped. A very attractive
introduction, floriferous but not
the easiest to grow.
(Storey/Oxtoby, UK, 1996) (KM)

Jim Hawkins
Single H2 Bush
Tube and *sepals* pink. *Corolla*
petals lilac pink. The upright
growth is very strong and the
plant as a whole is extremely
attractive.
(Stiff, UK, 1996) (BAK)

Jim Missin
Double H2 Bush
Tube and *sepals* white. *Corolla*
petals magenta and white at the
base. Large flowers. *Foliage*
attractive lime green and yellow.
A foliage 'sport' from 'Bow Bells'.
(Missin, Belgium, 1994)
(MO)(ALD)(ASK)

Jimmy Cricket
Single H2 Bush
An encliandra-type plant that has
small pink and white flowers.
Foliage very dainty.
(Strickland, UK, 1997) (KM)(LB)

Jim's Gold
Single H2 Bush
Tube and *sepals* amaranth-rose.
Corolla petals lavender pink. The
flowers are of medium size and are
freely produced. *Foliage* golden
yellow. This plant is a 'sport' from
'Lady Kathleen Spence'.
(Willment, UK, 1998) (ISL)

Jingle Bells
Single or Semi-Double H2
Trailer
Tube and *sepals* red, the latter
being rather broad and held a
little above the horizontal.
Corolla petals white with red
veining. Small to medium-sized
flowers. Rather lax growth that
will produce a bush with supports
or a good hanging container.
(USA) (ISL)(BRE)(WAY)(STM)
(RIV)(FUC)(OLI)

Joan Christina
Single H2 Bush
Tube and *sepals* pale pink.
Corolla petals lavender. The
medium-sized flowers are freely
produced. Good, strong, upright
growth.
(RIV)

Joan Cox
Single H2 Bush
Tube and *sepals* light pink.
Corolla petals lilac pink. The
small to medium flowers are
produced very freely throughout
the season. A really excellent
cultivar with upright-facing
flowers. (FUC)

Joan Fischer
Semi-Double H2 Bush
Tube and *sepals* pink and white.
Corolla petals white. The
medium-sized flowers are freely
produced on strong, upward-
growing stems.
(RIV)

Joan E. Caunt
Single H2/3 Bush
Tube and *sepals* rose red, tipped
with green. *Corolla* petals deep
purplish pink, edged with fuchsia
purple, and veined red. Medium-

sized flowers. *Foliage* darkish
green. Makes a good upright
bush of about 18in (45cm) in the
hardy border.
(Caunt, UK, 1994)
(SIL)(RKY)(KM)

Joan Jewel
Single H2 Bush
Tube and *sepals* crimson. *Corolla*
petals magenta. The growth is very
strong, self-branching and upright.
Will make a superb Standard.

Jo Anne Fisher
Double H2 Bush
Tube and *sepals* creamy white.
Corolla petals are white, veined
with pink. Strong upright growth.
(FEN)(RKY)(POT)

Joan Paxton
Single H2 Bush
Tube and *sepals* pink. *Corolla*
petals white and slightly flared.
Good, strong, self-branching,
upward-growing bush.
(Lorimer, UK, 1995)
(CL)(SIM)

Joan Spencer
Single H2 Trailer
Tube and *sepals* white. *Corolla*
petals magenta. The flowers are
large and are freely produced on
naturally trailing stems.
(CHA)(FOX)

Joan Walters
Double H2 Bush
Tube and *sepals* rose red. *Corolla*
petals open purple maturing to
magenta with light violet in the
centre. Large but prolific blooms
with an unusual shape.
(Forward, UK, 1997)
(WV)(FUC)(GLE)(ISL)

Joel
Single H2 Bush
The upward-looking small flowers
have white *tubes* and *sepals*.
Corolla petals deep lilac. The
smallish flowers appear on self-
branching bushy plants. Extremely
prolific.
(Humphries, UK, 1993)
(LB)(PER)(ISL)

JEZEBEL

JIDDLES

JINGLE BELLS

JOAN WALTERS

JOAN PAXTON

Joe Nicholls
Double H2 Bush
Tube and *sepals* rose. *Corolla*
petals violet blue. This plant has
all the strength and characteristics
of its parent 'Westminster
Chimes' but with double flowers.
Very compact and bushy growth.
Should make an excellent
exhibition plant.
(Nicholls, UK, 1996)
(KM)

John Boy
Semi-Double or Double H2
Trailer
Tubes and recurving *sepals* bright
pink. *Corolla* petals violet in the
centre and violet and pink
marbled on the outer petals.
Growth is spreading. Ideal for
baskets in sheltered positions.
(Goulding, UK, 1996)
(GOU)(RKY)(BRI)

John E. Caunt
Single H3 Bush
Tube and *sepals* red. *Corolla*
petals half flared and rosy
magenta. Excellent for the hardy
border. H and S: 1ft 6in (45cm).
(Caunt, UK, 1994)
(KM)

John Grooms
Double H2 Bush
Tube and *sepals* pink. *Corolla*
petals violet blue. The medium-
sized flowers are produced very
freely throughout the season.
Nice upright growth on self-
branching plants.
(Sinton, UK, 1995) (JAK)(FEN)
(WAR)(BRE)(STM)(EX)(ROU)
(RKY)(KM)(WAY)(RIV)(CLI)
(ISL)(OLD)(LOK)

Johnny
Semi-Double H2 Bush
Tube short and red. *Sepals* heavy,
upturned, rose-coloured. *Corolla*
petals white and pink with a blue
overcast and heavy red veining at
the base. Small flowers but very
heavy blooming. Growth upright
and bushy.
(Brown and Soules, USA, 1952)
(LOK)

John Ridding (Syn *Firecracker*)
This triphylla-type fuchsia is a
breakthrough in that it has
variegated *foliage* of dark olive-
green and cream. A 'sport' from
'Thalia' it has the typical flowers
of long red/orange *tubes* and
trumpet-shaped *sepals* and
corolla. A superb cultivar well
worth seeking out and trying.
(Fuchsiavale Nurseries, UK,
1998) (RID)

John Suckley
Semi-Double H2 Trailer
Tube and *sepals* pink. *Corolla*
pale blue. The medium-sized
flowers are freely produced. The
natural trailing habit makes it an
ideal plant to use in hanging
baskets.
(Suckley, UK, 1966) (BAK)

John Waugh
Single H2 Trailer
Tube and *sepals* creamy white.
Corolla petals salmon orange.
Medium-sized flowers. Very free-
flowering. *Foliage* very attractive.
Being a good trailer, it is excellent
for hanging containers although it
can be rather brittle.
(D. Clark, UK, 1988) (STM)

Jon Oram
Single H2 Bush.
Tube and *sepals* rhodonite red.
Corolla petals violet-purple.
Medium-sized flowers. Very
profuse and showy. Upright bush
and vigorous growth.
(J. Day, UK, 1988) (ISL)(LOK)

Jopie
Double H2 Trailer
Tube and *sepals* of this large-
flowered fuchsia are dark carmine
rose. *Corolla* petals plum purple.
A very attractive colour
combination carried on naturally
trailing stems.
(Giessen, Holland, 1993) (HYDE)

Joyce Adey
Double H2 Bush
Tube and *sepals* dark rose.
Corolla petals open violet and
mature to light purple. The

medium-sized blooms open
simultaneously creating a very
stunning effect.
('Dusted Pink' × 'Ruby Wedding')
(Forward, UK, 1997)
(WV)(FUC)(GLE)(ISL)

Joyce Forward
Single H2 Trailer
Tube and *sepals* pink. *Corolla*
petals scarlet. The medium to
large single flowers are carried on
naturally trailing stems and will
make a very attractive basket.
Foliage mid-green on the upper
surfaces and green flushed with
red on the lower.
('sport' of 'Coachman')
(Forward, UK, 1989)
(FUC)(GLE)(ISL)

Joyce Maynard
Double H2 Trailer
Tube is light pink with crimson
stripes. *Sepals* are blush pink with
green tips. *Corolla* petals are
white with pink splashes from the
base. Prefers shade for the best
colour but this graceful plant
trails under the weight of the
flowers. Multi-flowering from
most of the leaf axils.
(Varley, UK, 1997)
(MO)(JAK)

Joyce Storey
Single H2/3 Bush
Tube and fully up *sepals* red.
Corolla petals pink. The small to
medium-sized flowers are held
erect. It arguably makes a better
plant than its parent 'Pink
Fantasia' by holding its lower
leaves. Has a very long flowering
period. It might well be hardy in
some of the more favoured areas.
(Storey, UK, 1999) (KM)

Joyce Wilson
Double H2 Bush
Tube and *sepals* rosy pink.
Corolla petals white, veined with
pink. The smallish flowers are
produced in quantity and
continuously on an upright self-
branching plant.
(Wilson, UK, 1994)
(ISL)(SIM)

JOHN E. CAUNT

JOHN GROOMS

JOYCE FORWARD

JOYFUL JOANNE

Joyful Joanne
Double H2 Lax Bush
Tube pale pink, striped with
green. *Sepals* pink, tipped with
green on top and pink with a
white stripe on the underside.
Corolla petals violet and are paler
at the base – almost pink near the
tube. The petals mature to a
reddish purple. Growth is rather
lax for a bush so it will need
some supports for the fairly
heavy flowers.
(Allsop, UK, 1998) (ROO)
(*See* photograph on page 127.)

Jubilee
Double H2 Bush
Tube and *sepals* white. *Corolla*
petals are bright red and edged
with dark tyrian rose fading to
lighter shades at the base. The
large flowers are freely produced
for their size. Growth strong
upright bush.
(Reiter, USA, 1953)
(BRI)

Jubilee Quest (*see* **Angelina**)
Single H2 Bush
Tube and *sepals* shell pink.
Corolla petals darker pink with
distinctive edging. A very
attractive flower carried on an
upright self-branching bush.
Certain to be a show winner.
(Wilkinson, UK, 1997)
(LB)(BRE)(ROO)(ALD)(ISL)

Judith Louise
Single H2 Bush
Tube cream. *Sepals* pink. *Corolla*
petals cerise. An easy plant to
grow and one that will give great
satisfaction with its abundance of
flowers.
('Lye's Unique' × 'Other
Fellow')
(Barnes, UK, 1995)
(FOX)(ROU)(CHA)

Judith Mitchell
Double H2 Bush
Tube and *sepals* pink/white.
Corolla petals deep violet with
rosy streaks. The medium-sized
flowers are freely produced.
(ARC)

Julchen
Single H2 Bush
Tube short and like the upswept
sepals creamy white. The *corolla*
petals tangerine orange.
Peripheral and multi-flowering, its
habit is upright and self-
branching. Excellent for tubs or
the border.
(Gotz, Germany, 1986)
(ROU)(WV)(ROO)(HYDE)

Julie
Semi-Double H2 Trailer
Tubes and *sepals* of this naturally
trailing fuchsia neyron rose.
Corolla petals the same
colouring. An attractive medium-
sized flower that does well in
hanging containers.
(FEN)(RIV)

Jump for Joy
Double H2 Trailer
Tube and *sepals* white. *Corolla*
petals purple. Excitingly rich,
contrasting colours. Another fine
large double from this prolific
hybridizer.
(Garrett, USA, 1997)
(CLI)(HYDE)(SMI)

June Spencer
Single H2 Trailer
Tubes and recurving *sepals* white.
*Corolla*s cup-shaped, mauve
maturing to pink with marbled
petals. Growth is rather spreading
and therefore more suitable for
hanging pots, baskets or window-
boxes.
(Goulding, UK, 1998)
(GOU)(HYDE)

Juno 1
Double H2 Bush
Tube and *sepals* red. *Corolla*
lavender purple. Medium-sized
flowers. Freely produced with
rolled-back corolla. Upright
growth.
(Hazard and Hazard, USA, 1930)
(BAK)

Juno 2
Single H2 Trailer
Tube and *sepals* white tipped
with green. *Corolla* petals dark

red, fading to bright red with
maturity. *Foliage* large, light
green. Naturally trailing
growth.
(Kennett, USA, 1966) (BAK)

F. juntasensis
Single H1 Species
Tube rose to flesh-coloured.
Sepals reddish. There are no
petals. Very few flowers are
produced but those that do
appear come in terminal clusters.
Vine-like shrub, usually epiphytic.
A collector's item.
(Kuntze, Bolivia, 1898)
(GOU)(HYDE)

Justine Ann
Single H2 Bush
The small single flowers have
white *tubes*. *Sepals* white flushed
with pink and a deeper pink
underneath. *Corolla* petals deep
rose edged with magenta. Very
free-flowering. The upright
growth is short-jointed. Should be
a good exhibition variety.
(Kirby, UK, 1995) (JAK)(FEN)
(BRE)(ALD)(CLI)(ISL)

Just William
Single H2 Bush
Tube and *sepals* cardinal red.
Corolla petals also cardinal red
but with roseine purple at the
base of each petal, and maturing
to mallow purple. The growth is
as a small but bushy upright.
Would probably make an
excellent bonsai plant.
(R. Holmes, UK, 1996)
(ROO)

K

Karen Bradley
Single H2 Bush
Tube and *sepals* rose pink.
Corolla petals flowing pink or
deep rose. The medium-sized
flowers are produced in quantity
on good, strong, compact
bushes.
(Hanson, UK, 1998)
(JAK)(ARC)(ISL)

JUBILEE QUEST

JULCHEN

JUNE SPENCER

JUSTINE ANN

Karen Isles
Single H2 Bush
Perfect flowers. An encliandra-type fuchsia with dark red *tubes* and recurving *sepals*. *Corolla* petals also dark red. The growth is upright, self-branching and sturdy. Looks well in mixed tubs and as a miniature Standard.
(Strickland, UK, 1997)
(KM)(LB)(BLA)

Karen Louise
Double H2 Bush
Tube and *sepals* pink. *Corolla* petals also pink. Very large blooms for a double – a lovely pink self. Growth upright and self-branching.
(E. Holmes, UK, 1978)
(LOK)

Kate Harriet
Double H2 Trailer
The very large double flowers have red *tubes* and *sepals*. *Corolla* petals ruby red. The natural growth is as a trailer so will make a good basket.
(Stiff, UK, 1991)
(FOX)(RKY)(CL)(BRE)(CHA)
(PER)(BEL)(BAK)(ROO)
(RIV)(HYDE)(GLE)

Kath Van Hanegam
Single H2/3 Bush
Tubes small, dark red. *Sepals* horizontal with aubergine overtones. *Corolla* petals dark aubergine. The small to medium flowers are produced in profusion. Small and neat, self-branching bush. Excellent plant for the rockery. H: 1ft (30cm).
(Carless, UK, 1998)
(GOU)(ROO)

Kathy Louise
Double H2 Trailer
Tube carmine red. *Sepals* carmine with a crêpe effect on the underside. They are long, broad and curl up over the tube. *Corolla* a beautiful shade of soft rose. Large blooms. *Foliage* glossy dark green. Growth very vigorous and naturally trailing. Frequent stopping necessary to

obtain a good bushy plant.
(Antonelli, USA, 1963)
(LB)(PER)(ROO)(RIV)(HYDE)

Katie Coast
Single H2 Bush
Tube and *sepals* white overlaid with scarlet. *Corolla* petals turkey red. Upright bushy plant that is very showy.
(R. Holmes, UK, 1995)
(OLD)(RIV)

Katie Elizabeth Ann
Double H2 Bush
Tubes and *sepals* white flushed with rose. *Corolla* petals shell pink flushed with rose. A delicate and very attractive plant with small-sized flowers.
(D. Clarke, UK, 1997)
(WAR)

Katie Lu
Single H2 Bush
Tube and *sepals* light red to purple. *Corolla* petals bright purple with edges to light purple. The medium-sized blooms are profusely produced.
(McLaughlin, USA, 1994)
(SMI)

Katie Reynolds
Semi-Double H2 Bush
Medium sized blooms with white *tube* and *sepals* which are flushed with pink. The petals in the *corolla* are white. Beautifully shaped blooms. Medium green *foliage*.
(Gordon Reynolds, UK, 2000)
(BLA)

Katie's Double
Double H2 Bush
Tube and *sepals* red. *Corolla* petals red and purple with longer petals in the centre. A real beauty.
(McLaughlin, USA, 1997)
(ISL)(HYDE)(SMI)

Katie's Gem
Single H2 Lax Bush
Tube pale pink and striped with red. *Sepals* pink on top and deeper pink underneath. *Corolla* petals purple-violet with pink at

the base and slight red veining. The flowers hang in clusters. Growth is as a strong, self-branching but lax bush that will also make a good basket.
(Allsop, UK, 1998) (ROO)

Katinka
Single H2 Bush
Encliandra-type fuchsia with larger than average 'perfect' flowers. *Tubes, sepals* and petals bright scarlet. Growth is shrubby, self-branching and strong. Excellent for mini-standards, fans, and so on.
(Goedman, Holland, 1989)
(CL)(KM)(FEN)(RKY)(LB)
(GOU)(ROO)

Katjan
Single H2 Bush
Tube and *sepals* dull red. *Corolla* petals a duller red. The flowers are small but very profuse with three or four to each leaf axil. Suitable for use as a small Standard, bonsai or small upright bush.
(*magellanica* × *lycioides*)
(Carless, UK, 199?) (ROO)

Katy James
Single H2 Bush
Tube is short, rose-coloured. *Sepals*, horizontally held, are white tipped with green and flushed with pink on the underside. *Corolla* petals lilac blue flushed with white at the base. On maturity the petals flare to a rounded bell-shape and darken to a deeper purplish pink colour. The plant is bushy and self-branching with many buds in each leaf axil. A must for the show bench.
(Wilkinson, UK, 1999) (KM)

Kay Riley
Double H2 Trailer
Tube and *sepals* white. *Corolla* petals deep pink and streaked with white. The large blooms are carried on strong trailing growths.
(Riley, USA, 1994)
(FOX)(FEN)(RKY)(LB)(GOU)
(ROO)

KATE HARRIET

KATH VAN HANEGAM

KATHY LOUISE

KATIE COAST

KATJAN

KATY JAMES

Keesje

Keesje
Single H2 Lax Bush
The small single flowers have red *tubes*, *sepals* and *corolla* petals. Growth is rather horizontal but is self-branching. Worth trying in a hanging pot.
(Peters-Vingerh, Holland, 1991)
(MO)(ISL)

Kegworth Beauty
Single H2 Bush
Tube long, white. *Sepals* short, waxy white. *Corolla* petals amaranth rose. The flowers are small but are freely produced over a long period. Growth upright, bushy and short-jointed.
(H. Smith and Pacey, UK, 1974)
(WV)(ASK)

Kelly Jo
Single H2 Bush
Tube and *sepals* rose red. *Corolla* petals cyclamen purple. The flowers are borne in profusion and it should make an excellent show plant.
(R. Holmes, UK, 1996)
(CL)(ROO)(OLD)(SIM)

Kempenaar
Single H2 Bush
Tube and *sepals* orange. *Corolla* petals also orange. A delightful, glowing, bushy plant that proudly displays its medium-sized flowers.
(Deelkens, Belgium, 1996)
(HYDE)

Ken Birch
Double H2 Bush
Tube and *sepals* crimson. *Corolla* petals white. Floriferous upright bush well within the show category.
(Ron Holmes, UK, 1998) (OLD)

Kenny Holmes
Single H2 Bush
The long *tube* and *sepals* pale scarlet. *Corolla* petals scarlet. The upright self-branching growth produces a very attractive bush.
(Holmes, UK, 1981)
(WV)

Keystone
Single H2 Bush
Tube pink. *Sepals* baby pink tipped with green, with a deeper pink underneath. *Corolla* baby pink – almost a pink self. Medium-sized blooms quite free and longish. Growth medium upright and bushy.
(Haag, USA, 1946)
(BAK)(OLI)

Kim Wright
Double H2 Bush
Tube long, thin and pink. *Sepals* long and pink. *Corolla* petals violet with large pink veining. Largish blooms of carnation form – best colour develops in the sun. *Foliage* deep green. Growth medium upright – makes a good bush.
(J.A. Wright, UK, 1976)
(FOX)(FEN)(CHA)(WHE)
(FUC)(GLE)

Kingswood Gem
Semi-Double H2 Lax Bush
Tube and *sepals* rose pink. *Corolla* petals lilac. The flowers are of medium size but freely produced. Growth is as a self-branching lax bush. Looks lovely in hanging containers.
(Wells, UK, 1989) (ROO)

Kleine Sandra
Single H2 Lax Bush
This encliandra-type fuchsia has perfect flowers. *Tubes* and swept-back *sepals* pink maturing to red. *Corolla* petals spreading and with the same colouring. Growth is neat, upright and self-branching. Ideal when used in large containers or mixed hanging baskets.
(Schlikowey, Holland, 1998)
(GOU)

Kocarde
Single H2 Bush
Tube, *sepals* and *corolla* petals all orangey pink. The growth is fairly strong upright.
('Kwintet' × 'Cardinal')
(de Groot, Holland, 1981)
(BRY)

Komeet
Single H2 Bush
Tube is short and red. *Sepals* also red and very long. *Corolla* petals purple changing to red lilac with maturity. Medium-sized flowers with red stamens. *Foliage* medium to dark green. Good, upright, bushy growth.
(De Groot, Holland, 1970)
(FEN)(EX)(OLI)

König der Nacht
Double H2 Trailer
Tube and *sepals* rose red. *Corolla* petals violet purple. The medium-sized flowers are freely produced on naturally trailing branches. A good basket or hanging pot can easily be grown.
(Rapp, Germany, 1985)
(HYDE)

Kopjes
Double H2 Bush
Tube and *sepals* neyron rose. *Corolla* petals pale lilac pink with dark violet edging. The blooms are small. A very compact, bushy plant that will be ideal for use in smaller pots.
(Weston, UK, 1996)
(SIM)

Koralle (Synonymous with **Coralle**)
Triphylla-Type H1 Bush
Tube long, thin and tapering. *Sepals* short, salmon orange. *Corolla* also salmon orange. *Foliage* deep sage green with veins of a slightly paler shade and an overall velvety sheen. The leaves are fairly large. Growth is upright and very vigorous. The flowers are carried terminally (at the ends of each lateral).
(*F. triphylla* × *F. fulgens*)
(Bonstedt, Germany, 1905)
(FOX)(FEN)(BRE)(BRI)
(WV)(BAK)(BLA)(RIV)(BRY)
(GLE)(OLI)(SIM)

132

KEMPENAAR

KEN BIRCH

KINGSWOOD GEM

KOMEET

KÖNIG DER NACHT

KORALLE

L

La Bianca
Single H2 Lax Bush
Tube and *sepals* white tipped with green with a faint green stripe. *Corolla* petals white flushed with the faintest pink. The flowers of medium size are freely produced. Growth is rather lax so this will make a bush with supports or can be used in hanging containers.
(Tiret, USA, 1950) (BAK)

Laddie
Double H2 Bush
Tube light carmine. *Sepals*, that arch back, also light carmine with white stripes down the middle. *Corolla* petals light purple. The blooms are large and fairly free for their size. *Foliage* large, medium green. Growth is medium upright and bushy.
(L.A. Wright, UK, 1980) (BRY)

Lady Boothby
Single H3 Bush
Tube crimson, short and thin. *Sepals* crimson, short and broad and held almost horizontally. *Corolla* blackish purple, slightly pink at the base of the petals and veined with cerise. *Foliage* darkish green and finely serrated. Growth is upright and very vigorous, with very long branches and considerable length between the nodes. A climber, it will cover an archway in a season. H and S: 36in–48in (90–120cm)
('*F. alpestris*' × 'Royal Purple')
(Rafil, UK, 1939)
(SIL)(LB)(ARC)(FIS)(KM)(OLI)
(BAK)(WV)(STM)(EX)(CL)(ROO)
(ASK)(SIM)(ISL)(BRI)(CLI)(OLD)

Lady Dorothy
Single H2/3 Bush
Tube, *sepals* and *corolla* are all bright vermilion. This is a 'sport' from 'Beacon' with the same growth and habit. *Foliage* is the same colour but without the ation.
('sport from 'Beacon')
(Robinson, UK, 1980)
(BUR)(BRY)

Lady Framlingham
Double H2 Bush
Tube of this medium-sized flower cream. *Sepals* pink. *Corolla* petals deep lilac. A strong, upright-growing and self-branching plant.
(1997) (POT)

Lady in Pink
Double H2 Bush
Tube and *sepals* light pink and *corolla* petals shell pink. A delightful colour combination. The medium-sized flowers are freely produced on well-branched plants.
(Sinton, UK, 1996) (ROU)(LB)
(WAY)(WAL)(FUC)(ISL)

Lady Patricia Mountbatten
Single H2 Lax Bush
Tube and *sepals* white. *Corolla* petals blue. Growth is rather lax but it is an extremely showy plant. (Sister seedling of 'Border Queen' × 'Lady Kathleen Spence')
(D. Clark, UK, 1985)
(SIL)(FEN)(ROU)(RKY)(KM)
(CL)(BRE)(WAY)(STM)(EX)
(ARC)(CHA)(WV)(WAL)(PER)
(ROO)(RIV)(CLI)(ASK)(WHE)
(FUC)(GLE)(ISL)(OLD)

Lady Rebecca
Double H2 Bush
Tube very short and pink. *Sepals* broad, pink with a crêped appearance on the undersurface. *Corolla* petals bluish lilac and heavily veined with pink at the base. The medium-sized blooms are freely produced. *Foliage* mid-green with serrated edging. Growth is upright, strong and vigorous.
(E. Holmes, UK, 1983) (LOK)

Lambada
Single H2 Bush
Tube and *sepals* pinky white. *Corolla* petals mallow purple. Growth is upright and compact. The flowers are fairly small but prolific. Good show bench variety.
(Gotz, Holland, 1993)
(ROU)(KM)(LB)(BRE)(MO)
(ROO)(FUC)(BLA)(ISL)

Lamplight
Single H2 Lax Bush
Tube and *sepals* neyron rose. *Corolla* petals glowing red, pink and white at the base. The large-sized flowers hang in clusters. They resemble the old-fashioned street lights.
(Brigadoon Fuchsias, UK, 1995) (BRI)

Lancashire Lad
Double H2 Bush
Tube and *sepals* red. *Corolla* petals white veined with pink. The medium-sized flowers are produced in profusion.
(Sinton, UK, 1994) (FOX)(FEN)
(ROU)(WAR)(CL)(BRE)(WAY)
(STM)(CHA)(ROO)(RIV)(FUC)
(ISL)
(*See* photograph on page 137.)

Land van Beveren
Single H2 Trailer
Tube and long *sepals* waxy white. *Corolla* carmine. *Foliage* medium green. The natural growth of this very attractive coloured fuchsia is as a trailer.
(Saintenoy, Holland, 1988)
(WAR)(LB)(MO)(BUR)(WAY)
(STM)(EX)(ARC)(BRI)(WAL)
(PER)(ROO)(ALD)(HYDE)(CLI)
(FUC)(GLE)(ISL)(OLI)(SIM)

Larksfield Skylark
Single H2 Bush
Tube and *sepals* carmine. *Corolla* petals bright white. The medium-sized flowers are freely produced on upright, self-branching plants.
(Sheppard, UK, 1991)
(FEN)

L'Arlésienne
Semi-Double H2 Bush
Tube and long recurving *sepals* pale pink, tipped with green. *Corolla* petals white, veined pink and ageing to palest pink. The beautifully shaped long flowers are very freely produced. *Foliage* lightish green. Growth is upright and bushy.
(Colville, UK, 1968)
(LOK)

LADDIE

LADY DOROTHY

LADY IN PINK

LADY PATRICIA MOUNTBATTEN

LAMBADA

LAND VAN BEVEREN

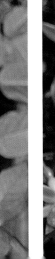

La Traviata
Double H2 Bush
Tube and *sepals* pillar-box red.
Corolla petals pale strawberry
pink veined and marked with
rose. The flowers are medium-
sized and freely produced.
Growth is upright and bushy.
(Blackwell, UK, 1967)
(BAK)(BRI)(RIV)(CLI)

Lau Lady
Double H2 Bush
Tube and *sepals* pale pink.
Corolla petals pink lavender. The
medium-sized flowers are
produced on upright-growing,
self-branching plants.
(OLI)

Laura Amanda
Double H2 Bush
Tube rose and *sepals* rose on the
upper surface and purple on the
lower. *Corolla* petals violet
streaked with magenta. *Foliage*
medium green. Fairly small
upright bush.
('Perky Pink' × 'Tutti-Frutti')
(Welch, UK, 1991)
(POT)

Laura's Treasure
Semi-Double H2 Trailer
Tube and *sepals* of this delightful
trailing plant white. *Corolla*
petals a delicate rose. The natural
trailing habit will provide you
with an excellent basket.
(Hutchins, UK, 1998)
(RKY)

Lavender Ann
Double H2 Trailer
Tubes and flyaway *sepals* rosy
pink. *Corolla* petals marbled
with violet, mauve and pink.
Growth is spreading and self-
branching. Most suitable for
wall baskets and hanging
pots.
(Goulding, UK, 1999)
(GOU)

Lavender Beauty
Semi-Double H2 Bush
Tube and *sepals* scarlet. *Corolla*
petals a beautiful shade of clear

lavender. The largish blooms are
freely produced. Growth is
upright.
(USA)
(FOX)(CHA)(PER)(HYDE)

Lavender Cascade
Single H2 Trailer
Tube and *sepals* white. *Corolla*
petals a delicate light lavender
shade. The medium-sized blooms
trail attractively and last over a
long period.
(SMI)(CHA)

Lazy Lady
Semi-Double H2 Trailer
Tube light red and the *sepals*
that are extra long and curly are
also light red. *Corolla* medium
blue, shading to light blue near
the sepals. The blooms are
medium-sized and are freely and
continuously produced. The
natural growth is as a trailer
so it will make a superb
basket.
(Martin, USA, 1960)
(BAK)(WV)(RIV)

Lechlade
Single H3 Bush
Tube, *sepals* and *corolla* red. A
hardy cultivar.
(Lechlade Garden Centre, UK,
1988) (FEN)

Lechlade Bullet
Single H1 Species Cross
Sepals pink, tipped with green.
Corolla petals cerise. The plant is
well named as the flower is
shaped like a bullet.
(J.O. Wright, UK, 1986)
(BRE)

Lechlade Fairy
Single H2 Bush
A small encliandra-type flower.
Tube and *sepals* pale pink.
Corolla petals small and also pale
pink. Thin willowy growth, the
appearance of which is enhanced
by the many small black berries
that are produced following the
flowering.
(J.O. Wright, UK, 1986)
(BRE)

Lechlade Gorgon
Single H1 Bush
A plant with huge leaves and
tiny flowers. *Tube* rosy purple.
Sepals also rosy purple but much
lighter at the tips. *Corolla* pale
mauve with erect and spreading
petals. The flowers are produced
in great quantities in terminal
branched panicles. Very similar
to sprays of lilac. *Foliage* long:
3½–5in (9–15cm) and deep green
with paler colouring
underneath. Growth can be
very rampant and virtually
uncontrollable if the plant is
given a free root run in warm
conditions.
(*F. arborescens* × *F. paniculata*)
(Wright, UK, 1985) (SIL)(FOX)
(KM)(CL)(BRE)(WAY)(EX)(ARC)
(CHA)(WV)(PER)(ROO)(HYDE)
(BRY)(CLI)(ASK)(FUC)(GLE)
(ISL)

Lechlade Maiden
Single H2 Bush
Tube longish, rather thick and
pink. *Sepals* very pale green but
darker at the tips. *Corolla*
petals, almost hidden by the
sepals, are pale peach pink.
Foliage medium green, soft with
velvety texture and large spear-
shaped leaves. Upright and
vigorous, very easy, but untidy
growing habit.
(J.O. Wright, UK, 1985)
(SIL)(BRE)(HYDE)(CLI)

Lemacto
Single H2 Bush
Tube short, orient pink. *Sepals*
orient pink on top and neyron
rose underneath. *Corolla* petals
orient pink. *Foliage* sap green.
Growth self-branching, medium,
upright. 'Sport' from 'Camelot'
raised by the finder.
('sport' from 'Camelot')
(Goulding, UK, 1984)
(RIV)

LANCASHIRE LAD

LAVENDER BEAUTY

LECHLADE BULLET

LECHLADE GORGON

L'Enfant Prodigue
Semi-Double H2/3 Bush
Tube and *sepals* cerise. *Corolla* petals royal purple. Very free-flowering. Excellent medium-sized bush for use in the hardy border. Also known as, or appears to be synonymous with, 'Enfant Prodigue', 'Prodigue' and 'Prodigy'.
('Ricartonii' ×)
(Lemoine, France, 1887)
(LOK)

Leonard von Fuchs
Single H2 Lax Bush
A terminal-flowering triphylla-type fuchsia. *Tube* orange. *Sepals* light green, drooping, with recurved tips. *Corolla* petals orange. *Foliage* reddish brown maturing to medium green. The growth is spreading and the plant appears to have a dislike of being 'stopped'. Could be useful in hanging containers.
(Strumper, Germany, 1989)
(GOU)(HYDE)

Leonora
Single H2 Bush
Tube, *sepals* and *corolla* petals all the same very soft pink colours. The flowers are bell-shaped and are produced in great profusion. Growth is strongly upright, bushy and self-branching. A superb single, especially with this colouring.
(Tiret, USA, 1960)
(BEL)

Les Hobbs
Single H2 Bush
Tube glossy crimson. *Sepals* glossy crimson on the upper surface and arch down one and a half times the length of the corolla. *Corolla* petals claret rose. The medium and compact flowers are very freely produced. *Foliage* darkish green. Growth is tall and upright and will make an excellent bush. The arching branches hang down with the weight of the flowers that are produced mostly at the terminals.
(L. Hobbs, UK, 1981) (BRI)

Lesley (Tri)
Single H1 Bush
Triphylla-type of fuchsia. *Tube* and *sepals* dark pink, waxy in texture. *Corolla* petals of the same colouring. Growth is strongly upright and arching – showing off its terminal flowers. Robust in appearance and growth. Ideal for large containers.
(Howard, UK, 1996)
(CL)(WV)(ROO)(ISL)(SIM)

Lesley
Double H2 Trailer
Tube and *sepals* dark red. *Corolla* petals dark reddish purple maturing to rosy red with rose centres. *Foliage* medium green. The growth is of a rather lax bush so will make a good trailer with training.
(Garrett, USA, 1989) (EX)

Lett's Delight
Double H2 Lax Bush
Medium-sized flowers freely produced throughout the season. *Tube* and *sepals* rose pink. *Corolla* lavender pink. *Foliage* medium green. The growth being rather lax permits use in baskets but can be used in pots provided supports are given.
(Goulding, UK, 1986) (GOU)
(FEN)(BRI)(WV)(OAK)
(POT)(FUC)(GLE)(OLI)

Leverhulme (Synonymous with Leverkusen)
Single H1 Bush
Triphylla-type single flower. *Tube* rose cerise with a distinctive bump in the middle. *Sepals* short and drooping rosy cerise. *Corolla* petals, hardly visible, also rosy cerise. Objects strongly to a change in atmosphere and will rapidly drop its flowers and buds should this occur. Numerous flowers are produced generally in the leaf axils as opposed to terminally.
(Hartnauer, Germany, 1923)
(FEN)(WAY)(STM)(EX)
(ARC)(JAK)(WV)(ASK)(SMI)
(OLD)(OLI)(SIM)(LOK)

Libra
Semi-Double/Double H2 Trailer
Tube pink. *Sepals* white on the top and pink on the underside. *Corolla* petals pale blue to lavender with splashes of pink. Large blooms fairly freely produced. Growth is as a natural trailer.
(Castro, USA, 1971)
(ISL)(SMI)

Liebestraum
Double H2 Bush
Tube and *sepals* white with a pink flush. *Corolla* pale lavender with white at the base and some deeper markings with splashes of palest pink. The largish flowers are freely produced. *Foliage*, dark green, sets off the upright-growing plants to perfection.
(Blackwell, UK, 1966) (BAK)

Liemers Lantaern
Double H2 Trailer
Tube and *sepals* of these large flowers deep rose. *Corolla* petals lilac rose. A delightfully named plant as the flowers hang down like a lantern.
(Giessen, Holland, 1983)
(BRI)(WV)(HYDE)

Li Kai Lin
Single H2 Trailer
Tube and *sepals* glistening white. *Corolla* petals light purple and mature to red purple. The superb colour combination and the trailing nature of growth makes this a very attractive proposition for basket work.
(Luther, UK, 1995)
(SIL)(BRI)(WV)(RIV)

Lilac
Single H2 Stiff Trailer
Tube and *sepals* light pink, tipped with green. *Corolla* petals pure lilac. The largish flowers are freely produced. Growth is as a low spreading bush. It only appears to want to grow horizontally – will make a basket but weights may be necessary.
(Haag and Son, USA, 1952)
(SIL)(BAK)

LEONARD VON FUCHS

LESLEY

LETT'S DELIGHT

LEVERHULME

Lilac Queen

Lilac Queen
Double H2 Bush
Tube and *sepals* bright crimson.
Corolla petals white flushed and
veined with lilac. Large blooms
freely produced. Growth upright
and bushy.
(Raiser and date unknown,
European) (BAK)(OLI)

Lillian Annetts
Double H2 Bush
Tube and *sepals* white. *Corolla*
petals powder blue overlaid with
pink and lilac. The small, petite
blooms are carried in profusion.
Excellent for show purposes
especially in the smaller pot
classes.
(Clark, UK, 1993) (FOX)(ROU)
(LB)(BRE)(MO)(BUR)(STM)
(BRI)(CHA)(PER)(ROO)(RIV)
(HYDE)(GLE)(ISL)(SIM)

Lilo Vogt
Triphylla-Type H1 Lax Bush
Tube quite long and pink. *Sepals*
pink tipped with green. *Corolla*
pink. The flowers are fairly small
for a triphylla-type but are very
freely produced. *Foliage* medium
to darkish green with a faint
purple sheen beneath. With
training, (weights) could be used
for hanging containers.
(Nutzinger, Austria, 1976)
(FOX)(ROU)(CL)(BRE)(STM)
(EX)(ARC)(BRI)(CHA)(HYDE)
(BRY)(CLI)(ASK)(GLE)(ISL)

Linda Copley
Double H2 Lax Bush
Tube and *sepals* clear pink.
Corolla petals also clear pink.
The largish flowers are freely and
continuously produced. Growth is
rather lax yet bushy. Should make
a good basket.
(Copley, USA, 1966) (CLI)

Linda Grace
Single H2 Bush
Tube and *sepals* candy pink.
Corolla petals of similar
colouring, flecked and edged with
darker pink. The short-jointed
growth and its floriferous nature
make this an excellent prospect

for the show bench.
(Wilkinson, UK, 1995)
(FEN)(KM)(BRE)(BUR)(JAK)
(WAL)(BLA)(ALD)(HYDE)(CLI)
(ISL)(SIM)

Lindsay Hendrickx
Single H2 Trailer
Tube and *sepals* of these medium-
sized flowers white. *Corolla*
petals violet purple. Another with
a delightful colour combination
that with its trailing habit will
make a good basket.
(Claes, Belgium, 1994)
(HYDE)

Lindsey Brown
Double H2 Bush
Tube pink as are also the *sepals*,
which have white tips. *Corolla*
petals white and veined with
pink. The natural growth is as an
upright and self-branching bush.
(Coupland, UK, 1994)
(BUR)(WV)

Lindsey Victoria
Semi-Double H2 Bush
Tube short, creamy white. *Sepals*
creamy white, flushed with pink.
Corolla petals deep pink to
fuchsia purple. *Foliage* with
distinct veins and serrated edging.
Self-branching bush.
('White Queen' self ×)
(Thornley, UK, 1981) (EX)

Linhope Sprite
Single H2 Trailer
Tube long, thin, rose bengal. *Sepals*
phlox pink and hang downwards.
Corolla petals a rich violet purple.
The medium-sized flowers are
produced continuously. *Foliage*
medium green with coarsely
serrated leaves and light red stems.
Growth as a trailer so will make a
good plant for hanging baskets or
pots.
(Ryle, UK, 1975) (CLI)

Lionel
Single H2/3 Bush
Tubes and *sepals* white with
green tips. *Corolla* light mauve.
Foliage small and carried on self-
branching plants. This small-

flowered plant is very similar to
one found in 'Logan Gardens'
and may prove to be just as
hardy.
(Morris, UK, 1998)
(MO)(FEN)

Lisa Jane
Single H2 Lax Bush
Tube and *sepals* white. *Corolla*
petals lavender. The medium-
sized flowers are carried on
rather lax branches. Will make a
reasonable bush plant with
supports but might be better
displayed in hanging pots or
baskets.
(WHE)

Lisa Rowe
Double H2 Bush
Sepals pink suffused, tipped with
white. They are slightly green on
the outside and flushed with
pink on the inside and recurve
back to the tube. The fully
double *corolla* has dark blue
petals with some petaloids that
are blue fused with pink and
with red veins. A strong,
upright-growing bush.
(Clark, UK, 1998)
(SIL)(WAL)

Little Baby
Single H2 Bush
Tube and *sepals* rose. *Corolla*
petals violet with a darker edge
to each petal and paler pink at
the base. The small flowers are
very freely produced. The natural
growth is as a small upright and
self-branching bush.
(Chatters, UK, 1997)
(ROO)

Little Catbells
Single H2/3 Bush
Has small encliandra-type flowers.
Tube short and white. *Sepals* small
and rose-coloured. The petals in
the small *corolla* also white and
change to rose. *Foliage* medium to
light green and very willowy. The
berries that follow the flowers
(and which should be left on the
plant) are jet black.
(Travis, UK, 1980) (LB)

140

LILLIAN ANNETTS

LILO VOGT

LINDA GRACE

LITTLE BABY

Little Cutie
Single H2 Trailer
Tube long, light pink with deeper veins. *Sepals* pink with white on top with light green tips. *Corolla* petals purple with light reddish purple at the base. Smallish flowers. *Foliage* light green with red stems. A natural trailer.
(Palko, USA, 1976)
(BRY)

Little Darling
Double H2 Bush
Tube and *sepals* waxy white. *Corolla* petals white with a pink flush. Upright-growing plant.
(EX)

Little Gene
Single H2 Bush
Tube short and carmine. *Sepals* also carmine. *Corolla* petals deep campanula violet. The medium-sized flowers are flared and freely produced. Upright, self-branching growth.
(Baker, UK, 1970) (BAK)

Little Snow Queen
Single H2 Trailer
Tube and *sepals* white with a faint touch of green on the *sepals*. *Corolla* petals white with smooth edges. *Foliage* dark green. A natural trailer.
(Franck, Holland, 1991)
(CHA)(HYDE)

Little Witch
Single H2 Bush
A very graceful novelty fuchsia of the semi-paniculate type. *Tubes* and *sepals* pale lilac. *Corolla* a darker violet. The growth is upright, strong and slender. *Foliage* medium to dark green.
(de Graaff, Holland, 1989)
(RKY)(KM)(CL)(LB)(EX)(GOU)
(HYDE)

Liza Todman
Double H2 Trailer
Tube ivory white. *Sepals* white on top and white rippled with red underneath, with green tips. *Corolla* petals aster violet marbled and flushed with pink and white, maturing to violet with white marbling and aster violet flush. The medium-sized blooms are fully flared and fluffy. A very attractive natural trailer that will make an excellent basket.
(Allsop, UK, 1998) (ROO)

Logan Woods
Single H2/3 Bush
Tube red. *Sepals* white blushed pink with green tips on the upper surfaces and carmine with green tips on the lower surfaces. *Corolla* petals violet with a pink base and vein. The flowers are small. *Foliage* also rather small.
(Found at Logan Botanic Gardens) (SIL)(BEL)

Lolita
Double H2 Trailer
Tube and *sepals* white tinted with rose and tipped with green. *Corolla* petals porcelain-blue ageing to lilac with maturity. Natural growth is as a trailer.
(Tiret, USA, 1963) (BAK)(RKY)
(EX)(BRI)(WV)(RIV)(ASK)(ISL)
(OLI)

Long Distance
Single H2/3 Bush
Triphylla-type. Single terminal flowering. *Tube*, *sepals* and *corolla* all carmine. Good, strong, upright growth. Useful, with its long, willowy branches when growing topiary shapes.
(de Cooker, Holland, 1993)
(ISL)

Look East
Single H2 Bush
Tube short and white. *Sepals* flushed white with green tips. *Corolla* petals open bishop's violet and mature to imperial-purple. Saucer-shaped blooms. Very floriferous and attractive. *Foliage* mid-green. The plant is self-branching and short-jointed. Best bloom colour is produced with filtered light.
('Florence Mary Abbott'×)
(P. Heavens, UK, 1987)
(BLA)(GOU)

Lorna Fairclough
Single H2 Trailer
Sepals of this trailing fuchsia pale pink. *Corolla* petals deep pink. The medium-sized flowers are freely produced and will make an excellent full or half basket.
(Hanson, UK, 1998)
(JAK)(ARC)(BLA)

Lorelei
Single H2 Bush
Tubes and *sepals* pink. *Corolla* petals also pink although of a slightly darker shade. This small-flowered plant is a very attractive proposition for showing in small pots.
(Fix, UK, 1996)
(FEN)(MO)(PER)(ROO)(BLA)
(RIV)

Loreley
Single H2 Bush
Tube and *sepals* the palest pink. *Corolla* petals white. The flowers are quite small and are carried on a compact upright bush.
(Gotz, Germany, 1991)
(PER)(ROO)(OLD)

Lorna Robertson
Double H2 Lax Bush
Sepals deep pink with a frosty white blush. *Corolla* petals violet with a pink and silver blush. The upright growth is semi-lax and self-branching. The compact growth makes it suitable for pot or basket work.
(A 'sport' from 'Dollar Princess')
(Robertson, UK, 1997)

Lorna Swinbank
Single H2 Bush
Very attractive small-flowered cultivar. *Tube* and *sepals* white flushed with pink. *Corolla* palest violet blue. *Foliage* medium green. The natural growth is upright and self-branching. A superb small bush can be achieved quite quickly.
(Fleming, UK, 1990) (BRE)
(STM)(ARC)(WV)(ROO)
(RIV)(HYDE)(BRY)(CLI)(ISL)
(OLI)(SIM)(LOK)

LITTLE CUTIE

LITTLE SNOW QUEEN

LITTLE WITCH

LORELEI

LORELEY

LORNA SWINBANK

Los Angeles
Single H2 Bush
Tube and *sepals* waxy coral-apricot. *Corolla* petals deep orange suffused with vermilion. Large flowers, carried in clusters, free and produced over a long period. *Foliage* lush green. Growth upright and vigorous.
(Evans and Reeves, USA, 1938)
(BRY)

Lottie Hobby Variegata
Single H3 Bush
This 'sport' from a species hybrid has the typical small enclandra-type flowers. *Tube* and *sepals* crimson. *Corolla* petals dark crimson. *Foliage* a combination of green, red and yellow making a very attractive novelty. Not as vigorous as its parent and rather slow to start.
(Hybrid × *F. bacillaris*) (SIL)

Louise Foster
Single H2 Trailer
Tube of this medium-sized flower is light pink. *Sepals* pink and there are numerous petaloids that are lilac with blushed pink at the base. *Corolla* petals are lavender maturing to pale lavender. With its very attractive colouring and its lax habit of growth, this is an ideal plant for use in hanging containers.
(Foster, UK, 1998) (WAR)

Louise Nicholls
Single H2 Bush
Tube short and white in small flowers. *Sepals* pale pink and tipped with green. *Corolla* pale pink and cylindrical, the petals having darker edges. Easy to shape for the show bench as it is self-branching and quite compact. *Foliage* mid-green, does not stain with age. A good plant in a 5in (13cm) pot can be grown in five or six months.
(Nicholls, UK, 1999) (KM)

Louisiana
Double H2 Trailer
Tube and long *sepals* white, flushed with pink. *Corolla* petals

pink. The natural trailing habit of these large flowers makes the plant ideal for use in hanging baskets.
(BRI)

Lovable
Double H2 Lax Bush
Short *tube* and broad *sepals* deep red. *Corolla* petals orchid pink and veined with a deeper pink. The large blooms are fairly freely produced. *Foliage* small for the size of the flower and the plant. Growth is lax bush or trailer; it will need supports as a bush plant.
(Erickson, USA, 1963)
(BAK)(RIV)(ASK)

Lovely Linda
Single H2 Trailer
Tube and *sepals* waxy white. *Corolla* rose pink. The natural growth is as a trailer and the abundance of flowers will provide a superb basket.
(Allsop, UK, 1998)
(LB)(BRE)(ROO)

Love's Reward
Single H2 Bush
The small to medium sized flowers are produced in great quantity throughout the season. *Tube* and *sepals* are white. *Corolla* petals violet blue. *Foliage* medium green. Growth is short and self-branching. A superb cultivar especially for the smaller pots on the show bench.
('Estelle Marie' × 'Carol Roe')
(Bambridge, UK, 1996)

Lower Raydon
Semi-Double/Double H2 Bush
Tube and *sepals* pink. *Corolla* petals purple. The growth is strong, upright and self-branching. Will make an excellent plant for the patio container.
(Stiff, UK, 1994) (BAK)

F. loxensis
Single H1 Species Hybrid
Tube fairly long, narrow and deep orange. *Sepals*, which are quite long, pointed and wide-spreading, are orange with green tips. The short petals in the

corolla are also orange. *Foliage* quite large, mid-green in colour and has a velvety texture with a light purple stem. Quite strong, upright growth.
(*F. splendens* × *F. fulgens*) (CL)

Loxhore Angelus
Single H2 Bush
Tube long, tapering, pale magenta in colour. The sharp-pointed *sepals* are scarlet on the upper surface and bright orange on the reverse. *Corolla* petals pale magenta with a dark red band down the centre. A strong growing plant that is short-jointed. *Foliage* dark green on an upright-growing bush.
(Seedling of 'Fanfare')
(J.O. Wright, UK, 1991) (SIL)

Loxhore Choralle
Single H2 Bush
A triphylla-type. *Tube* strong, red, tapering. *Sepals* also a very strong red with darkening towards the tips. The small petals in the *corolla* a vivid red. There is a very distinctive white stigma. *Foliage* is light green with a velvety texture, overlaid with a darker green with red/brown veining.
(*F. triphylla* × *F. boliviana* var. 'Pink Trumpet')
(J.O. Wright, UK, 1994) (SIL)(BRE)

Loxhore Clarion
Single H2 Bush
Tube and *sepals* deep pink. *Corolla* petals purplish red. The small to medium flowers are borne horizontally. The growth is rather lax so will require regular pinching and training.
(J.O. Wright, UK, 1995) (RIV)

Loxhore Cotillon
Single H2 Bush
Sepals and *tube* deep pink. *Corolla* petals vivid purple-red with an orange base. The small to medium flowers are carried on long, jointed, lax-growing bushes that will need frequent pinching to acquire a good shape.
(J.O. Wright, UK, 1995)
(SIL)(BRE)(BRI)

LOVELY LINDA

F. LOXENSIS

LOS ANGELES

LOXHORE CHORALLE

LOXHORE COTILLON

Loxhore Herald
Single H2/3 Bush
Tube and *sepals* shiny red.
Corolla petals purple. The flowers
are of medium size and freely
produced throughout the season.
Foliage mid-green on a very
hardy upright bush that grows to
around 3ft (90cm) in height.
(*F. Hatschbachii* × *F. magellanica*
var. *alba*)
(J.O. Wright, UK, 1984)
(SIL)

Loxhore Mazurka
Single H2 Bush
Tube strong pink. *Sepals*
spreading, reddish on the upper
surface and orange below.
Corolla a vivid red. The small
flowers are clustered at the
branch ends. *Foliage* is of
medium size and the growth is as
an upright bush.
(J.O. Wright, UK, 1994)
(SIL)(ROU)(CL)(BRE)(BRI)

Loxhore Minuet
Single H2 Bush
Tube and upper surface of the
sepals pink, the lower surfaces
being reddish orange. *Corolla* a
deep purplish-black. The small
flowers are profuse and are
carried on an upright, short-
jointed bush. Will make an
excellent exhibition plant either
as a small Standard or as a
bush.
(J.O. Wright, UK, 1995)
(SIL)(ROU)(BRE)(BEL)(ROO)
(ISL)

Loxhore Operetta
Single H2 Bush
Tube dark pink with the half-
down *sepals* pink vignetting to
near white and tipped with green
on the upper surface and pale
rose on the lower surface. *Corolla*
petals bright rose pink with an
orange base and slight orange
edging. The small flowers are held
out straight and clustered at the
branch tips. *Foliage* medium-
sized. Growth as a lax bush.
(J.O. Wright, UK, 1994)
(SIL)(BRE)

Loxhore Posthorn
Single H2 Lax Bush
A long, triphylla-type flower.
Tube long, thin, tapering and off-
white vignetting to pale pink at
the *sepals* that are reddish pink
on the upper surfaces and
carmine underneath. *Corolla*
petals are brilliant scarlet and
flower in terminal racemes.
Foliage large mid- to dark green.
Rather lax growth.
(J.O. Wright, UK, 1994)
(SIL)(BRE)

Loxhore Tarantella
Single H2 Bush
Tube glossy red. *Sepals* that curl
back onto the tube are magenta
on the upper surface and deep
rose on the reverse. The *corolla*
petals are clear violet with a
white base and red veining.
Foliage mid-green with dark red
veins and stems. Rather lax and
willowy growth.
(*F. regia* × 'White Spider')
(J.O. Wright, UK, 1994)
(SIL)(BRE)

Lubbertje Hop
Semi-Double H2 Bush
Tube and *sepals* white with a
slight flush. *Corolla* petals
aubergine red. A very attractive
combination of colouring.
(Bieje, Holland, 1992)
(HYDE)(ISL)

Lucy
Single H2 Bush
Tube and *sepals* pink. *Corolla*
petals a slightly different shade of
pink. The flowers are quite small
but freely produced. Could be
described as being a slightly
bigger 'Eleanor Leytham'.
(Stiff, UK, 1996)
(BAK)(FEN)(RKY)(PER)
(ROO)

Lucy Harris
Single H2 Bushy
Tube and *sepals* neyron rose.
Corolla petals pure white with
slight rose veining at the base of
the petals. Each petal is sharply
pointed. The medium-sized

flowers are very freely produced.
Upright and bushy growth.
(Pacey, UK, 1988) (SIL)(WV)

Lucy Locket
Single H2 Bush
Tube and *sepals* waxy, white
tipped with green and turned up.
Corolla petals deep rose pink-
edged with rose purple, the petals
fading to white at the base. A
medium-sized bloom that is very
free-flowering. Strong, upright
and spreading growth.
(Kirby, UK, 1996)
(JAK)(FEN)(EX)(ROO)(RIV)
(ISL)

Luscious
Double H2 Lax Bush
Tube and *sepals* dark red, the
latter being very wide. *Corolla*
petals dark wine and red marbled
with orange. Very large blooms,
fairly free for their size, but long-
lasting and rather fluffy. *Foliage*
dark green with red veins.
Growth, lax bush or trailer.
(Martin, USA, 1960)
(FOX)(RKY)(BRI)(CHA)
(GLE)

Lye's Elegance
Single H2 Bush
Tube waxy white with faint
touch of yellow. *Sepals* waxy
cream. *Corolla* petals rich cerise.
The flowers are of medium size,
very free, and produced early in
the season. Upright and bushy
growth.
(Lye, UK, 1884)
(SIL)(FEN)(RKY)(BRE)(RIV)
(CLI)(ASK)

Lye's Own
Single H2 Bush
Tube and *sepals* waxy white.
Corolla pinkish lilac. The
medium-sized flowers are freely
produced early in the season and
last throughout. *Foliage* medium
green. Growth is strong, bushy
and upright. Well worth trying as
a Standard.
(Lye, UK, 1871) (FEN)(RKY)
(BRE)(EX)(BEL)(BAK)(RIV)(CLI)
(ASK)(ISL)(OLI)

LOXHORE MAZURKA   LOXHORE MINUET

LOXHORE OPERETTA   LOXHORE TARANTELLA

LYE'S ELEGANCE   LYE'S OWN

Lynda

Lynda
Double H2 Trailer
Tube pale pink. *Sepals* extra long, pale pink. *Corolla* petals marbled violet. The flowers are large and fairly free. Growth as a natural trailer.
(Tiret, USA, 1970) (CLI)

Lynette 1
Double H2 Bush
Tube and *sepals* rich red. *Corolla* white blotched with red. Medium-sized blooms freely produced for a double. Growth upright.
(E. Holmes, UK, 1981)
(LOK)

Lynette 2
Double H2 Lax Bush
Tube white. *Sepals* long and twisted pinwheel fashion, white flushed with pink. *Corolla* petals white. Flowers very full, large and free. Could be described as a double 'White Spider'. Growth lax bush or trailer.
(Thornley, UK, 1961) (LOK)

M

Maarten Toonder
Single H2 Trailer
Tube and *sepals* white with green tips. *Corolla* petals white to rose. The medium-sized flowers are freely produced on naturally trailing branches.
(Krom, Holland, 1993) (HYDE)

Madame Butterfly
Double H2 Lax Bush
Tube and *sepals* red. *Corolla* petals white. Medium-sized blooms. Similar in form to 'Pink Quartette' only with larger blooms. Fairly free. Growth is as a lax bush.
(Colville, UK, 1964) (LOK)

Madame van der Strasse
Single H2/3 Bush
Tube and *sepals* light reddish cerise. *Corolla* petals white, veined and flushed with cerise.

Medium-sized blooms very freely produced. Growth is as an upright bush – a good bedding plant.
(Hazard and Hazard, USA, 1930) (OLI)

Maddy
Double H2 Trailer
Tube and *sepals* strawberry red. The petals in the *corolla* are pure white. Large, densely petalled blooms. Short-jointed trailing growth.
(Storvick, USA, 1995)
(CLI)(SMI)

Madeleine Sweeney
Double H2 Bush
Tube and *sepals* rose. *Corolla* petals lilac. The medium-sized flowers are produced early in the season on strong-growing and vigorous plants.
(Sinton, UK, 1996)
(FEN)(ROU)(BRE)(WAY)(STM)(WAL)

Maesy-y-Groes
Single H3 Bush
Similar to Mrs Popple but with upswept *sepals*. *Tube* and *sepals* scarlet, *corolla* a dark purple.
H: 3ft (90cm)
(Jones, UK, 1992)
(RKY)(KM)

Mag Americana Elegans
Single H3 Bush
A very hardy spreading bush with flowers that have red *sepals* and purple *corollas*. This will make an excellent low bush. H: 2ft (60cm)
(SIL)(KM)(CL)

Magellanica Argentia
Single H3 Bush
Single flowers with red *sepals* and purple *corolla*. Growth is as a typical Magellanica.
(OLI)

Magellanica var. Ballochmyle
Single H3 Bush
Tube and *sepals* intense red. *Corolla* petals intense purple. Quite large flowers for a Magellanica but the growth is the

usual straggly type. (Section *Quelusia*)
(CL)

Magellanica var. Comber
Single H3 Bush
Sepals scarlet. *Corolla* petals violet purple. Small flowers. *Foliage* smallish light olive green. Growth upright bush to about 2ft (60cm).
(SIL)

Magellanica var. Discolor
Single H3 Bush
Single flowers. *Tube* and *sepals* deep pinky red. *Corolla* petals are mauve.
(KM)(CL)

Magellanica Gracilis Tricolor
Single H3 Bush
Sepals red. *Corolla* petals purple. Small flowers but very freely produced. *Foliage* variegated cream, green and pink with red veining. Suitable as a hedge. H: to 3ft (90cm)
(Potney, UK, 1840)
(SIL)(CL)(ALD)

Magellanica var. Logans Wood
Single H3 Bush
Tube and *sepals* pinkish white. *Corolla* petals purple. *Foliage* small with less rampant growth than usual.
(KM)(CL)

Magellanica var. Longipedunculata
Single H3 Bush
Typical Magellanica-type growth with very long flowers with lilac-mauve petals in the *corolla*.
(SIL)(KM)(CL)

Magellanica Prostrata
Single H3 Low Bush
Tube and *sepals* a dull red. *Corolla* petals violet with a red base, ageing to reddish purple. Flowers are bell-shaped. *Foliage* is mid-green with pale veins and reverse. Growth is as a low spreading bush.
(Scholfield, UK, 1841)
(SIL)(BUR)

148

LYNETTE 1
MAGELLANICA VAR. BALLOCHMYLE

MADELEINE SWEENEY
MAGELLANICA VAR. DISCOLOR

MAGELLANICA VAR. COMBER

Magellanica var. Rosea
Single H3 Bush
A natural hybrid of *F. lycioides* and *F. magellanica*. *Tube* and reflexing *sepals* red. *Corolla* petals rosy purple. Very vigorous.
(*F. lycioides* × *F. magellanica*)
(SIL)(CL)

Magellanica var. Sharpitor
Single H3 Bush
Tube and *sepals* mauve. *Corolla* petals pink. *Foliage* is very attractive, small, and coloured pink, green, cream. Hardy.
(National Trust, UK)
(SIL)(CL)(ARC)(GOU)(HYDE) (ASK)

Magellanica Tricolor
Single H3 Bush
Pendant single. *Tubes* and *sepals* bright red. *Corolla* dark violet. Bushy and spreading growth. *Foliage* is variegated – green and yellow with a clear contrast. ('sport' from 'Magellanica Gracillis')
(FOX)(CHA)(GOU)(HYDE) (GLE)

Magellanica Variegata
Single H3 Bush
Sepals red. *Corolla* petals purple. The flowers are small. *Foliage* pale green, cream-edged and has a red hue to the young growing tips. Reddish brown stems. Low-growing bush. H: 18in (45cm)
(SIL)(ROU)(RKY)(GOU) (RIV)(HYDE)

Magenta Flush
Double H2 Bush
Tube spinel red. *Sepals* also spinel red and tipped with green. *Corolla* petals magenta rose, flushed with rose red. The large flowers are freely produced for their size. *Foliage* dark green with serrated edging. Good, strong, upright growth.
(Gadsby, UK, 1970)
(BRY)(FOX)(CHA)(WV) (CL)

Magic Flute
Single H2 Trailer
Tube very thick waxy white. *Sepals* white-tipped with chartreuse. *Corolla* petals clear coral rose and white near the *tube*. The medium-sized flowers are freely produced and early in the season. *Foliage* bright green. A naturally trailing fuchsia that will do well in hanging baskets.
(Handley, UK, 1975)
(SIL)(FEN)(JAK)(WV)(RIV) (BRY)(CLI)(SIM)(LOK)

Maike
Single H2 Bush
Tube and *sepals* pale pink. *Corolla* petals are pink. Upright growth. Little-known German cultivar raised by Bogemann in 1981.
(Bogemann, Germany, 1981) (WAY)(EX)

Malou
Double H2 Trailer
Tube and *sepals* rose-coloured. *Corolla* petals violet rose. The medium-sized flowers are freely produced on naturally trailing stems.
(Claes, Belgium, 1993) (HYDE)

Mandarin
Semi-Double H2 Lax Bush
Tube and *sepals* pale salmon pink, tipped with green. *Corolla* glowing orange carmine. Largish blooms and heavy. Free-flowering. *Foliage* dark leathery green. Growth lax bush or a trailer.
(Schnabel, USA, 1963) (BAK) (FOX)(RKY)(BRE)(STM)(ARC) (BRI)(CHA)(ROO)(RIV)(CLI) (GLE)(ISL)(OLI)

Mandi
Single H1 Bush
Triphylla-type. The long *tubes*, short *sepals* and petals are all orange. The flowers appear in terminal whorls in large numbers. Growth is bushy and upright. Does best when kept out of full

sun – in a shaded border or in patio tubs.
(Bielby/Oxtoby, UK, 1994) (KM) (RKY)(CLI)(LB)(BEL)(MO) (PER)(GOU)(ROO)(ISL)(FOX) (EX)(CHA)

Maori Maid
Double H2 Trailer
Tube and *sepals* red. *Corolla* petals purple. The large blooms are freely produced for their size. A natural trailer so this plant will make a good basket.
(Tiret, USA, 1966)
(FEN)(RIV)(HYDE)

Marcus Graham
Double H2 Bush
Tubes slim, white to flesh pink. *Sepals* salmon or pink, long and broad. *Corolla* a delicate shade of salmon. *Foliage* medium green, lighter beneath. Growth is very strong and is most suitable for large bushes or Standards. A very versatile and attractive fuchsia.
(Stubbs, USA, 1985)
(FOX)(FEN)(RKY)(KM)(WAR) (CL)(LB)(BRE)(WAY)(EX) (ARC)(JAK)(BRI)(CHA)(WV) (WAL)(PER)(BAK)(GOU)(ROO) (RID)(ALD)(OAK)(RIV)(HYDE) (BRY)(CLI)(ASK)(WHE)(FUC) (GLE)(ISL)(SMI)(OLD)(OLI) (SIM)(LOK)

Mardi Gras
Double H2 Bush
Tube and *sepals* red. *Corolla* petals dark purple and heavily mottled with pink. Large blooms of striking colour contrast. Fairly freely produced. Growth as an upright bush. Vigorous.
(Reedstrom, USA, 1958) (BAK) (FOX)(FEN)(STM)(BRI)(CHA) (RIV)(GLE)

Margaret Beavis
Semi-Double H2 Bush
Tube and *sepals* bright pink. *Corolla* petals are cherry red. The blooms are of medium size and are produced continuously over a long season.
(OLI)

MAGIC FLUTE

MALOU

MANDI

MAORI MAID

Margaret Davidson
Double H2 Bush
Tube rosy red. *Sepals*, also rosy
red, are long and held upright.
Corolla is pink heavily veined
with crimson and with an
outstanding picotee laced edging.
Extremely long red pistil and
stamens. *Foliage* dark. Easy
upright grower.
(Day, UK, 1992)
(ISL)(LOK)

Margaret Hazelwood
Single H2 Bush
Stiffly erect flowers. *Tube* short
and deep pink. *Sepals* also deep
pink. *Corolla* petals very pale
lilac-purple, almost white. Very
floriferous with multiple flowers
from each leaf axil. Responds
well to pinching and looks
striking planted out in the
border. Probably not hardy, so
care will be needed in the
autumn.
(Storey, UK, 1996)
(KM)(MO)(ROO)(ISL)

Margaret Kendrick
Double H2 Bush
Tube and *sepals* red. *Corolla*
petals white. This fuchsia can best
be described as an upright
'Swingtime'. Good, strong growth
with medium to large flowers.
Worth trying as a Standard.
(Sinton, UK, 1995)
(FEN)(ROU)(FUC)(ISL)

Margaret's Pearl
Double H2 Bush
Tube and *sepals* white. *Corolla*
petals pure white. The large
flowers are produced quite freely.
Not readily available.
(EX)(BRI)

Margery Blake
Single H3 Bush
Tube and *sepals* scarlet. *Corolla*
solferino-purple. The flowers are
very small but are continuously
and prolifically produced. Growth
upright, bushy and hardy.
(Wood, UK, 1950)
(SIL)(RKY)(EX)(BAK)(RIV)
(BRY)

Margharita
Double H2 Bush
Tube pale pink. *Sepals* are of
good firm texture and are of the
palest creamy pink. *Corolla* petals
are white. The medium to large
flowers are freely produced. The
fully double centre petals are
folded into tubes and the outer
petals are pleated. Strong, upright
and bushy habit.
(V. Miller, UK, 1970)
(RIV)

Maria Merrills
Double H2 Bush
Tube white flushed with pale
pink. *Sepals* are white flushed
with pale pink on the upper
surfaces but dark pink on the
lower. *Corolla* petals white
veined with rose and with
streaks of rose in the centres. It
is a very floriferous and
attractive plant.
(Caunt, UK, 1989)
(FOX)(KM)(BRE)(EX)(CHA)
(WV)(PER)(RIV)(CLI)(GLE)
(OLI)

Marietta
Double H2 Bush
Tube carmine. *Sepals* broad,
upturned and bright carmine.
Corolla petals dark magenta-red
with splashes of carmine on the
outer petals, and maturing to
dark clear red. Large blooms, free
for size. Growth upright.
(Waltz, USA, 1958)
(STM)(RIV)

Marijt
Single H2 Lax Bush
Tube light flamingo. *Sepals* also
light flamingo on the upper
surfaces but poppy red on the
lower. *Corolla* petals light scarlet
maturing to light currant red. A
self-branching, lax, upright bush
or will make a trailer.
('Mrs Lovell Swisher' ×)
(Bremer, Holland, 1987)
(PER)

Marissa
Single H2 Bush
Tube and *sepals* deep magenta

rose. *Corolla* petals deep robin
red. A very delightful colour
combination with flowers that are
freely produced on good, strong,
upright-growing branches.
(Veen, Holland, 1995)
(HYDE)

Marjory Almond
Double H2 Trailer
Tubes ivory white. *Sepals*
spreading and pale pink. *Corolla*
centre dark tuna orange with
salmon marbling on outer petals.
Growth is arching and versatile.
Excellent for use in hanging
baskets or in tubs.
(Goulding, UK, 1996)
(RIV)(CLI)

Marlea's Vuurbol
Double H2 Bush
Tubes red and of medium length.
Sepals spreading and also red.
Corolla petals ruby red. Growth
is strong and upright. Makes a
splendid patio plant in large
tubs.
(Michiels, Holland, 1995)
(GOU)

Marlies
Double H2 Trailer
Sepals deep rose. The petals in
the fully double *corolla* are white
veined with rose. A natural
trailer, this plant will make an
excellent basket.
('Swingtime' × 'Celebrity')
(van de Beek, Holland, 1986)
(EX)(WV)

Mars
Semi-Double H2 Trailer
Tube short, thick, rose pink.
Sepals also short and thick, pink
on the outside and rose on the
inside. *Corolla* petals cardinal
red with edges and base a lighter
red. Medium-sized blooms. An
early bloomer. The natural
growth is as a trailer, self-
branching and will make an
excellent basket with a minimum
of assistance.
(Handley, UK, 1977)
(CLI)

MARGERY BLAKE

MARIA MERRILLS

MARGARET HAZELWOOD

MARISSA

MARIJT

Martin's Catherina
Single H2 Bush
Tubes small and green ripening to
ruby red. *Sepals* green turning to
ruby. *Corolla* petals dark
aubergine to dark oxblood red.
Its habit is that of a miniature.
Novelty value only. Best growing
in small pots.
(Beije, Holland, 1992) (GOU)

Martin's Choice
Single H2 Stiff Trailer
Tube short and brick-red
coloured. *Sepals* green-tipped and
downward pointing. *Corolla*
petals yellow. The plant is very
floriferous. The growth is
spreading but, although stiff, will
make an unusual and attractive
display in a hanging container.
(Beije, Holland, 1999)
(GOU)

Martin's Cinderella
Single H2 Bush
Tubes short and waxy white.
Sepals also white. The petals in
the cup-shaped *corolla* aubergine.
Growth is strongly upright and
will benefit from early pinching.
Excellent in garden tubs or other
large containers.
(Beije, Holland, 1998)
(GOU)

Martin's Double Delicate
Semi-Double or Double H2
Stiff Trailer
The short *tubes* and fully
recurved *sepals* are pale pink.
Corolla petals mauve with a
darker lace edging. Growth is
spreading but will look good in
a hanging container. Best when
sheltered from full wind and
sun.
(Beije, Holland, 1999)
(GOU)

Martin's Yellow Surprise
Single H1 Bush
Triphylla-type growth. *Tube*
and *sepals* green-yellow. *Corolla*
petals also green-yellow. Large
felty leaves. Spreading branches.
Not very floriferous – a
novelty.

(Beije, Holland, 1995) (FOX)
(FEN)(RKY)(KM)(LB)(BRE)(MO)
(EX)(CHA)(GOU)(BLA)(HYDE)
(LOK)

Martinus
Double H2 Trailer
The *tube* and *sepals* white.
Corolla petals white, flecked with
rose. A delightful medium-sized
flower that is carried on naturally
trailing branches.
(Giessen, Holland, 1995)
(BLA)(HYDE)

Marty
Double H2 Trailer
Tube and *sepals* pink. *Corolla*
petals orchid pink. Large blooms
fairly freely produced. Growth as
lax bush or trailer.
(Tiret, USA, 1962) (BAK)(BRI)

Mary Caunt
Double H2 Lax Bush
Tube and *sepals* rose madder.
Corolla has pointed, lavender
petals. The natural growth is as a
rather lax bush. Easy to grow.
(Caunt, UK, 1996) (KM)

Mary Ellen Guffey
Double H2 Trailer
Tube dark rose. The fully up wide
sepals are red to rose on the
upper surface and pink on the
lower surface with reflexed tips.
Corolla petals pink maturing to
orchid pink. The flowers are large
and freely produced. *Foliage* dark
green on the upper surface and
medium green on the lower.
Natural trailer so will make a
good basket.
(Stubbs, USA, 1989)
(MO)(EX)(BEL)(RIV)

Mary Fairclo
Single H2 Trailer
A deep pink self. *Tube*, *sepals* and
petals are all deep pink. The
medium-sized blooms are freely
produced. *Corolla* shaped like a
Christmas bell provides a real
novelty. Growth is trailing. Will
make a very attractive basket.
(Fairclo, USA, 1955)
(RKY)(GOU)

Mary Reynolds
Double H2 Trailer
Tube and *sepals* rhodonite-red.
The petals in the fully double
corolla are violet. The natural
trailing habit makes this an
excellent fuchsia for use in
hanging containers.
('Angel's Flight' × 'Royal
Velvet')
(Reynolds, UK, 1976) (BLA)

Mary's Beauty
Double H2 Trailer
Tube and *sepals* of this large-
flowered fuchsia are dark pink.
The petals in the fully double
corolla are white with red
veining. A superb basket variety
with its natural trailing habit.
(Garrett, USA, 1997)
(HYDE)(SMI)

Mary Thorne
Single H2/3 Bush
Tube and *sepals* turkey red.
Corolla petals are violet, scarlet
at the base and ageing to purple.
The medium-sized flowers are
very freely produced. *Foliage*
large, darkish green. Growth is
upright, bushy and hardy in the
Midlands. Makes a delightful
bush plant.
(Thorne, UK, 1954)

Mary Walker
Double H2 Bush
Sepals of this delightful plant
cardinal red. *Corolla* petals violet
fading to purple giving a two-
tone effect. The numerous flowers
are carried on strong, upright-
growing bushes.
(R. Holmes, UK, 1997)
(OLD)

Mary Wright
Double H2 Bush
Tube bright pink. *Sepals* also
bright pink arch back to the tube.
Corolla petals also bright pink.
Medium-sized blooms. *Foliage*
medium green, large. Growth is
tall, upright and bushy. Best
colour develops in the sun.
(J.A. Wright, UK, 1980)
(CLI)(WHE)

154

MARTIN'S YELLOW SURPRISE

MARY ELLEN GUFFEY

MARY THORNE

MARY WALKER

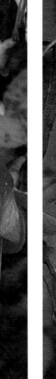

Master Rhys
Double H2 Bush
Tube and *sepals* waxy red.
Corolla petals deep purple
splashed with pink. The medium-
sized flowers are fairly freely
produced. Good, strong, upright
growth and will make a good
Standard.
(Brigadoon Fuchsias, UK, 1994)
(BRI)

Matador
Single H2 Bush
Tube and *sepals* pink. *Corolla*
petals purple. The medium-sized
flowers have intense colour.
(J.A. Wright, UK, 1979)
(SIL)(BRI)

Matthew Morrison
Single H1 Bush
Triphylla-type with flesh-pink
tubes and spreading *sepals*.
Corolla petals salmon orange
with pale pink marbling. Irregular
in outline. The flowers are freely
produced. Growth is stiffly
upright. Ideal when seen in patio
tubs or as temporary visitors in
the border.
(Beije, Holland, 1999) (GOU)

Mauve Lace
Double H2/3 Bush
Tube and *sepals* red. *Corolla*
petals mauve. Large blooms are
continuously produced. *Foliage*
dark green. Growth upright and
bushy. H: 2ft–2ft 6in (30–45cm).
Hardy in southern England.
(Tabraham, UK, 1974)
(SIL)(FEN)(RIV)

Maybejo
Double H2 Bush
Tube and *sepals* white. *Corolla*
petals violet blue. *Foliage* darkish
green. Fairly large flowers. A very
pretty cultivar.
(BRI)

Mayfayre
Double H2 Bush
Short *tube* and the very broad
sepals red. *Corolla* petals white
shaded carmine. Largish blooms.
The petals have rolled edges and

are freely produced. Growth
upright.
(Colville, UK, 1967) (LOK)(EX)

May Rogers
Double H2 Bush
Tubes and long spreading *sepals*
ivory white. Peach-coloured outer
petals and rich salmon inner ones.
Growth strong and arching. Ideal
for strong bushes in garden tubs.
(Goulding, UK, 1996)
(CHA)(WV)(HYDE)

Maytime
Double H2 Trailer
Tube and *sepals* rosy pink.
Corolla petals are lilac. The large
blooms are fairly freely produced.
The trailing habit makes it an
ideal plant for large hanging
baskets.
(Tiret, USA, 1965)
(RKY)(GLE)

Mazarine
Double H2 Lax Bush
Tube and *sepals* white. *Corolla* is
deep blue splashed with white
and pink. The medium-sized
blooms are produced very freely
for a double. Growth is rather lax
upright.
(J. Brough, UK, 1986) (CLI)

Meditation
Double H2/3 Bush
Tube and *sepals* red. *Corolla*
petals creamy white veined with
carmine. Medium-sized flowers
are produced very early and
freely. Growth is upright and
bushy. Hardy in southern
districts.
(Blackwell, UK, 1956) (SIL)(LOK)

Melanie
Single H2 Stiff Trailer
Tubes and *sepals* dark red. The
sepals open horizontally when
mature. *Corolla* petals very dark
aubergine. Growth is strong and
rather spreading. Best when
contained within patio tubs.
(Bogemann, Germany, 1990)
(RKY)(LB)(BRE)(BAL)(EX)
(ARC)(CHA)(WAL)(PER)(RID)
(RIV)(HYDE)(CLI)

Mephisto
Single H2/3 Bush
Sepals of this hardy fuchsia
scarlet. *Corolla* petals deep
crimson. The flowers are small
but are produced in great
quantity. Extremely vigorous
growth.
(*F. lycioides* × 'Mrs W Rundle')
(Reiter, USA, 1941)
(WV)(FUC)

Merlin
Single H2/3 Bush
Tube short, thin, bright red.
Sepals short, bright red and
tipped with green recurve at the
tips. *Corolla* petals deep purple
flushed with pink and with pink
veining. The small flowers have
pink stamens and pistils. *Foliage*
dark green with small, narrow,
serrated leaves. Growth self-
branching, tall, upright and
bushy.
(Adams, UK, 1982)
(SIL)(CL)(EX)(BRY)(SMI)

Mexicali Rose
Single H2 Lax Bush
Tube and *sepals* creamy and long.
Corolla petals bright carmine.
Free-growing plant that carries its
flowers on arching branches. Very
attractive.
(Machado, USA, 1962)
(BRI)(BRY)(LOK)

Michael
Double H2 Lax Bush
Tube and *sepals* white flushed
with pink. *Corolla* petals white
veined pink. This is a 'sport' from
'Annabel' and is identical to it
apart from the very attractive
yellow-green *foliage*.
(Barker, UK, 1988) (SIL)(RKY)
(BRI)(WV)(RIV)(POT)(CLI)(ASK)
(SMI)

Michel Schwab
Single H2 Lax Bush
Tube soft red. *Sepals* red orange
with yellow tips. *Corolla* petals
bright red. Growth is as a lax
bush.
(Schwab, Holland, 1994)
(ROO)

MAYFAYRE

MEDITATION

MELANIE

MERLIN

Microphylla/Quercetorum
Single H3 Bush
Encliandra-type single flower.
'Perfect'. *Tubes*, *sepals* and
corolla red. *Foliage* is dark green
and it is shrubby by habit.
Another easy one to grow and
to train.
(Breedlove, 1969)
(CL)(KM)(GOU)

Midnight
Single H2 Bush
Tube and *sepals* scarlet. *Corolla*
petals very deep purple – almost
black. A well-named cultivar that
carries its medium-sized flowers
on strong, upright, self-branching
stems.
(FEN)(RKY)

Mien Kuypers
Single H2 Bush
Tube and *sepals* red. *Corolla*
petals aubergine. The flowers are
of medium size, and carried on
strong and upright bushes.
(de Groot, Holland, 1997)
(HYDE)

Miep Aalhuizen
Triphylla-type H1 Bush
A terminal-flowering triphylla-
type fuchsia that has long thin
tubes, short *sepals* and *corolla*,
all a delightful shade of lavender.
Foliage medium to dark green
with a slight purple hue on the
reverse. Growth is upright and
very strong.
(de Graaff, Holland, 1987)
(CL)(KM)(BRE)(MO)(EX)(GOU)
(HYDE)(ISL)(OLI)(SIM)

Milena
Semi-Double H2 Bush
The short *tube* and the *sepals* are
light rose with darker stripes.
Corolla petals are rose pink to
light violet. The medium-sized
flowers are freely produced on
strong, upward-growing bushes.
(Dietrich, Germany, 1994)
(MO)

Millennium
Double H2 Trailer
Tube and recurving *sepals* red

with green tips. The petals in the
fully double *corolla* are red, blue
and white. The large flowers are
very freely produced. A natural
trailer, this will make a superb
basket.
(Smith, USA, 1998)
(CLI)(HYDE)(ISL)(SMI)

Mimi
Single H2 Bush
Tube and *sepals* rose-coloured.
Corolla petals rose and white.
The medium-sized flowers are
very freely produced on upright-
growing bushes.
(HYDE)

Miniature Jewels
Single H3 Bush
An encliandra-type plant with the
typical small leaves and small
flowers. *Tube* and *sepals* rosy
pink. *Corolla* petals also the same
delightful colouring.
(Francesca, USA, 1976) (LB)

F. minata
Single H1 Bush
Tubes, *sepals* and *corolla* petals
of these small flowers, are red.
Foliage also very small so this
plant will make a delightful small
pot exhibit.
(Finder and date unknown)
(HYDE)

***minimiflora* (*F. thymifolia* ssp.)**
Single H3 Bush
Tube whitish to reddish. *Sepals*
red with white edges. *Corolla*
petals white to red. One of the
tiniest of flowers, borne solitary
in the leaf axils. Upright, and
strong-growing shrub.
(Hemsley, Mexico, 1880)
(EX)

Minnesota
Semi-Double H2 Bush
Tube and *sepals* ivory, flushed
with rose. *Corolla* petals deep
purple shaded carmine. The
medium-sized blooms are freely
produced. Very similar to 'Rose
of Castille'. Upright growth.
(Garson, USA, 1938)
(BAK)(WV)

M.I.R.
Single H2 Trailer
Tube and *sepals* orange rose. The
corolla petals also orange rose.
The small flowers are freely
produced on a natural trailing
plant.
(Baarda, Holland, 1988)
(BRI)

Miss Aubrey
Double H2 Trailer
Tubes and horizontally held
sepals ivory white with a touch of
pink. The *corolla* petals rosy red
with pink marbling. Growth is
spreading and amenable. Ideal for
hanging pots and baskets.
(Stubbs, USA, 1993)
(RKY)(EX)(BRI)(RID)(HYDE)
(CLI)(SMI)

Miss Debbie
Double H2 Trailer
Tubes pale pink. *Sepals* spreading
and also pale pink. *Corolla* petals
pale lilac with pink marbling. Its
natural habit is to spread and it
is self-branching. Another
excellent plant for the hanging
containers.
(Stubbs, USA, 1993)
(JAK)(RKY)(EX)(WV)(PER)
(ROO)(RID)(RIV)(FUC)(SMI)

Miss Lye
Single H2 Bush
Tube and *sepals* ivory white.
Corolla petals magenta-rose. The
medium-sized flowers are freely
produced from early in the
season. Upright and bushy
growth. One of 'Lye's' lesser
known raisings.
(Lye, UK, 1870)
(SIL)(CLI)

Miss Marilyn
Single H2 Bush
Tube and *sepals* white. *Corolla*
petals plum purple. The medium-
sized blooms are very eye-
catching.
(Fix, UK, 1994)
(ISL)(FOX)(ROU)(BRE)
(CHA)(PER)(ROO)(ALD)
(GLE)

MIEN KUYPERS

MIEP AALHUIZEN

F. MINATA

MISS MARILYN

MISS AUBREY

Miss Muffet
Double H2/3 Bush
Tube and *sepals* deep pink.
Corolla petals white, lightly
veined with pink. Small very full
double flowers. *Foliage* deep
green. Dainty, upright very
dwarf plant only achieving a
spreading height of 4–6in
(10–15cm). Excellent for the
rockery but would be lost in a
garden border. Hardy in
southern counties.
(Tabraham, UK, 1988)
(BRI)(BEL)(ROO)(RIV)(HYDE)

Miss San Diego
Double H2 Bush
Tube and *sepals* dark rose.
Corolla petals open purple with
outer petals half size and striped
red-purple. An interesting colour
combination and well worth
growing.
(Garrett, USA, 1995) (SMI)

Mistoque
Single H2 Bush
Tube and *sepals* white edged with
rose. *Corolla* light blue tinged
with light pink at the base of each
petal. *Foliage* medium green. The
growth habit is upright and
bushy. Quite floriferous.
(UK, 1978) (SIL)(FOX)(STM)
(CHA)(RIV)(GLE)

Mme Eva Boye
Single H2 Bush
Tube and *sepals* pale cerise.
Corolla petals a mixture of
parma violet, violet, and fuchsia
purple. The flowers are of
medium size and are very freely
produced.
(Lemoine, France, 1908) (BAK)

Mollie Edwards
Single H2 Bush
Tube red and *sepals* are rose with
green tips. The petals in the
corolla are white veined with red.
The blooms are produced early in
the season and are prolific. The
colours are held well in bright
light. Self-branching, small,
upright bush.
(Edwards, UK, 1998) (ROO)

Molly
Double H2 Bush
Tube and large horizontal *sepals*
white. The petals in the full
double *corolla* light purple to
blue. The flowers are very large
and yet are freely produced.
(Dietrich, Germany, 1994)
(HYDE)

Molly Chatfield
Double H2 Bush
Tube and *sepals* white with a red
edging. *Corolla* petals white. The
flowers are of medium size and
are freely produced.
(RIV)(ARC)

Money Spinner
Single H2 Trailer
Tube and *sepals* neyron rose. The
underside of the sepals is slightly
darker. *Corolla* petals imperial
purple. Large flowers are very
freely produced and very showy
with their rich colouring. Early-
flowering. Growth is as a trailer.
Excellent basket.
(Lockyer, UK, 1974)
(BAK)(CLI)(SMI)(LOK)

Monica
Semi-Double H2 Bush
Tube and *sepals* cerise. *Corolla*
petals pink. Medium-sized flowers
freely produced.
(FOX)(CHA)(GLE)

Monica Dare
Single H2 Bush
Triphylla-type fuchsia with
flowers carried in terminal
bunches. *Tubes* and short, flared
sepals bright orange. *Corolla*
petals brownish orange. Growth
is sturdily upright and self-
branching. Very floriferous and
showy.
(Goulding, UK, 1999)
(GOU)

Monteray
Single H2 Bush
Tube and *sepals* white flushed
with pink. *Corolla* petals bright
vermilion shaded orange.
Medium-sized flowers freely
produced. *Foliage* lightish green.

Growth upright and sturdy.
(Greene, USA, date unknown)
(BRI)(RIV)(WHE)

Monty Python
Single H2 Lax bush
Triphylla-type fuchsia. *Tubes*
long, bright orange. *Sepals* and
small petals also bright orange.
Terminal-flowering after the
initial flush. Growth is strong and
spreading, self-branching. Looks
at its best in mixed tubs or in
large, fully round baskets.
(Van Den Bergh, Holland, 1994)
(GOU)(HYDE)

Moondance
Single H2 Bush
Tube and *sepals* white with pink
flushing. *Corolla* petals pale lilac
and pink. *Foliage* very dark and
shows up the best colouring of
the flowers. Good, strong, sturdy
upright growth.
(Fix, UK, 1999) (PER)

Mordred
Single H2 Bush
Tube long, narrow, flesh-
coloured. *Sepals* long, thin,
recurving and pink. *Corolla* dull
red with a faint hint of blue. The
flowers are largish, long, thin and
bell-shaped. Very free-flowering.
Foliage quite large. Growth is
self-branching, lax upright with
long internodes.
(Goulding, UK, 1983)
(CLI)

Morecott
Double H2 Bush
Tube and *sepals* white. *Corolla*
petals soft lilac/lavender. The
flowers are of large size and are
fairly freely produced.
(ARC)

Morning Cloud
Double H2 Bush
Tube and *sepals* white flushed
with pink. *Corolla* also white
with pink shading. The medium-
sized flowers are freely
produced.
(RKY)(ARC)(BRI)(CHA)(GLE)
(ISL)

MOLLY

MONTY PYTHON

MISS SAN DIEGO

MISTOQUE

MOONDANCE

Morning Mist
Single H2 Lax Bush or Trailer
The long *tube* and *sepals* orange
pink. *Corolla* petals orange-red
suffused with purple. The long
and large flowers are very freely
produced.
(Berkeley Hort Nursery, USA,
1937) (RIV)

Morrells
Double H2 Bush
Tube crimson. *Sepals* rose red
with neyron rose on the inside.
Corolla petals lavender violet
lightly veined with neyron rose.
The medium-sized blooms rather
squarish in shape. *Foliage* dark
green. Growth is upright and
vigorous but will require regular
stopping to make a well-shaped
bush.
(Hobbs, UK, 1977) (BAK)

Morton Smith
Single H2 Bush
Tube and *sepals* creamy white.
Sepals held horizontally. *Corolla*
petals violet, veined with pink
and maturing to rosy purple.
Good upright-growing plant with
a self-branching habit.
(Smith, UK, 1989) (WHE)

Mr P.D. Lee
Single H2 Bush
Tube and *sepals* carmine.
Corolla petals dark purple. A
strong, vigorous, upright-
growing plant.
(WHE)

Mrs Harrison
Single H1 Bush
Triphylla-type fuchsia. *Tube*,
sepals and *corolla* petals dark
orange. *Foliage* bronze. Strong,
upright growth with the flowers
held in terminal bunches.
(ROU)

Mrs Janice Morrison
Single H2 Bush
Tubes ivory. *Sepals* horizontally
held, pink. *Corolla* petals mauve
to magenta. Small cups. The
flowers are held upwards and
outwards on stiffly upright, self-
branching growth. Certainly a
show type fuchsia.
(Beije, Holland, 1997) (GOU)

Mrs J.D. Fredericks
Single H2 Bush
Tube and *sepals* salmon pink.
Corolla petals a darker pink.
Flowers are of medium size, very
profuse and borne in clusters.
Foliage light green. Growth
upright and extremely vigorous.
(Evans and Reeves, USA, 1936)
(SIL)(ROO)(BRY)(CLI)

Mrs Lawrence Lyons
Semi-Double H2 Bush
Tube and *sepals* rosy pink.
Corolla petals pale fuchsia
purple. The medium-sized
blooms are produced in great
profusion. Growth is upright
and bushy. Will make an
excellent bush or shrub
specimen plant.
('sport' of 'Nonpareil')
(Reiter, USA, 1952) (BAK)

Mrs W. Rundle
Single H2 Lax Bush
The very long *tube* and reflexing
sepals flesh pink. *Corolla* petals
rich orange vermilion. The
flowers are large and quite long.
Foliage light green. Growth is
rather lax for a bush but will
make a very good weeping
Standard.
('Earl of Beaconsfield' × 'Lady
Heytesbury')
(Rundle, UK, 1883)
(ARC)(BAK)(RIV)(OLI)

Mrs W.P. Wood
Single H3 Bush
Tube and *sepals* pale pink.
Corolla petals pure white.
Flowers are very small but
profuse. *Foliage* small, lightish
green. Growth is upright and
bushy. Much too vigorous for
cultivation under glass. A superb
plant for permanent growing in
the hardy border.
(Wood, UK, 1949) (FOX)(ROU)
(RKY)(KM)(BRE)(STM)(EX)
(ARC)(CHA)(HYDE)(CLI)(GLE)
(ISL)(OLI)(LOK)

Multa
Single H2 Lax Bush
Tube and *sepals* red. *Corolla*
petals purple. Small flowers but
very free. Growth lax bush. Very
easy grower. Makes an excellent
basket.
(Van Suchtelen, Holland, 1968)
(CLI)(FEN)(BRE)(PER)(ROO)
(RIV)(FUC)(GLE)(ISL)
(OLI)

Mutter's Tag (Mothers Day)
Single H2 Trailer
Tube and *sepals* red. *Corolla*
petals mauve. Trailer suitable for
baskets.
(Rapp, Germany, 1993)
(EX)

My Delight
Single H2 Bush
Tube short and red. *Sepals* long,
deep rose red, tapering to a long
point. *Corolla* petals pale lilac
very lightly veined deep pink.
Medium-sized flowers with a
cylindrical shape. *Foliage* is
yellow-green with lanceolate
leaves.
(Hall, UK, 1982)
(CLI)(WV)

My Ding a Ling
Double H2 Bush
Tube and *sepals* white flushed
pink. *Corolla* petals dark purple
streaked pink. Large blooms are
presented on strong, vigorous
growth.
(Forward, UK, 1993)
(WV)(FUC)(GLE)(ISL)

My Eve
Single H2 Trailer
Tube and *sepals* claret rose.
Corolla petals beetroot purple.
A profuse flowerer. The natural
trailing habit makes it an ideal
plant for growing in hanging
containers.
(Holmes, UK, 1997)
(OLD)

MRS J.D. FREDERICKS

MULTA

Myra Baxendale
Double H2 Bush
Tube and *sepals* red. *Corolla*
petals bluish purple. Strong
upright growth with a self-
branching habit. *Foliage* light
olive with red veining. A very
attractive plant.
(WAL)

My Reward
Double H2 Trailer
Tube and *sepals* pale lavender.
Corolla opens violet and matures
to light purple. Another very
large double that will do well in
hanging containers.
(Forward, UK, 1993)
(WV)(FUC)(GLE)(ISL)

Mystery
Single H2 Bush
Tube and *sepals* red. *Corolla*
petals also red. Good, strong,
upright-growing and self-
branching plant.
(FEN)

Mystique
Single H2 Bush
Tube white and *sepals* also white
but edged with rose. *Corolla*
petals lilac blue tinged with light
pink. A strong, upright-growing
plant with a self-branching habit.
(FEN)(ROU)(ASK)

My Trisha
Single H2 Bush
Tube and *sepals* crimson. *Corolla*
petals violet purple veined with
red. An extremely prolific
bloomer over a very long season.
A superb, upright, bushy, self-
branching growth.
(Holmes, UK, 1998)
(OLD)

My Valentine
Double H2 Trailer
Tube and *sepals* dark pink.
Corolla petals light pink. A very
attractive medium-sized double
that will, with its natural trailing
habit, make a good basket.
Foliage dark green.
(Martin, USA, 1964)
(RIV)

N

Nancy Darnley
Double H2 Bush
Tube and *sepals* white flushed
pink. *Corolla* petals ruby red
splashed with pink at the base.
Very early to come into flower
and the double flowers are
produced quite freely.
(Bielby/Oxtoby, UK, 1994)
(FOX)(KM)(MO)(CHA)(WV)

Nancy Scrivener
Single H2 Bush
Tube and *sepals* white. *Corolla*
petals burgundy. Medium-sized
flowers freely produced.
(Hewitson, UK, 1995)
(LB)(ARC)(BLA)(RIV)

Nanny Ed
Double H2 Bush
Tube and *sepals* red. *Corolla* petals
purple. The growth is strong and
upright, the medium-sized flowers
being quite freely produced.
(Sinton, UK, 1993) (ROU)(BRE)
(BUR)(WAY)(WAL)(RIV)
(CLI)(FUC)(ISL)(OLI)

Naomi Adams
Double H2 Stiff Trailer
Tube and *sepals* white. *Corolla*
petals open purple veined red and
with outer petals flushed pink
with a cream base and wavy petal
edges. *Foliage* dark green. The
growth is rather stiff trailing but
will make a good basket and also
a bush if given supports.
('Bicentennial' × 'Sebastopol')
(Redfern, UK, 1987) (WV)

Natalia
Double H2 Trailer
Tube and *sepals* red. *Corolla*
petals light pink splashed with
red. The large-sized flowers are
freely produced. The natural
trailing habit makes this an ideal
plant for the hanging basket.
(BRI)

Native Dancer
Double H2 Trailer
Tube and *sepals* bright red.

Corolla petals deep purple. Large
blooms freely produced for the
size of the flower. Growth is lax
bush or trailer.
(Tiret, USA, 1965)
(BAK)(FEN)(RKY)(WV)(ISL)

Naughty Nicole
Double H2 Lax Bush
Tube white. *Sepals* pale pink.
Corolla petals pale violet splashed
with pink. The flowers are large
and borne in profusion. A lax
upright, this will require supports
for the heavy flowers. Will make
a good hanging basket. A real
eye-catcher.
(Allsop, UK, 1998)
(LB)(MO)(ROO)

Neige
Double H2 Bush
Tube, *sepals* and *corolla* petals are
all white. An upward-growing
compact bush that has the merit of
being very early in its flowering.
(GLE)

Nellie Lavrijsen
Double H2 Bush
Tube and *sepals* bright red.
Corolla petals white with pink
mottling. An upright bushy plant
that demands attention.
(Brantz, Belgium, 1996) (HYDE)

Neville Young
Double H2 Trailer
Tube short, thin, shell pink tinged
with green. *Sepals* long, apple
blossom pink cover the tube and
the ovary. *Corolla* petals shell
pink. The blooms are medium to
large. *Foliage* mid-green. Growth
is naturally trailing.
('sport' of 'His Excellency')
(Young, UK, 1982) (ASK)

Nicky Veerman
Single H2 Bush
Tube and *sepals* white. *Corolla*
petals very pale pink. The flowers
are held outwards near the
branch ends. Growth stiffly
upright and free-branching.
Looks well in window-boxes.
(Franck, Holland, 1994)
(ROO)(HYDE)

MY TRISHA

NANNY ED

MY REWARD

NICKY VEERMAN

NAUGHTY NICOLE

Nicola
Single H2 Bush
Tube cerise. *Sepals* also cerise are
fully reflexed and fold back hiding
the tube. *Corolla* petals violet
purple, paler at the base and
veined with cerise. The medium-
sized blooms are freely produced.
The petals are held flat. Growth is
upright, self-branching, and
bushy.
('Swanley Gem' × 'Citation')
(Dalgliesh, UK, 1964) (BAK)

F. nigricans × F. gehrigeri
A naturally occurring hybrid with
long-tubed red flowers.
(KM)

Niki Nicky
Double H2 Trailer
Tube pink and *sepals* a deeper
pink. *Corolla* petals rich purple
with deep pink at the base,
marbled and splashed with pink.
They mature to reddish purple
splashed with pink. Growth is
naturally trailing so will make a
very eye-catching basket.
(Allsop, UK, 1996) (ROO)

Nikki
Single H2 Bush
Tube and *sepals* pale flesh pink.
Corolla petals a deeper shade of
salmon rose. The medium-sized
flowers are freely produced on a
plant that is very easy to grow.
Growth is upright and bushy.
('sport' from 'Elizabeth'
(Whiteman))
(Head, UK, 1979) (RIV)

Nimue
Single H2 Bush
Tube is short and has a flesh-pink
colouring. *Sepals* are pale flesh to
cream on top and pink on the
undersurface. They are held
horizontally away from the tube
and are narrow. *Corolla* petals
pink to mauve with a pronounced
darker blue edge on each petal.
The flowers are rather small when
first opening but mature to larger.
Very free-flowering. Growth
upright, bushy and self-
branching.

(Goulding, UK, 1983) (GOU)
(BRI)(CHA)(WV)(ROU)(RIV)
(FUC)(GLE)(ISL)

Niobe
Semi-Double H2 Trailer
Tube and *sepals* pale rose flushed
with pale pink. *Sepals* upturned
and twisting. *Corolla* petals
Tyrian rose. The blooms are
medium-sized and are very freely
produced. A natural trailer that
will make a superb basket.
(Reiter, USA, 1950) (BAK)(RIV)

Niula
Single H2 Bush
This inter-specific hybrid has a
long *tube* and tiny *sepals* that are
dull purple. The small *petals* are
black-purple. Flowers in racemes
and doesn't mind being pinched.
An interesting cross that might
even make the show bench
though it is worth growing just
for its fascinating flowers.
(*F. nigricans × F. crassistipula*)
(Tickner, UK, 1996)
(KM)(CL)(MO)(ISL)

No Name
Double H2 Bush
Tube and *sepals* white. *Sepals*
white on the outside and pink
inside. *Corolla* petals deep violet
fading with maturity. The largish
flowers are freely produced.
Growth is upright and bushy.
(Baker, UK, 1967) (BAK)

Norfolk Belle
Double H2 Bush
Tube and *sepals* white with pink
blushing. *Corolla* petals white.
Upright, self-branching growth.
Makes a good patio plant.
(FEN)

Norfolk Ivor
Semi-Double H2 Bush
Tube short and ivory-coloured.
Sepals white with a hint of pink.
Corolla petals lavender blue to
pink. Growth is strong and highly
versatile. Will make a good
Standard.
(Goulding, UK 1984) GOU)(FEN)
(RKY)(PER)(ROO)(HYDE)(ISL)

Norman Mitchinson
Single H2 Bush
Tube and *sepals* white with a hint
of pink. *Corolla* petals violet and
occasionally marbled with white
and pink. Growth is upright and
self-branching. The *foliage* is
medium green. A versatile and
attractive plant.
(Ryle, UK, 1976)
(GOU)(RIV)(CLI)

Nunthorpe Gem
Double H2/3 Bush
Tube and *sepals* bright red. *Corolla*
petals deep purple. The flowers are
of medium size. *Foliage* mid-green.
One for the hardy border.
(Birch, UK, 1970) (SIL)(FEN)
(EX)(ARC)(BRI)(RIV)(HYDE)

Obconica
Single H2/3 Bush
Encliandra-type. *Tube*, *sepals* and
petals all white. The tiny flowers
are borne singly in the leaf axils.
Following the flowers there will
be black shiny berries. *Foliage*
lightish green with strong bushy
and upright growth.
(Breedlove, Mexico and Central
America, 1969) (SIL)(CL)(GOU)

Obcylin
Single H2/3 Bush
Encliandra-type. *Tubes* short
peach-coloured. *Sepals* spreading,
of the same colouring. The petals,
which flare in the *corolla*, are
slightly darker in colouring. The
plant produces many flowers.
Growth is self-branching and may
be used for many purposes.
Prefers cooler conditions.
(Beije, Holland, 1999)
(GOU)

Oetnang
Double H2/3 Bush
Tube and *sepals* pink. *Corolla*
petals maroon. Growth is upright
and bushy. An Austrian
introduction.
(RKY)(OLI)

NIULA

NIKI NICKY

NUNTHORPE GEM

NORFOLK IVOR

OBCONICA

Oklahoma
Double H2 Trailer
Tube and *sepals* white. *Corolla* petals magenta pink. The large flowers are fairly freely produced on naturally trailing stems.
(BRI)

Old Rose
Double H2 Bush
Tube carmine rose. *Sepals* and *corolla* petals neyron rose. The medium-sized blooms have twenty large and seven small petals. Best colour in the shade. Growth is tall and bushy.
(Pugh, UK, 1976)
(BRY)(RIV)

Olive Davis
Double H2 Trailer
Tube and *sepals* deep pink. *Corolla* petals blue fading to mauve and flecked with pink. An extremely floriferous plant with very lax growth. Excellent for hanging pots or baskets.
(Bellamy, UK, 1995)
(BLA)

Omeomy
Double H2 Stiff Trailer
Tube pale pink. *Sepals* long, narrow and upturning also pink. *Corolla* dianthus purple overlaid with coral pink marbling. The flowers are large and tightly formed. *Foliage* medium green. Growth is rather stiff for a basket but the trailing effect can be achieved with weights.
(Kennett, USA, 1963)
(CLI)(CHA)(RIV)(HYDE)
(OLI)

Opalescent
Double H2 Bush
Tube and *sepals* china rose. *Corolla* petals pale violet blended with opal and rose. Largish blooms freely produced. The weight of the blooms will require some support to be given to the stems. Growth is upright and willowy.
(Fuchsia-la, USA, 1951)
(BRY)(ARC)(BRI)(WV)
(LOK)

Orange Belle
Single H2 Trailer
The medium-sized blooms have *tubes*, *sepals* and *corolla* petals that are all reddish orange. The flowers are produced quite freely on naturally trailing branches.
(E. Brown, UK, 1996)
(OLI)

Orange Flame
Single H2 Bush
Tube and *sepals* pink. *Corolla* petals salmon. Natural growth is as an upright bush.
(Handley, UK, 1960)
(FEN)(BLA)(OLI)

Orange Mirage
Single H2 Trailer
Tube and *sepals* salmon. *Corolla* petals smoky orange with touches of salmon. *Foliage* light green. The natural trailing growth makes this another ideal plant for the hanging baskets.
(Tiret, USA, 1970)
(FEN)

Orange Queen
Single H2 Bush
Tube and *sepals* rose. *Corolla* petals bright orange. Good, strong, upright, self-branching growth. A delightful plant.
(Jones, UK, 1960) (FOX)(FEN)
(RKY)(EX)(CHA)(CLI)

Orangey
Single H2 Bush
Tube, *sepals* and *corolla* petals orange. A compact, bushy plant.
(Reedstrom, USA, 1962)
(FEN)(RKY)

Orang U Tan
Single H2 Bush
Tube short, thin, cream coloured. *Sepals* small, thin, slightly recurving, are cream flushed with light orange on the upper surface with deeper orange on the lower. *Corolla* petals a lovely shade of orange. The flowers are very small but are very freely produced. *Foliage* light green. Growth is tall and upright.
(Adams, UK, 1982) (BRY)

Oriental Sunrise
Single H2 Lax Bush
Tube short, thin, light orange. *Sepals* light orange tipped with green on top and darker orange underneath – star-shaped. *Corolla* dark orange. The medium-sized flowers are freely produced. *Foliage* medium green with red veining and stems. Growth is rather stiff for a trailer but can be encouraged by the use of weights to fill a basket.
(Soo Yun, USA, 1976) (WAY)
(WV)(WAL)(HYDE)(CLI)(ASK)
(WHE)(SMI)(OLI)(SIM)

Orphan Annie
Single H2 Bush
A small growing plant of very unusual colour and shape. The *tube* fairly long, thin and of a strong pink. *Sepals* green. The petals in the four-petalled *corolla* dark purple and there is a yellow pistil. *Foliage* delicate and of a fairly pale green. A plant that can be described as 'different' but well worth a try. You might even feel that it is one raised by a committee.
(Bielby/Oxtoby/McManus/Tickner, UK, 1999) (MO)

Orwell High
Double H2 Bush
Tube and *sepals* pinky orange. *Corolla* petals red and orange. The strong, upright and self-branching growth makes this an ideal plant for larger pots and patio tubs.
(Goulding, UK, 1988)
(RIV)

O'So Sweet
Double H2 Lax Bush
Tube and *sepals* rose and light pink. *Corolla* petals magenta maturing to light magenta. The large, compact blooms give a great display.
(Forward, UK, 1993)
(CHA)(WV)(HYDE)(FUC)
(GLE)

O'SO SWEET

OMEOMY

ORIENTAL SUNRISE

Our Brenda
Single H1 Lax Bush
Triphylla-type. A rich candy pink
self (*tube*, *sepals* and *corolla* all
of the same colouring). The *sepals*
are held out at right angles to the
tube. Large, vivid blooms are
produced in quantity on lax
upright growth. Well-suited to
hanging containers in which the
blooms show themselves off with
stunning effect.
(Willment, UK, 1997) (ISL)(HYDE)

Our Joyce
Single H2 Bush
Tube and *sepals* crimson. *Corolla*
petals cyclamen purple. A good,
strong, upright and self-branching
bush.
(Holmes, UK, 1999) (OLD)

Our Topsy
Single H2 Bush
Tube and *sepals* crimson.
Corolla petals lilac purple. The
semi-erect blooms are freely
produced.
(R. Holmes, UK, 1995)
(CLI)(RIV)(OLD)(OLI)

P

Pabbes Teudebel
Single H2 Lax Bush
Tubes medium to long, pale pink.
Sepals pink with green tips and
open to the horizontal. *Corolla*
petals a darker pink. Spreading
habit needs 'pinching' to get
bushiness. Unusual and attractive
in hanging pots.
(Koerts, Holland, 1993)
(SIL)(RKY)(GOU)

Pabbes Tudebekje
Single H2 Bush
A single of the intermediate type.
The long *tubes* and spreading
sepals glossy scarlet. *Corolla*s tiny
and white. Growth is sturdy.
Early pinching out will be useful.
Makes an excellent summer
bedding plant.
(Koerts, Holland, 1990)
(CHA)(HYDE)

Pacific Grove
Double H2 Bush
Tube and *sepals* dark crimson.
Corolla petals Bishop's violet
with smaller petals outside
crimson. Fairly large blooms
quite freely produced. Growth is
upright and quite tall and
vigorous.
(Niederholzer, USA, 1947)
(BAK)(BRI)(RIV)

Pam Plack
Single H2/3 Bush
Tube and *sepals* white with
reflexed tips. *Corolla* opens a
light shade of lilac pink maturing
to a deeper shade of pink. Profuse
flowers. *Foliage* medium-sized,
light green. Strong upright
grower. H: 36in (one metre). A
'sport' from 'Margaret Brown',
this delightful plant has proved
itself to be very similar in its
hardiness and multiple flowering.
('sport' from 'Margaret Brown')
(Plack, UK, 1998) (CL)

Panache
Single H2 Bush
Tubes of medium length and, like
the shorter *sepals* and *petals*,
pink. Flowering is between
paniculate and triphylla-type.
Growth is strong and spreading.
Very suitable for growing in large
pots or patio tubs.
(de Graaff, Holland, 1991) (GOU)

Pan America
Double H2 Trailer
Tube and *sepals* red. *Corolla*
petals very pale pink. The large
flowers are very freely produced.
The lax growth and weight of
flowers make it a candidate for
hanging containers.
(Reiter, USA, 1940) (BAK)

Pangea (Tri)
Single H2 Bush
Single of the terminal-flowering
sort, long, bulbous *tubes*, short
sepals and *corolla* petals bright
orange. Growth is upright.
Foliage mid-green. Prefers filtered
light. Makes a good pot plant for
show purposes.

(Van der Post, Holland, 1993)
(MO)

Pantomime Dame
Double H2 Trailer
Tube and *sepals* magenta. *Corolla*
petals white veined with magenta.
Large blooms on strong trailing
growths. Easily fills large baskets.
(Forward, UK, 1993)
(WV)(FUC)(GLE)(ISL)

Panyella Prince (Enc)
Single H2 Bush
Encliandra-type. *Tube* and *sepals*
red-purple. *Corolla* petals light
purple. Strong upright-growing
plant. Rather out of the ordinary.
(Drapkin, USA, 1988)
(CL)(LB)(BRE)(ISL)

Parkstone Centenary
Double H2 Bush
Tube and *sepals* light pink.
Corolla petals purple to
red/purple. Growth is strongly
upright and self-branching.
(Forward, UK, 1995)
(WV)(FUC)(GLE)(ISL)

Parliament
Double H2 Trailer
Tube and *sepals* white and dark
rose. *Corolla* petals purple with
rose stripes. The large blooms are
fairly freely produced and the
natural trailing habit makes this a
good plant for baskets.
(Southall, Australia, 1997) (HYDE)

Party Time
Double H2 Trailer
Tube and *sepals* white fused pink.
Corolla petals light purple marbled
pale lilac. Very strong grower with
large flowers. Will easily fill a large
basket – a natural trailer.
(Forward, UK, 1993)
(WV)(FUC)(GLE)(ISL)

F. parviflora
Single H1 Bush
Species. Single flowers. *Sepals*
spreading, red and slightly hairy.
Corolla petals coral red. The
flowers are very small.
(Lindley, Mexico, 1827)
(BAK)(ROO)

PANTOMIME DAME

PARLIAMENT

PAM PLACK

PANYELLA PRINCE

PARTY TIME

Pasadena
Double H2 Bush
Tube and *sepals* deep rose.
Corolla petals snowy white and
lightly veined with pink. The
large, flaring blooms are freely
produced. *Foliage* light green.
Growth is upright and
vigorous.
(Evans and Reeves, USA, 1938)
(BRY)

Pathétique
Double H2 Lax Bush
Tube and *sepals* dark red. *Corolla*
petals white, veined with carmine.
Large blooms fairly free. Very
similar to 'Swingtime'. Growth as
lax bush.
(Blackwell, UK, 1952) (LOK)(EX)

Patie Sue
Double H2 Bush
Tube and *sepals* of this medium-
sized flower deep pink. *Corolla*
petals light pink. Strong, upright,
bushy with good self-branching
habit.
(Sinton, UK, 1994)
(FEN)(WAR)(CL)(BRE)(STM)
(BRI)(ROO)(FUC)(GLE)(ISL)

Pat Meara
Single H2 Bush
Tube and *sepals* pale rose pink.
Corolla petals veronica blue with
a white band down the centre.
Medium to large flowers that
sometimes appear as semi-
doubles. Very free-flowering.
Open saucer-shape. Growth
upright and bushy – resents
overwatering and overpotting.
(V.V. Miller, UK, 1962)
(BAK)(EX)(RIV)(LOK)

Patricia
Single H2 Bush
Tube and *sepals* waxy pale salmon.
Corolla petals rosy cerise. Smallish
flowers but freely produced.
Growth upright and bushy.
(Wood, UK, 1940) (SIL)(FEN)
(BAK)(BLA)(RIV)(BRY)

Patricia Joan Yates
Double H2 Stiff Trailer
Tubes sturdy and ivory white.

The flared *sepals* pale salmon.
Corolla petals marbled salmon
and pink. Growth is spreading
and strong. Most suitable for
wall and fully round baskets.
(Goulding, UK, 1998)
(GOU)(HYDE)

Patty Lou
Double H2 Bush
Tube and *sepals* dark rose.
Corolla petals purple and veined
with red. The upward-growing
habit makes an ideal bush plant
for the patio tub.
(Roach, USA, 1990) (EX)

Paula Bayliss
Single H2/3 Bush
Tube and *sepals* red. *Corolla*
petals lavender pink. Medium-
sized flowers continuously
produced. *Foliage* dark green.
Tall, upright-growing plant with a
self-branching habit. Considered
hardy in the south of England.
(Tabraham, UK, 1974) (OLI)

Paula Jane
Semi-Double H2 Bush
Tube venetian pink. *Sepals* curving
upright and covering tube are
carmine rose. *Corolla* beetroot
purple changing to ruby red as the
medium-sized flowers develop. Pale
pink flush at base of petals. *Foliage*
medium green. Growth upright
and bushy. Very free flowering.
(Tite, UK, 1975)

Paul Berry
Single H1 Bush
Triphylla-type single fuchsia. The
very long *tube*, *sepals* and *corolla*
petals orange.
(Reiman, Holland, 1991)
(SIL)(KM)(LB)(MO)(HYDE)

Pauline McFarland
Double H2 Trailer
Tube and *sepals* white, streaked
with pale pink. *Corolla* petals
purple maturing to red/purple.
Profuse quantity of large flowers.
Very attractive plant for use in
baskets.
(Pearson, USA, 1996)
(ISL)

Pauline Rawlings
Double H2 Bush
Tube and *sepals* pale flesh pink.
Corolla petals rich pink but
deeper at the base. Medium-sized
blooms very freely produced.
Foliage dark green. Growth
upright and bushy.
(Bridger, UK, 1959)
(LOK)

Paul Meredith
Single H2 Bush
Tube and *sepals* rose. *Corolla*
petals violet. The strong upright
and bushy growth carries good
quantities of medium-sized
flowers.
(Holmes, UK, 1994)
(RIV)

Paulus
Single H2 Bush
Tube pink. *Sepals* light red with
green tips. *Corolla* petals blood
red. Very eye-catching upright-
growing bush.
(Krom, Holland, 1994)
(LB)(MO)(HYDE)(ISL)

Peace
Double H2 Bush
Tube and *sepals* white tipped
with green. *Corolla* petals white
with a very pale pink line on each
main petaloid. The very freely
produced flowers are of medium
size. Growth is upright. Like all
whites it needs careful cultivation.
(Thorne, UK, 1968)
(BAK)(FOX)(BRI)(CHA)(RIV)
(HYDE)(CLI)(FUC)(GLE)(ISL)

Peaches and Cream
Single H2 Bush
Encliandra-type fuchsia with
perfect flowers. *Tubes* salmon.
Sepals spreading, green. *Corolla*
petals pale tangerine. Growth is
spreading and self-branching.
Ideal when grown in small pots
or used in fuchsia 'topiary'.
(Robson, UK, 1997)
(ROO)

PASADENA

PATRICIA JOAN YATES

PAULUS

PEACHES AND CREAM

Peachy
Double H2 Trailer
Tube and *sepals* pale pink, tinged with darker pink. *Corolla* petals pink, mottled with lavender and maturing to orangey pink. The large blooms are freely produced and the plant is deservedly very popular for use in baskets.
(Stubbs, USA, 1992)
(JAK)(LB)(FOX)(FEN)(ROU) (RKY)(BRE)(EX)(BRI)(CHA) (PER)(BEL)(GOU)(BLA)(RID) (ALD)(RIV)(HYDE)(CLI)(ASK) (FUC)(ISL)(SMI)

Peachy Keen
Double H2 Trailer
Tube and *sepals* rose. *Corolla* petals salmon-orange. Largish blooms fairly freely produced. Growth is as a natural trailer.
(Tiret, USA, 1967)
(BAK)(BRI)(WV)(RIV)

Peacock
Double H2 Bush
Tube and *sepals* scarlet, the latter very broad. *Corolla* petals rich violet-blue. Medium-sized blooms freely produced. Lovely vivid contrast between sepals and petals – hence the name. *Foliage* dark green and shiny. Growth is upright and bushy.
(Colville, UK, 1981)
(LOK)(BRI)

Pearl Farmer
Single H2 Bush
Tube and *sepals* carmine. *Corolla* petals amethyst violet. Upright bushy growth.
(Pacey, UK, 1982) (FEN)

Pearly Gates
Double H2 Lax Bush
Tube and *sepals* light red-purple. *Corolla* petals light purple. Large blooms with half-flared petals. Remarkably rich colouring.
(Forward, UK, 1993)
(WV)(FUC)(GLE)(ISL)

Pearly King
Double H2 Trailer
Tube and *sepals* pink. *Corolla* petals light purple. The flowers

are quite large and freely produced. The naturally trailing habit makes a good basket.
(WV)(FUC)(GLE)

Pearly Queen
Semi-Double H2 Bush
Tube red. *Sepals* red outside tipped with green and pink on the underside. They are held horizontally. *Corolla* petals have a pearly sheen that spreads from the base changing to light blue halfway up. Smallish flowers, very delicate, held up and out at right angles. Very freely produced. Growth upright and very bushy.
(Dyos, UK, 1980) (EX)

Pebble Mill
Semi-Double H2/3 Bush
Tube and *sepals* pink. *Corolla* petals violet blue. Upright bushy growth well worth trying as a hardy in the garden.
(Johnson/Laburnum, UK, 1987) (FEN)

Peggy King
Single H2/3 Bush
Tube and *sepals* rosy red. *Corolla* petals peony-purple. Small flowers but very free. Growth upright, bushy and hardy.
(Wood, UK, 1954)
(SIL)(FOX)(CL)(BUR)(STM) (ARC)(BRI)(CHA)(BAK)(RIV) (BRY)(WHE)(FUC)(GLE)(ISL)

Penny
Single H2 Trailer
Little-known red self (i.e. red *tube*, *sepals* and *corolla*) cultivar with bronze *foliage* especially on the young growth. Similar in many respects to 'Autumnale'. Natural trailer and excellent for basket work. Small flowers compensated for by the delightful foliage.
(Clapton Court Gardens, UK, 1985) (RIV)

People's Princess
Single H2 Bush
Tube and *sepals* light pink.

Corolla petals pale violet flecked darker and with light purple edging. A good upward-growing, self-branching bush.
(BRE)(ARC)

Percy Holmes
Single H2 Bush
Tube thin, azalea pink. *Sepals* azalea pink on the outside and scarlet inside and tipped with green. *Corolla* petals rhodonite-red, nasturtium red at the base. The medium-sized flowers are freely produced. *Foliage* is large and lush.
('Coachman' × 'Sunset')
(Holmes, UK, 1960)
(RIV)

Percy Thorpe
Single H2 Bush
Tube and *sepals* crimson. *Corolla* petals aster violet, veined with red. The medium-sized flowers are borne in profusion. A good, strong, upright and self-branching bush.
(Holmes, UK, 1999)
(OLD)

Periwinkle
Single H2 Bush
Tube and long recurved *sepals* pink. *Corolla* petals medium lavender blue. The medium-sized flowers are free and long. Growth is upright and willowy.
(Hodges, USA, 1961)
(WAY)(CHA)(GLE)

Perle Mauve
Semi-Double H2 Bush
Tube and *sepals* pink. *Corolla* petals mauve. Bushy upright growth.
(Rozain-Boucharlet, France, 1913) (EX)

Peter Grange
Single H2 Bush
Tube and *sepals* pink. *Corolla* petals lavender pink. Delightful medium-sized flowers produced in vast numbers. Ideal plant for the show bench.
(Stiff, UK, 1995) (BAK)

PEARLY GATES

PEGGY KING

PEOPLE'S PRINCESS

Peter James
Double H2/3 Bush
Tube and *sepals* red. *Corolla* petals pale pink, veined with red. Upward-growing bushy plants that are considered to be hardy from the Midlands southwards.
(Rolt, UK, 1990)
(SIL)(RKY)(KM)(ROO)
(RIV)

Peter Pan
Single H2 Lax Bush
Tube and upturned *sepals* pink. *Corolla* petals orchid and lilac. The largish flowers are prolifically produced. The flowering starts early and is continuous. The growth is very lax – really a trailer. Useful for hanging containers or trailing over the edge of patio tubs.
(Erickson, USA, 1960)
(SIL)(RKY)(BRE)(WV)(BRY)

F. petiolaris
Species H1 Bush
Tube very long and thin, narrowly funnel-form, dark pink. *Sepals* pink to pale pink and sometimes tipped with green. *Corolla* bright rosy pink. The flowers are produced in the leaf axils. *Foliage* a dull medium green. The leaves are quite large. Best when grown under warmer greenhouse conditions.
(Colombia and Venezuela)
(KM)(CL)(GOU)

Petit Four
Single H2 Bush
Tube and *sepals* pink flushed with aubergine. *Corolla* petals dark aubergine. The small flowers are very striking in their appearance. Mid-green *foliage*. An upright-growing bush that will make a good half-standard.
(de Graaff, Holland, 1992)
(SIL)(RKY)(WV)(HYDE)

Pharaoh
Single H2 Bush
Tube and edge of *sepals* rose bengal. *Sepals* white tipped with green. *Corolla* petals plum purple fading to ruby red. Medium-sized

flowers freely produced. Good, strong, upright growth.
(Need, UK, 1965) (LOK)(BRI)

Phillip Paul
Double H2 Trailer
Tube reddish purple. *Sepals* reddish purple with green tips – the underside has a crêped effect. *Corolla* petals very deep purple with slight red veining at the base. Holds its colour well even when mature. *Sepals* curl back to the *tube* showing the whole of the *corolla*. Although the blooms are small they are very freely produced. The naturally trailing growth makes this a super plant for hanging containers.
(Allsop, UK, 1998) (ROO)

Pick of the Pops
Double H2 Bush
Tube and *sepals* neyron rose, tipped with green. *Corolla* petals rose pink. Large blooms freely produced. Growth is upright and bushy.
(W. Jones, UK, 1960) (FEN)(OLI)

Piet Heemskerke
Single H1 Trailer
Terminal-flowering single. *Tubes* long, thin, pale tangerine. The short *sepals* and *corolla* also pale tangerine. Growth is naturally pendant and looks at its best when viewed at eye level in hanging containers. Well worth growing.
(Franck, Holland, 1990)
(ISL)(EX)

Pink Beacon
Single H2/3 Bush
Tube and *sepals* pink. *Corolla* petals magenta pink. Growth is upright and bushy.
(Raiser and date unknown)
(STM)

Pink Cornet
Single H1 Bush
An interspecific hybrid. *Tube* pink, paler at the base. *Sepals* pink and slightly darker underneath. *Corolla* petals rosy carmine. Very vigorous in its growth.
(*F. boliviana* var. *alba* ×

F. boliviana)
(Wright, UK, 1981) (CL)

Pink Domino
Double H2/3 Trailer
Tube and *sepals* red. *Corolla* petals bright pink. The medium-sized blooms are freely produced. *Corolla* very full. Pendulous growth so will make a good basket. Considered to be hardy in the southern part of the United Kingdom.
(Tabraham, UK, 1978) (KM)

Pink Fandango
Semi-Double H2 Bush
Tube and *sepals* rosy carmine. *Sepals* broad and long. *Corolla* petals start rosy carmine shading to magenta with carmine edges. Medium-sized blooms freely produced. Growth upright and bushy. Makes an excellent Standard quite quickly.
(Lockyer, UK, 1979) (LOK)

Pinkhaze
Double H2/3 Bush
Tube and *sepals* a beautiful shade of pink. *Corolla* petals pink but heavily splashed with blue. The largish fully double flowers are freely produced considering their size. Good, strong, upright and vigorous growth. H: 2ft–2ft 6in (60–75cm). Considered to be hardy in the south of England.
(Tabraham, UK, 1984) (RIV)

Pink la Campanella
Single H2 Trailer
Small to medium-sized flowers. *Tube* pale carmine. *Sepals* pale carmine shading to darker at the tips on the upper surface and white on the lower surface. *Corolla* magenta maturing to carmine. *Foliage* medium green. The growth is really rather stiff for a trailer but it will make a very good basket with assistance.
(Hansom, UK, 1988)
(SIL)(FEN)(WAR)(LB)(WAY)
(STM)(EX)(ARC)(JAK)(BRI)
(CHA)(WV)(PER)(BAK)(ROO)
(RID)(BRY)(CLI)(WHE)(FUC)
(GLE)(SMI)(OLD)(OLI)

PETER PAN

F. PETIOLARIS

PETIT FOUR

PHILLIP PAUL

PINK LA CAMPANELLA

Pink Pineapple
Double H2 Bush
Sepals white with a hint of pink.
Corolla petals white with pink
shades. Foliage light green. Good,
strong, upward growth.
(ASK)

Pink Slipper
Single H2 Trailer
Tube white with very faint pink
tinge. Sepals pale pinkish white
with green tips and stand out
horizontally. Corolla petals pink
with slight veining at the base.
Medium-sized flowers, free.
Growth is naturally trailing. Self-
branching.
(Rye, UK, 1975) (LOK)

Pinto de Blue
Double H2 Lax Bush
Tube and sepals a sparkling
white. Corolla petals a rich blue.
Huge blooms that are very
floriferous for their size. Very eye-
catching.
(Antonelli, USA, 1995) (GOU)
(FOX)(FEN)(BRI)(CHA)(ROO)
(RIV)(HYDE)(GLE)(ISL)(SMI)

Pin Up
Semi-Double H2 Trailer
Tube and sepals pure white.
Corolla petals bright pink. The
medium-sized blooms are freely
produced. A natural trailer that
will make a good basket.
(Kennett, USA, 1968)
(RIV)

Piper
Double H2 Bush
Medium-sized blooms. Tubes and
sepals white tinged with pink.
Corolla petals pure white with
smooth petal edges. Foliage mid-
green. Upright-growing bush that
will make a good Standard.
Prefers cool conditions.
(Howarth, UK, 1985) (SIL)(FEN)
(WAR)(BUR)(BRI)(WV)(OAK)
(RIV)(OLI)

Piper's Vale
Triphylla-Type H1 Bush
A true terminal-flowering
triphylla-type. The long tube and

short sepals pink. Corolla petals a
darker shade of pink. Foliage
medium green. The flowers are
produced profusely. Growth is
strong but is suitable for both
upright growth or in hanging
containers.
(Stannard, UK, 1992) (RKY)
(KM)(CL)(LB)(GOU)(ROO)
(HYDE)(ISL)

Pixie Variegata
Single H3 Bush
Tube and sepals of this 'sport' of
'Pixie' scarlet. Corolla petals
violet. Could be a reversion to
'Graf Witte' from which 'Pixie'
was itself a 'sport'.
(SMI)

P.J.B. (Pippa)
Double H2 Bush
Tube and sepals deep crimson.
Corolla petals magenta-burgundy.
Medium-sized blooms. Medium
upright to lax bushy type of
growth. Suitable for hanging
containers.
('Royal Velvet' × 'Swingtime')
(P.J. Bradley, UK, 1986) (CL)
(BRE)(ARC)(CHA)(PER)(ROO)
(RIV)(FUC)(GLE)(SIM)(OLI)

Plum Perfect
Semi-Double H2 Trailer
Tube and sepals light pink and
rose. Corolla petals open purple,
maturing to red purple.
Medium-sized blooms are
freely produced early in the
season. A natural trailing
variety that will make a good
basket.
(Pearson, USA, 1967)
(ISL)

Poacher
Triphylla-Type H1 Lax Bush
Terminal-flowering. Tube long,
pink. Sepals almost white.
Corolla rosy pink. Growth is
spreading and rather elegant.
Foliage medium to dark green.
An excellent fuchsia. In view of
its laxity of growth it could be
good for hanging containers.
(Stannard, UK, 1993)
(ISL)(ROO)(HYDE)

Polly Oliver
Single H2 Trailer
Tube and rather wide sepals white.
Corolla petals pale lilac veined
with pink. Foliage dark green with
dark pink stems. A natural trailer
that will produce a superb basket.
(Oliver, UK, 1987) (FEN)

Polychinelle
Double H2 Bush
Tube and sepals white with blush
pink. Tube quite long. Sepals
deep pink underneath, short and
green-tipped. Corolla petals matt
purple shading to pink at the
base. The medium-sized flowers
are freely produced. Growth is
upright and bushy.
(Holland – date and raiser
unknown)

Polynesia
Double H2 Trailer
Tube and sepals salmon. Corolla
petals salmon orange. Large
blooms fairly freely produced.
Natural trailer that will rapidly
fill a hanging container.
(Tiret, USA, 1966) (EX)(BRI)

Popely Pride
Double H2 Lax Bush or Trailer
Tubes are ivory. Sepals pale pink
and sweep back like steers' horns.
Corolla petals a subtle shade of
mauve to magenta. A highly
versatile habit best suited to
hanging containers.
(Goulding, UK, 1997)
(GOU)(BRI)(CHA)(HYDE)

Port Arthur
Semi-Double H2/3 Bush
Tube and sepals red. Corolla
petals are purple. Old cultivar
suitable for the hardy border.
(Story, UK, 1869) (ROU)(STM)
(ARC)(BRI)(CHA)(BAK)(RIV)
(BRY)(GLE)(OLI)

Port Royal
Single H2 Bush
Medium-sized flowers. Tube and
sepals scarlet. Corolla petals
purple streaked with pale purple.
Very vigorous bush-type growth.
(BRI)

PINTO DE BLUE

PIPER'S VALE

POACHER

POPELY PRIDE

Postman
Double H2 Bush
Tube and *sepals* dull pink.
Corolla petals smoky blue
splashed with red. Makes a good
upright bush or a Standard.
(L. Wright, UK, 1980) (CLI)
(FOX)(FEN)(BRE)(STM)(CHA)
(RIV)(GLE)(ISL)(OLD)(OLI)

Powder Pink
Double H3 Bush
Tube and *sepals* red. *Corolla*
petals pink. A strong, upright-
growing bush that is probably
hardy in most districts.
(RIV)

President B. Gaucher
Single H2 Bush
Tube and *sepals* pink. *Corolla*
petals dark violet. *Foliage*
medium green. Good strong
bush-type growth.
(Masse, France, 1989) (EX)

President B.W. Rawlins
Single H2 Trailer
Tube and *sepals* white. The
underside of the *sepals* is flushed
pink. *Corolla* petals purple
blended with rose. The medium-
sized flowers are freely produced.
Natural cascading growth.
(Thorne, UK, 1966)
(FEN)(RIV)(BAK)(BRY)

President George Bartlett
Semi-Double H2 Bush
A strong upright-grower with
small to medium-sized semi-double
flowers. *Tube* and *sepals* rich
cardinal red. *Corolla* opens dark
violet purple and ages to a rich
ruby red. *Foliage* dark green and
glossy. Easy to grow in pots and
tubs. Makes a good plant for the
show bench or in the hardy border.
('Dollar Princess' × 'Cotta Vino')
(Bielby/Oxtoby, UK, 1997)
(FOX)(FEN)(ROU)(KM)(LB)(BRE)
(MO)(EX)(JAK)(CHA)(PER)
(ROO)(ALD)(CLI)(HYDE)(ISL)

President Roosevelt
Double H2 Bush
Tube medium length, coral red.
Sepals reflexing, also coral red.

Corolla dark violet blue. The
flowers are small but they are
freely produced. *Foliage* medium
green with serrated edges. Growth
is upright, bushy and vigorous.
(Garson, USA, 1942) (BRY)(FEN)
(WAY)(STM)(CHA)(HYDE)
(BRY)(GLE)

Preston Field
Single H2 Bush
Tube and *sepals* carmine striped
red. *Corolla* petals dark violet
blue. The flowers are of medium
size but are freely produced.
Foliage vibrant golden/yellow/
green. A beautiful plant to grow.
(Cathcart, UK, 1995) (SIL)(LB)

Pretty in Pink
Single H2 Bush
Tube and *sepals* white with pink
shading. *Corolla* petals a delicate
lilac pink. Profuse medium-sized
flowers. *Foliage* light green,
complementing flower colouring
beautifully.
(Raiser and date unknown)

Pretty Paige
Single H2 Trailer
Tube white and *sepals* pale pink
tipped with pale green. *Corolla*
petals pale lilac with a deeper
edge to each petal. Light mauve
veining. Very free-flowering.
Growth self-branching and
compact trailer.
(M. Allsop, UK, 1996) (ROO)

Priscilla Spek
Semi-Double H2 Lax Bush
Tube is long, thin and white.
Sepals upturned, pale pink. *Corolla*
petals deep pink with irregular
petal margins. With its spreading
habit, this fuchsia does best when
used in hanging containers.
(Beije, Holland, 1998)
(GOU)

F. procumbens* var. *argentius
Single H2 Low Bush
Species. *Tube* greenish yellow, red
at the base. *Sepals* green tipped
with purple. Reflexed completely
back onto the *tube*. No *corolla*.
Blue pollen. Small heart-shaped

leaves that are variegated silvery
green and lighter at the edges.
Creeping growth.
(Finder unknown, New Zealand)
(SIL)(CL)

***F. procumbens* variegated**
Typical description of the
flowering of this '*procumbens*'
'sport' with the exception that
the *foliage* has a definite silver
variegation.
(Finder and date unknown)
(EX)(CLI)

Profusion
Single H3 Bush
Tube and *sepals* scarlet. *Corolla*
petals violet purple. Small flowers
that are very freely produced.
Growth is low but bushy and
very hardy.
(Wood, UK, 1938)
(FOX)(FEN)(EX)(CHA)(WHE)

Prostrata
Single H2 Low Bush
Tube and *sepals* dull red.
Corolla petals violet. The flowers
are very small but borne in
profusion. Growth low and
spreading. Aptly named plant
that could be of use in the border
or on rockeries. (Correct name
could be '*F. magellanica* var.
prostrata')
(Scholfield, UK, 1841)
(RIV)

Prove Thyself
Single H2 Bush
Encliandra-type. *Tube* and
sepals cream. *Corolla* petals
orangey-pink. Largish strong
flowers.
(GOU)(ISL)

Purbeck Mist
Double H2 Bush
Tube and *sepals* frosty white.
Corolla petals deep dusky rich
mauve-pink. Large flowers. The
blooms remain tight and are of
good substance. Excellent for
containers. Bushy upright
growth.
(Swinbank, UK, 1993)
(KM)(BRI)(WV)

PRESIDENT GEORGE BARTLETT

PRESIDENT ROOSEVELT

POSTMAN

PRETTY PAIGE

PROSTRATA

Purple Emperor
Semi-Double H2 Bush
Tube and *sepals* crimson. *Corolla*
petals violet. Good, strong,
upright bush. Very prolific.
Excellent grower.
(Endicott, UK, 1970)
(CLI)(LOK)

Purple Graseing
Semi-Double H2 Bush
Tube and *sepals* red with splashes
of purple. *Corolla* petals light
purple with pink splashes. Bushy
upright plant.
(seedling of 'Purple Gem')
(J.A. Wright, UK, 1980) (ASK)

Purple Lace
Double H2/3 Bush
Tube and *sepals* red. *Corolla*
petals purple. Large blooms that
are profuse for a double. *Foliage*
dark green. Growth upright and
bushy with a strong branching
habit. Hardy in southern
counties.
(Tabraham, UK, 1974) (RIV)

Purple Patch
Single H2 Bush
Tube and *sepals* crimson. *Corolla*
petals very dark purple. Flowers
are of medium size and increase
with age. Strong, upright, bushy
growth. Easy to grow.
(Sinton, UK, 1995) (LB)(ROU)
(BRE)(BUR)(WAL)(PER)(GLE)
(ISL)(SMI)(OLI)

Putney Pride
Double H2 Lax Bush
Tube and *sepals* flesh pink to
cream. *Corolla* petals purple.
Medium-sized flowers produced
in profusion. The lax growth
makes it ideal for use in hanging
containers.
(Raiser unknown, UK, 1993)
(POT)

Q

Queen Esther
Single H2 Bush
Tube and *sepals* white. *Corolla*

petals violet. Good, upright,
bushy plant.
(FOX)(CHA)(GLE)

Queen Mabs
Single H2 Lax Bush
Tube thin, crimson with creamy
striping. *Sepals* crimson crêped on
the inside and tipped with green.
Corolla petals cyclamen purple and
neyron rose at the base. The large
flowers are square-shaped. Semi-
trailer so will make a good basket.
(Holmes, UK, 1976)
(BAK)(RIV)

Queen of Hearts
Single H2/3 Bush
Corolla petals deep mauve flushed
with pink. The medium-sized
flowers are very freely produced.
Growth is upright and bushy.
Hardy in southern counties.
(Tabraham, UK, 1974)
(SIL)(BRY)

Queen of Sheba
Single H2 Bush
Tube, *sepals* and *corolla* petals all
aubergine. The medium-sized
flowers are freely produced.
Certain to be popular on the
show bench with this colouring.
('sport' from 'Cotta Vino')
(Willment, UK, 1999) (ISL)

Queens Park
Double H2 Bush
Tube and *sepals* rich waxy red.
Corolla petals parma-violet.
Large blooms very free and of
good substance. Growth is
upright and bushy.
(Thorne, UK, 1959)
(BAK)(FEN)(RKY)(BRI)
(BRY)

Queen Victoria
Double H2 Bush
Tube and *sepals* pale pink.
Corolla petals purple carmine.
Large flowers that are fairly
freely produced. *Foliage* medium
green. Responds well to
'pinching' and will make a good
upright bush.
(Smith, UK, 1843)
(BRI)(BAK)(BRY)

R

Rachel Craig
Double H2 Trailer
Tube and *sepals* rose. *Corolla*
petals white with broad pink
veining. The large-sized flowers
are produced quite freely.
Foliage is yellow green and the
plant will make an excellent
basket.
(P. Eaton, UK, 1996)
(WAR)

Rachel Sinton
Double H2 Trailer
Tube and *sepals* red. *Corolla*
petals pink. Large blooms freely
produced on a neat compact
plant that naturally trails. A very
attractive hanging container
variety.
(Sinton, UK, 1993) (FOX)
(BRE)(BUR)(WAY)(BRI)
(CHA)(FUC)(GLE)(ISL)(OLD)
(OLI)

Radings Gerda
Single H2/3 Bush
Encliandra-type. 'Perfect'
flowers with small, single
blooms. *Tubes*, *sepals* and *corolla*
petals all lavender blue. Growth
is stiffly upright and shrubby. A
slow starter but one that is
attractively different. Best
grown in medium to large pots
to give the necessary root
space.
('*Fuchsia*' × '*Bacillaris*')
(Reiman, Holland, 1984)
(GOU)

Rading's Mapri
Single H1 Bush
Species hybrid. *Tube* longish,
sepals small, both scarlet with
green tips. *Corolla* petals
vermilion.
(*F. magdalenae* × *F. pringsheimii*)
(Reiman, Holland, 1986) (KM)

PURPLE PATCH

RACHEL SINTON

QUEEN OF SHEBA

Rading's Marjorie
Single H2 Lax Bush
'Perfect' flowers. Single.
Encliandra-type. *Tubes* waxy
white with mauve overtones.
Sepals spreading dark pink or
mauve. Flared *corolla* pale pink.
Growth is shrubby and self-
branching. Looks well in hanging
containers – especially with other
plants.
(Reiman, Holland, 1980) (GOU)

Rading's Mia
Single H2 Bush/Trailer
Encliandra-type. 'Perfect' flowers.
Single. *Tube, sepals* and the flared
corolla petals all pink. The
growth spreads horizontally,
joints are short and leaves are
holly-like in appearance. Looks
best in hanging containers.
(Reiman, Holland, 1986)
(PER)(GOU)

Rading's Michelle
Single H2 Lax Bush
Encliandra-type. 'Perfect' flowers.
Tubes pink and *sepals* very pale
pink. *Corolla* petals also very pale
pink. Growth is spreading and
self-branching. Very versatile
plant. One for mixed tub
planting.
(Reiman, Holland, 1986)
(SIL)(WV)(HYDE)

Raintree Legend
Semi-Double H2 Bush
Tube white with pale phlox pink
overcast. *Sepals* white with a faint
brushing of pink at the base and
absinth tips. *Corolla* petals white.
The flowers are of medium size,
compact, very profuse and appear
over a long season. *Foliage*
smallish with fine serrations on
the edges. Upright bushy and self-
branching.
(Foster, USA, 1975) (CLI)(FOX)
(ARC)(CHA)(RIV)(GLE)

Rakastava
Double H2 Trailer
Tube and *sepals* glossy white with
green streaks and cyclamen pink.
Corolla petals white with
cyclamen pink veining. Large

fully double flowers. The natural
trailing habit will present a
superb basket.
(Blackwell, UK, 1969) (ISL)(RIV)

Ralph Oliver
Semi-Double/Double H2 Bush
Tubes and spreading *sepals* white.
Corolla petals white with
magenta marbling, the inner
petals being magenta. Strong
upright habit makes this an ideal
subject for planting in large patio
tubs.
(Goulding, UK, 1997)
(GOU)(RKY)(HYDE)

Ralph's Delight
Double H2 Trailer
Tube ivory white. *Sepals* arched
like wings, white with a pink
reverse. *Corollas* densely petalled,
dark plum maturing to rich
magenta. The natural growth is
as a trailer so will make an
excellent basket.
(Goulding, UK, 1997)
(GOU)(CHA)(HYDE)

Rambo
Double H2 Bush
Tube and *sepals* pale rose.
Corolla petals rose lilac with
darker veins. *Foliage* dark green.
Growth is as a medium upright.
(Franck, Holland, 1989)
(BRY)(EX)(ARC)(BRI)(BLA)

Raspberry Punch
Double H2 Bush
Tube and *sepals* pale orange.
Corolla petals raspberry red. The
large flowers are produced quite
freely. Natural upward-growing
bush-type plant.
(Riley, UK, 1992)
(EX)(WV)(RID)

Raspberry Sweet
Double H2 Trailer
Tube and *sepals* white blushed
light pink. *Corolla* petals
magenta. Large flowers with
picotee edging to the petals. A
natural trailer that will make an
excellent basket. Most attractive.
(Forward, UK, 1993)
(WV)(FUC)(GLE)(ISL)

Raspberry Twist
Semi-Double H2 Trailer
Tube and *sepals* pink. *Corolla*
petals imperial purple. Largish
flowers very freely produced for
their size. Delightful colouring.
Will make a large basket.
(Pearson, USA, 1997)
(ISL)

Ratae Beauty
Single H2 Lax Bush
Tube and *sepals* waxy white.
Corolla petals currant red. A
compact self-branching and
spreading bush, that with its lax
habit will make a good hanging
pot or wall basket.
(Green, UK, 1975) (WV)

Ratcliffe Beauty
Single H2 Bush
The *tube* and *sepals* scarlet rose.
The petals in the *corolla* are
violet blue. The upright growth is
strong and self-branching.
(Gadsby, UK, 1974) (WHE)

Ravenslaw
Single H2/3 Bush
Tube and *sepals* red. *Corolla*
petals also red. An upright hardy
bush that can be produced quite
quickly. H and S: approx. 1ft 6in
(45cm)
(Donald, UK, 1986) (KM)

Raymond Scopes
Double H2 Bush
Tube and spreading *sepals* dark
pink. *Corolla* petals marbled with
shades of russet and red. Growth
is immensely strong. Will make
excellent Standards.
(Goulding, UK, 1995) (BRI)

Rebecca Sinton
Single H2 Bush
Tube and *sepals* pink and rose.
Corolla petals red shaded red-
purple. *Foliage* variegated yellow
and light green flushed with
carmine. A delightful upward-
growing bush plant.
(Sinton, UK, 1992) (FOX)(FEN)
(RKY)(WAR)(BRE)(BUR)
(PER)(RIV)(CLI)(ASK)(GLE)
(ISL)(OLI)

RADING'S MIA

RALPH OLIVER

RASPBERRY SWEET

REBECCA SINTON

Red Ace
Double H2 Bush
Tube and *sepals* post-office red.
Corolla petals Indian lake. The
medium-sized blooms are
produced quite freely. Growth is
upright and bushy.
('Rufus' × 'Herald')
(Roe, UK, 1983) (SIL)(BRI)(SMI)

Redbridge in Bloom
Single/Semi-Double H2 Lax Bush
Tube pale peach. *Sepals* peach
and slightly darker underneath.
Corolla petals smoky orange
streaked with peach. A very free-
flowering plant. Although a lax
upright-growing plant it will
make a very good half basket.
(Allsop, UK, 1998) (ROO)

Red Jacket
Double H2 Trailer
Tube and long, upturned *sepals*
bright red. *Corolla* petals pure
white. Large, fluffy blooms with
long buds. Very freely produced.
Growth is as a natural trailer and
will quickly make an excellent
basket.
(Waltz, USA, 1958) (BAK)(RKY)
(EX)(ARC)(WV)(RIV)

Red Petticoat
Single H2 Bush
Sepals and *tube* rose bengal.
Corolla petals cyclamen purple. A
compact, self-branching bush.
Foliage is light green with
scalloped edges.
(Soo Yun Field, USA, 1978)
(WV)(RIV)

Red Ribbons
Double H2 Lax Bush
Tube and extremely long *sepals*
red. *Corolla* petals stark white.
Large blooms freely produced. The
blooms curl up to form a Christmas
bow. Growth lax bush or trailer. A
little smaller than 'Texas
Longhorn' but a much better plant.
(Martin, USA, 1959) (EX)(BAK)

Red Rover
Single H2 Bush
Tube and *sepals* red. *Corolla* petals
purple flushed with red. Medium-

sized flowers freely produced.
Growth medium upright bush.
(Hazard and Hazard, USA)
(GOU)(ISL)

Red Sunlight
Single H2 Bush
A single of the intermediate type.
Long *tubes* and short *sepals* like
the *corolla* petals all bright
crimson (almost fluorescent).
Growth spreading. This cultivar
does well in large mixed tubs or
as a specimen plant.
(Moerman, Holland, 1991)
(CL)(RKY)

Red Wing
Single to Semi-Double H2 Trailer
Tube and long *sepals* red. *Corolla*
petals plum-purple. Large flowers
fairly free. The buds are
unfortunately reluctant to open
under adverse conditions. A natural
trailer, will make a good basket.
(Tiret, USA, 1949) (LOK)

Regal
Single H2 Bush
Tube, *sepals* and *corolla* petals all
rose madder. The flowers are of
medium size and are freely
produced. Growth is extremely
strong upright. This plant could
be used as a greenhouse climber
as it insists on growing straight
up the central stem with few or
no side shoots.
(An American introduction but
raise and date unknown) (LOK)

F. regia
Single H1 Semi-climbing Shrub
Flowers solitary in upper axils
and rather small. *Tubes* and
sepals deep red. *Corolla* petals
purplish. Red anthers and
yellowish or reddish stigma.
(Vandelli, Brazil, 1825) (SIL)

Reinholt Leuthardt
Single H1 Bush
A triphylla-type fuchsia with the
flowers carried terminally. *Tubes*
medium-length and short *sepals*
both bright waxy red. *Corolla*
petals the same colour. An
upright and self-branching fuchsia

that gives of its best when grown
in sunny conditions.
(Goulding, UK, 1999)
(GOU)

Remembrance
Semi-Double H3 Bush
This 'sport' from 'Edith' with
pink *corolla* petals will be an
excellent addition to the back of
the hardy border. Like its
'parent', it is a very good hardy
that will easily attain a height of
about 4ft (120cm).
(Gubler, UK, 1995) (SIL)(KM)
(CL)(LB)(RIV)(POT)

Rene Schwab
Single H2 Bush
Tube and *sepals* dark red with
green tips to the *sepals*. *Corolla*
petals dark red. Good, strong,
upward growth on self-branching
plants.
(Schwab, Holland, 1995) (HYDE)

Rhapsody
Double H2 Bush
Tube and *sepals* deep blood red.
Corolla petals white. Medium-
sized blooms are freely produced.
Growth is upright and bushy.
(Blackwell, UK, 1965)
(CLI)(LOK)

Rhombifolia
Single H3 Bush
Tube and *sepals* scarlet-cerise.
Corolla petals purple. The flowers
are quite small but very freely
produced. *Foliage* mid-green,
carried on strong upright growth.
Considered to be a seedling from
'Ricartonii'.
(Lemoine, France)
(SIL)

Richard John
Single H2 Trailer
This is one of two *foliage* 'sports'
from 'Waveney Gem'. *Tubes* and
sepals white. *Corolla* petals pink
with a hint of mauve. Very
floriferous. *Foliage* a delightful
green with yellow margins. Will
make a good show specimen.
(Wye, UK, 1998)
(GOU)(ARC)(HYDE)

RED ACE

REDBRIDGE IN BLOOM

RED SUNLIGHT

F. REGIA

RICHARD JOHN

Richard John Carrington
Single H3 Bush
Tube and *sepals* bright cerise, curling back and slightly twisting. *Corolla* petals blue-violet veined with cerise. The flowers are of medium size. *Foliage* starts light green aging to dark green. Upright bushes that are excellent for the hardy border. H and S: approx. 18in (45cm).
(Birch, UK, 1991) (SIL)(FEN)

Richita
Single H2 Bush
Tube and *sepals* carmine rose. *Corolla* petals aster violet maturing to cyclamen purple. A good bush plant.
(Hall, UK, 1979) (CLI)

Rikste
Single H2 Bush
Tubes and *sepals* pink. *Corolla* petals pale pink. Medium upright.
('Lampadaria' × 'Ting a Ling')
(Bogemann, Germany, 1982)
(BRY)

Rita Kolk
Single H2 Trailer
Tube and *sepals* white. *Corolla* petals red. The small flowers are carried in abundance.
(Schwab, Holland, 1997) (HYDE)

Roberts
Double H2 Bush
Tube and *sepals* red. *Corolla* petals pink. Growth is strongly upright.
(RIV)

Robin Hood
Double H3 Bush
Tube and *sepals* bright glowing red. *Corolla* petals deep crimson maturing to rich self red. Very large blooms for a hardy that are carried on exceptionally strong stems. Growth upright, bushy and self-branching.
(Colville, UK, 1966)
(SIL)(CLI)(SMI)

Robin Pacey
Single H2 Bush
Sepals roseine purple. *Corolla*

petals campanula violet. Growth is upright and self-branching. The large flowers are of excellent shape.
(Pacey, UK, 1982) (FEN)

Rocket
Single H1 Bush
A triphylla-type fuchsia with the typical long *tubes* and trumpet-shaped *corolla*. *Tubes*, *sepals* and *corolla* all turkey red. *Foliage* dark green and deeply veined with red. One well worth trying.
('Gartenmeister Bonstedt' × 'Mrs Victor Reiter')
(Reiter, USA, 1942)
(ISL)(RIV)

Rocket Fire
Double H2 Bush
Tubes magenta. *Sepals* that have reflexed tips are dark rose on the upper surface and slightly lighter on the lower. *Corolla* has purple pleated outer petals and dark pink inner petals. *Foliage* dark green. The natural growth is as an upright bush. Good strong grower.
(Garrett, USA, 1989)
(MO)(FOX)(FEN)(ROU)(WAY)
(EX)(BRI)(CHA)(WV)(WAL)
(PER)(ROO)(BLA)(RIV)(HYDE)
(FUC)(GLE)(ISL)(OLD)
(OLI)

Rolt's Bride
Double H2 Trailer
Tube and *sepals* white. *Corolla* petals pink. A natural trailer with very vigorous growth. Will quickly make an excellent basket.
(Rolt, UK, 1996) (KM)

Rolt's Ruby
Double H2 Trailer
Tubes and *sepals* dark pink. *Corolla* petals aubergine. Very nice plant with medium-sized flowers that is naturally trailing and will form a good basket.
(Rolt, UK, 1996) (KM)(FOX)
(RKY)(LB)(EX)(ARC)(BRI)(CHA)
(ROO)(RIV)(POT)

Romany Rose
Single H2/3 Bush
Tube short, thick and pink. *Sepals* phlox pink. *Corolla* petals neyron rose. The medium-sized flowers are held semi-erect. Very prolific. Growth medium, upright and bushy. May be hardy in west of England.
(Hilton, UK, 1984)
(ISL)(STM)(LOK)

Ron Chamber's Love
Double H2 Trailer
Tubes medium-length, white. *Sepals* arched, orange/pink. *Corolla*s multi-layered, orange marbling to magenta. Habit spreading and self-branching. Excellent for half or wall baskets.
(Goulding, UK, 1997)
(GOU)(BRI)(HYDE)

Ron's Ruby
Single H2 Bush
Tube and *sepals* ruby red. *Corolla* petals also ruby red. Upright bushy growth with semi-erect blooms produced in great quantity.
(Holmes, UK, 1997)
(ALD)(WHE)(OLD)(BRE)

Ron Suttle
Double H2 Lax Bush
Tube and *sepals* coral pink. *Corolla* petals dark blue. Growth is rather lax but will make a good bush with some supports. Will also make a good hanging container. *Foliage* rather yellowish.
(Shaffery, UK, 1992) (ROO)

Ron Venables
Single H2 Bush
Tube waxy white. *Sepals* white slightly flushed with pink on the upper surfaces and white flushed rose-pink underneath. *Corolla* petals lilac shading at base, each petal edged rose purple. *Foliage* dark green. Strong upright grower. Free-flowering and should make a good exhibition plant.
(Kirby, UK, 1995) (JAK)

RICHARD JOHN CARRINGTON

ROBIN HOOD

ROCKET

ROCKET FIRE

ROLT'S RUBY

RON'S RUBY

Ron Ward
Single H2 Bush
Tubes and *sepals* red to purple.
Corolla petals white to pink.
Compact self-branching bush
with smallish flowers.
(Taylor, UK, 1997)
(BEL)

Rookie
Double H2 Bush
Tubes and *sepals* pale pink.
Corolla petals blue, lilac and
pink. Upright, bushy, self-
branching growth with medium-
sized flowers.
(Coupland, UK, 1997)
(BUR)

Roos Breytenbach
Triphylla-Type H1 Bush
Terminal-flowering triphylla.
Tube long and *sepals* small, both
orange red. *Corolla* has pleated
orange red petals. The flowers are
produced very prolifically
throughout the season. *Foliage*
medium to dark green.
(Stannard, UK, 1993)
(SIL)(KM)(CL)(BRE)(MO)(GOU)
(ROO)(HYDE)(ISL)

Rosamunda
Double H2 Bush
Tube and *sepals* dark pink.
Corolla petals white with deep
pink flushings. Largish blooms
freely produced. Growth is
upright and bushy.
(Colville, UK, 1966)
(LOK)

Rose Phenomenal
Double H2 Bush
Large flowers. *Tubes* and *sepals*
scarlet. *Corolla* petals rose mauve
lavender. A very strong upright
grower.
(Banks, UK, 1850) (BRI)

Rose van der Berg
Single H2 Bush
Tube and *sepals* pale pink.
Corolla petals bright reddish
orange. Smallish flowers freely
produced. Growth is upright and
bushy.
(Holmes, UK, 1989) (ROO)(RIV)

Rosea
Single H1 Bush
Tubes and reflexing *sepals* red.
Corolla petals rosy purple. A
very vigorously growing plant
that is possible a natural hybrid
of *F. lycioides* and *F. magellanica*.
(RKY)(KM)

Roslyn Lowe
Double H2 Trailer
Tube pinkish white with dull
green stripe. *Sepals*, horizontally
held, neyron rose on top and
carmine rose underneath. *Corolla*
petals open deep violet and
neyron rose maturing to violet
purple. The large fully double
flowers are very freely produced
for their size. A natural trailer so
will make an excellent basket.
Foliage matt green with lettuce
green undersides.
('Pink Marshmallow' × 'Midnight
Sun')
(Richardson, Australia, 1985)
(RIV)

Rosse Tricolor
Double H2 Trailer
Tubes and *sepals* of these
medium-sized flowers phlox rose.
Corolla petals magenta. The large
flowers are freely produced on a
naturally trailing plant.
(HYDE)

Ross Lea
Double H3 Bush
Tube and *sepals* scarlet. *Corolla*
petals royal purple with a dusky
rose base. One petal between
each sepal dusky pink with purple
splash. Small blooms. *Foliage*
mid-green with red stems. Hardy.
H: approx. 15in (38cm)
(Griffiths, UK, 1978) (SIL)

Rosy Bows
Double H2 Trailer
Tube and *sepals* flesh and rose.
Corolla petals are light rose.
Largish flowers. Naturally
trailing, it makes a good basket.
('Cheers' × 'Ruby Wedding')
(Forward, UK, 1996)
(CHA)(WV)(HYDE)(FUC)(GLE)
(ISL)

Rosy Morn
Double H2 Bush
Tube white tinged with green.
Sepals pink. *Corolla* petals are
smoky rose. Medium-sized
blooms very freely produced.
Growth strong, upright and
bushy.
(Colville, UK, 1973)
(BAK)(BRI)(LOK)

Rothbury Beauty
Double H2 Bush
Tube and *sepals* red. *Corolla*
petals coral pink, heavily flushed
with rose pink and cerise. Large
blooms.
(Ryle, UK, 1976)
(FOX)(STM)(CHA)(RIV)
(CLI)(OLI)

Royal Mosaic
Double H2 Trailer
Tube and *sepals* cream and pink.
Corolla petals open purple
variegated dark rose and mature
to red purple. Large flowers freely
produced. Natural trailer.
(Garrett, USA, 1991)
(FEN)(ROU)(BRE)(EX)(BRI)
(WAL)(PER)(RID)(RIV)(HYDE)
(ASK)(GLE)(ISL)(SMI)
(*See* photograph on page 193.)

Royal Orchid
Single H2 Trailer
Tube and extra long, wide,
spreading *sepals* are white, tinted
pale carmine. *Corolla* petals a
blend of orchid and blue shades,
fading to wine with maturity.
Large bell-shaped flowers, very
free. Growth is as a natural
trailer.
(Hodges, USA, 1962) (BRI)(RIV)

Royal Ruby
Double H2 Bush
Tube and *sepals* claret. *Corolla*
petals ruby red. The medium-
sized blooms are very freely
produced but appear rather late
in the season. Growth is upright,
self-branching and bushy.
(Gadsby, UK, 1968)
(FUC)(GLE)

ROOS BREYTENBACH

ROSEA

ROSY BOWS

ROSSE TRICOLOR

Royal Serenade
Double H2 Bush
Tube and *sepals* rosy red. *Corolla*
petals violet. *Foliage* yellowish
green with central veins and
stems a deep wine red. Growth is
upright, short-jointed and bushy.
(Clyne, UK, 1979) (WV)(RIV)

Royal Silk
Single H2 Bush
Tube and *sepals* red. *Corolla*
petals purple. Small to medium-
sized blooms freely produced.
Foliage bright golden with strong
upright growth.
(Sandringham, UK, 1985) (FEN)

Roy Castle
Double H2 Bush
Tube and *sepals* dark pink. *Corolla*
petals pink with lilac marbling.
Strong, upright, bushy plant.
(WV)

Rubicon
Double H2 Bush
Tube and *sepals* deep crimson.
Corolla petals deep purple. The
medium-sized flowers are
produced quite freely. Upright
bushy growth.
(ARC)

Russ Abbott
Double H2 Bush
Tube and *sepals* white and *corolla*
petals lilac blue. Growth is
compact and bushy.
(EX)

Ruth
Single H3 Bush
Tube and *sepals* rosy red. *Corolla*
petals purplish red. Medium-sized
flowers freely produced. Growth
upright and bushy. Hardy.
(Wood, UK, 1949) (SIL)

Ruth Brazewell
Semi-Double H2 Lax Bush
Tube short, the palest pink. *Sepals*
recurving are of the palest pink on
top and blush pink underneath.
Corolla petals pale pink with pink
picotee edging. Medium-sized
blooms very free. Lax upright.
(Day, UK, 1989) (BRY)(LOK)

Ruthie
Double H2 Bush
Tube and the short *sepals* white
and flushed pink on the inside.
Corolla petals violet-blue, the
small outside petals being fuchsia
pink. Medium-sized blooms very
freely produced. Growth is
upright and bushy.
(Brand, USA, 1951) (BAK)(RIV)

Ruth King
Double H2 Trailer
Tube pink of medium length and
thickness. *Sepals* pink, recurving.
Corolla lilac and white, compact.
The large blooms are freely
produced. *Foliage* medium green.
The natural growth is as a trailer.
An excellent plant for hanging
containers.
(Tiret, USA, 1967) (FOX)(FEN)
(BRE)(WAY)(STM)(EX)(ARC)
(CHA)(WV)(WAL)(BAK)(OAK)
(RIV)(HYDE)(BRY)(CLI)(GLE)
(OLI)

Rutland Water
Single H2 Bush
Tube rose bengal. *Sepals* rose
bengal tipped with green and held
horizontally. *Corolla* petals
amethyst violet veined rose
bengal. Medium-sized flowers
and very free-flowering. Growth
medium upright and makes a
good compact bush.
(Pacey, UK, 1981)
(ARC)(CHA)(BEL)(RIV)(CLI)
(ASK)(FUC)(GLE)(OLI)

Rutti Tutti
Double H2 Stiff Trailer
Tube and *sepals* white, pale
purple and rose. *Corolla* petals
light purple. A rather stiff trailer
or lax bush. Large flowers freely
produced.
(Garrett, USA, 1991)
(SIM)(CHA)(RIV)

S

Sally Bell
Single/Semi-Double H2/3 Bush
Tube and *sepals* bright red.

Corolla petals dark purple and
splashed with rose at the base.
The medium-sized upright-
growing bush has proved to be
hardy in parts of East Anglia.
('Tennessee Waltz' ×)
(Carr, UK, 1987) (RIV)

Sampan
Double H2 Lax Bush
Tube and *sepals* rose pink.
Corolla petals rosy red. The
largish blooms are freely
produced. Growth is as a lax
bush or trailer.
(Tiret, USA, 1965)
(BRI)(RIV)

Sampson Delight
Semi-Double H2 Bush
Tube and *sepals* carmine pink
with coral shading underneath.
Sepals are of medium size and
reflex back completely covering
the tube. *Corolla* petals rose red
streaked with coral. The
medium-sized blooms are slightly
flared and bell-shaped with deep
garnet anthers. *Foliage* large,
spinach green. Growth tall and
upright.
(Barrett, UK, 1980)
(FEN)(ASK)

Samson
Double H2 Trailer
Tube and *sepals* pink. *Corolla*
petals dark plum purple fading to
pink. The large flowers are freely
produced. *Foliage* variegated pale
green and pale yellow. Naturally
trailing in its habit so will make a
good basket.
(Peterson, USA, 1957)
(BAK)(BRI)(RIV)(BRY)

San Francisco
Single H2 Trailer
Very long *tube* and long *sepals*
carmine rose. *Corolla* petals
geranium lake. Very long
flowers, free and largish.
Growth is vigorous cascading.
Excellent for weeping Standards
or in all types of hanging
containers.
(Reiter, USA, 1941) (BAK)(BRY)

RUTH

ROYAL MOSAIC

RUTH KING

San Leandro
Double H2 Bush
Tube and *sepals* dark carmine.
Corolla petals magenta shading
to vermilion. Large blooms freely
produced. Growth is upright and
vigorous. Will make a superb
large specimen in larger pots.
(Brand, USA, 1949)
(BAK)(BRI)(WV)

F. sanctae-rosae
Single H1 Bush
Species. *Sepals* orange red.
Corolla petals orange red and the
petals are oblong and spreading.
The younger branches are
purplish red. A very lax upright
growth. Flowers well into the
autumn. (Native of Bolivia)
(Britton, Bolivia, 1890) (CLI)(CL)

Santa Clara
Double H2 Trailer
Short *tube* and white *sepals* are
variegated with rose. *Corolla*
petals very deep purple fading to
dark rose. Largish blooms are
fairly freely produced. *Foliage*
small and yellowish green. Growth
is naturally trailing. Excellent for
all types of hanging containers.
(Pennisi, USA, 1969)
(ISL)

Santa Cruz
Double H3 Bush
Tube crimson. *Sepals* dark
crimson, short and broad,
upturned to the tube. *Corolla*
rather dark crimson. *Foliage* large
and bronzed, ovate, serrated. The
natural growth is strongly
upright. The plant is very sturdy
and self-branching. H and S:
18–30in (45–75cm)
(Tiret, USA, 1947) (SIL)(FOX)
(RKY)(KM)(CL)(LB)(BRE)(STM)
(EX)(ARC)(BRI)(CHA)(WV)
(WAL)(BAK)(GOU)(ROO)(OAK)
(RIV)(HYDE)(BRY)(CLI)(ASK)
(WHE)(FUC)(GLE)(ISL)(SMI)
(OLD)(OLI)(SIM)

Santa Lucia
Double H2 Bush
Tube and broad spreading *sepals*
deep red. *Corolla* petals orchid

pink, with rose veining. The
outside petals are overlaid with
salmon rose. Large blooms free
for the size of the flowers.
Upright growth.
(Munkner, USA, 1956) (BAK)
(BRE)(ARC)(BRI)(WV)(GLE)
(OLI)(LOK)

Santa Monica
Double H2 Bush
Tube and *sepals* light red. *Corolla*
petals flesh pink streaked with
cerise. The flowers are large and
quite free for their size although
somewhat late. *Foliage* dark
green. Growth is tall, upright,
bushy and vigorous.
('Rolla' × 'Fascination')
(Evans and Reeves, USA, 1935)
(BAK)

Sarah Hadfield
Double H1 Bush
Tube thin, medium-sized and
carmine red. *Sepals*, held halfway below the horizontal, also
carmine red. *Corolla* petals as
near white as possible with
smooth edges. White petaloids.
Medium to large blooms. Small
upright-growing plant.
Continuous flowers are produced
from early in the season.
(J. Rowell, UK, 1986) (BEL)

Sarah Helen
Double H2 Bush
Tube and *sepals* white, turning to
pink. *Corolla* petals Tyrian
purple. The large blooms are very
full and are freely produced.
Growth is upright, self-branching
and bushy.
(Colville, UK, 1969) (BAK)(ROO)

Sarina
Single H2 Bush
Tube and *sepals* dark red. *Corolla*
petals aubergine. The natural
growth is as an upright bush.
(RIV)

F. scabriuscula
Species H1 Bush
The fairly small flowers are borne
solitarily in the upper leaf axils.
Tube and *sepals* bright red.

Corolla red. *Foliage* medium to
dark green. The natural growth is
as a low spreading shrub.
(Ecuador, 1845)
(CL)(KM)(GOU)

Scarlet O'Hara
Double H2 Bush
Tubes ivory and *sepals*
orange/red. *Corolla* petals scarlet.
The blooms, which are of
medium size, are held upward
and outward. Growth is bushy
and upright. Ideally suited as an
exhibition double.
(Shaffery, UK, 1997) (GOU)

Schiller 1
Double H2 Bush
Tube and *sepals* pale carmine.
Corolla petals bluish purple. The
medium-sized blooms are fairly
freely produced. Growth is
naturally upright and bushy.
(Reiter, USA, 1940) (KM)

Schiller 2
Single H2 Bush
Tube and broad, spreading *sepals*
blush white. *Corolla* petals
purplish and washed with white at
the base. A free-growing bushy
plant with rather a drooping habit.
A very old plant about the origins
of which there is some doubt.
(Banks, UK, *c.* 1860) (KM)

Schnabel
Semi-Double H2 Trailer
Tube and *sepals* salmon orange.
Corolla petals orange. The largish
flowers are very freely produced.
The colouring of the flowers is
very attractive. *Foliage* rather
large. Growth is vigorously
trailing.
(Antonelli, USA, 1971)
(BRY)(BLA)(EX)(OLI)

Schone Landaurin
Semi-Double H2 Lax Bush
Tube and *sepals* red. *Corolla*
petals violet blue. Growth is
rather lax so will make a bush
only with supports or could be
useful in hanging containers.
(Nutzinger, Austria, 1965)
(RIV)

F. SCABRIUSCULA

F. SANCTAE-ROSAE

SANTA CRUZ

Scion of Longleat
Single H2 Bush
Tube short, thin and red. *Sepals* long, very broad and have recurving tips are also red. *Corolla* petals open deep violet and mature to pale purple. The flowers are of medium size. *Foliage* dark green with a lighter green on the undersides. ('Swanley Gem' × 'Display') (Robertson, UK, 1985) (CHA)

Seaforth
Single H2 Bush
Tube short, thick and creamy white. *Sepals* creamy white with a slight rose flush. *Corolla* petals lilac pink deepening towards the edges. Large flowers but very floriferous. Growth upright and bushy.
(Need, UK, 1964)
(BAK)(RKY)(RIV)(BRY)

Sealand Prince
Single H3 Bush
Tube light red and quite thick. *Sepals* long, narrow and upturned, light red. *Corolla* violet purple fading to reddish purple. The medium-sized flowers are numerous. *Foliage* medium green. The natural growth is as an upright bush.
(Walker Bees Nursery, UK, 1967)
(SIL)(FOX)(ROU)(RKY)(KM)
(CL)(WAY)(STM)(ARC)(BRI)
(CHA)(ROO)(RIV)(HYDE)(BRY)
(ASK)(GLE)(ISL)(OLI)

September Morgen
Single H2 Bush
Tube and upswept *sepals* rose red. *Corolla* petals violet blue and open to a nice, square bell-shape. Upright, bushy growth that is easy to train.
(Eckbert, Germany, 1989) (KM)

Sharpitor
Single H3 Bush
Tube short, small and thin, pinkish white. *Sepals* pale pinkish white, short, fairly broad and well held out. *Corolla* very slightly darker than sepals. The flowers are small and compact. *Foliage* is the most redeeming feature of this plant being variegated pale cream and green, rather small and with serrated edging. Growth is upright and bushy. Thought to be a 'sport' of *F. magellanica* var. *molinae*. (National Trust, Sharpitor, UK, 1974) (FOX)(FEN)(ROU)(RKY) (KM)(WAR)(BRE)(MO)(WAY) (CHA)(WV)(PER)(BEL)(BAK) (ROO)(OAK)(RIV)(GLE)(SMI) (OLD)(OLI)

Sheila Joy
Single H2 Bush
Tube pale pink. *Sepals* white edged with pink. *Corolla* petals a brilliant white veined with pink. Growth is strong, upright and self-branching.
(ROO)

Sheila Mary
Double H2 Bush
Tube and *sepals* pale pink. *Corolla* petals are porcelain blue that deepens in full light. Upright, rather stiff but bushy growth. (Broughton, UK, 1995) (KM)(JAK)(ROO)

Sheila Steele
Double H2 Bush
Sepals and *tube* dark rose. *Corolla* petals white veined with dark rose. A compact upright bush. (Forward, UK, 1994) (WV)(FUC)(GLE)(ISL)

Shell Pink
Single H2/3 Bush
Tube and *sepals* pink. *Corolla* petals pale blue quickly changing to shell pink. The medium-sized flowers are very freely produced. Growth upright and bushy, spreading but dainty habit. Medium height only achieving 1ft 6in–2ft (45–60cm). Considered hardy in the south of England. (Tabraham, UK, 1975) (BRY)(BRI)

Shirley Halliday
Double H2 Lax Bush
Tube and *sepals* creamy white with a flush of pale purple to pink. The fully double *corolla* opens deep purple and matures to a rich red wine colour. Nice in pot or basket – the very large flowers are produced over a long period. (Bielby/Oxtoby, UK, 1996) (KM)(MO)(WAL)(ISL)

Showi
Double H2 Bush
Tube and *sepals* rose pink. *Corolla* petals delicate whitish pink. The smallish flowers are produced in great quantity. An excellent bush-type growth. Well-named. (Brigadoon Fuchsias, UK, 1998) (BRI)

Shugborough
Single H2 Bush
Tube and *sepals* pink. *Corolla* petals white. A very floriferous, upright, bushy plant. (Foster, UK, 1996) (FEN)(KM)(WAR)(JAK)(ROO)

Shy Lady
Double H2 Bush
Tube short, ivory white. *Sepals* broad, pointed, also ivory white. *Corolla* petals creamy ivory. With maturity the bloom changes colour into a delicate shade of pale peach. Medium-sized flowers very freely produced. *Foliage* dark green. Upright, bushy growth that is self-branching. (Waltz, USA, 1955) (CLI)(BRI)(WHE)(RIV)

Sian Diana
Double H2 Bush
Tube and *sepals* pale pink. *Corolla* petals violet with a whitish pink shading at the base. Strong, upright and self-branching growth. (Brigadoon Fuchsias, UK, 1998) (BRI)

Silver Breckland
Single H2 Bush
Tube very short and white. *Sepals* pink, lightening towards the base. *Corolla* petals silvery lavender open wide but not flat. *Foliage* dark green with strong stems growing upright. ('sport' from 'Breckland') (Oakleigh Nurseries, UK, 1995) (OAK)

SEALAND PRINCE

SHARPITOR

SEAFORTH

SHELL PINK

SHIRLEY HALLIDAY

Silver King

Silver King
Single H2 Lax Bush
Tube long, thin, red. *Sepals* red, held horizontally. *Corolla* petals white veined with rose red. Very large flowers with a cylindrical corolla. *Foliage* dark green deeply veined and serrated. Growth is lax upright. Excellent for all types of training.
(Hall, UK, 1982)
(CLI)

Silver Knight
Single H2 Lax Bush
Tube whitish pink. *Sepals* white with pink overtones and tipped with green. *Corolla* petals purple but much paler at the base. Medium-sized flowers are freely produced. Lax upright grower – needs staking for a bush or weighting for a basket.
(Released by F. Holmes, UK, 1989)
(BRY)

Simple Simon
Single H2/3 Bush
Tube pale pink. *Sepals* long and pale pink open to show the deep mauve petals in the *corolla* that mature with age to pink. The small flowers are produced in abundance. Another miniature hardy. Ultimate height achieved is in the vicinity of 6in (15cm). Excellent for rockeries or window boxes.
(Tabraham, UK, 1987)
(BRI)(RIV)

Simply Love
Single H2 Bush
Tube and *sepals* magenta pink. *Corolla* petals violet. The small flowers are produced in profusion.
(Large, UK, 1993)
(ALD)(OLI)

Simply Trish
Single H2 Bush
Tube and *sepals* pink. *Corolla* petals aubergine red. Easily shaped, self-branching cultivar especially good for training as a Standard.

('Hermiena' × 'Fenman')
(Large, UK, 1997) (ALD)

Sinton's Standard
Single/Semi-Double H2 Bush
Tube and *sepals* red. *Corolla* petals white. The upright growth will make a good bush plant quite quickly.
(Sinton, UK, 1996)
(ROU)(WAR)(BRE)(WAY)(STM)
(EX)(PER)

Sipke Arjen
Single H2 Bush
Encliandra-type fuchsia. *Tube* white. *Sepals* pale rose. *Corolla* petals open white and mature to pale rose with wavy edging. *Foliage* proportionately small on wiry stems.
(*F. microphylla* × *F. thymifolia*)
(Reimann, Holland, 1986)
(HYDE)

Sir Matt Busby
Double H2 Trailer
Tube and *sepals* red. *Corolla* petals white. The natural habit of this medium-sized flower is as a trailer so will make a good basket.
(Sinton, UK, 1998)
(FEN)(WAR)(BRE)(WAY)(STM)
(EX)(PER)

Slippery Horn
Single H2 Trailer
Tube long and white. *Sepals* pink. *Corolla* petals white with a pink blush. Quite floriferous. A natural trailer, it will make a good basket.
(Brouwer, Holland, 1991)
(EX)

Smile Girl
Single H2 Bush
Tube and *sepals* in shades of pink. *Corolla* petals lilac blue. Very free-flowering, self-branching, upright plant.
(Lewis, UK, 1996)
(PER)(ROO)(RIV)

Snowburner
Double H2 Lax Bush
Tube and *sepals* bright red.

Corolla petals white with red veining. Huge blooms that will need supporting are displayed on a lax bush. Will make a good basket but may need weights.
(Lockerbie, UK, 1975)
(MO)(FEN)(ROU)(BRE)(EX)
(BAK)(WAL)(PER)(BLA)(RIV)
(ISL)(HYDE)(SMI)

Snowdon
Double H2 Lax Bush
Tube and *sepals* pale pink. *Sepals* whiter on the upper surface. *Corolla* petals white with smooth edges. *Foliage* is golden and remains so throughout. Rather lax upright growth and will make a good basket.
(Howarth, UK, 1988)
(ROU)(WAR)(RIV)(WV)
(BRY)

Snowfall
Double H2 Lax Bush
Tube very long and white. *Sepals* long, slender and white, curving upwards to the tube. *Corolla* petals white with the faintest tinge of pink. Medium-sized blooms and very attractive. Lax growth makes it suitable for basket work.
(Bellamy, UK, 1985)
(BRI)(WV)

Snowfire
Double H2 Bush
Tube pink. *Sepals* wide, tapering and white. *Corolla* petals bright pink to coral, variegated with white in differing patterns. Medium-sized blooms. *Foliage* dark green. Good bushy upright growth.
(Stubbs, USA, 1978) (BAK)

Snowflake
Single H2 Trailer
Tube white. *Sepals*, which turn straight up, white with a pink tinge at the base. *Corolla* petals white. The flowers are of medium size, early and freely produced. Natural trailing growth will make a good basket.
(Walker and Jones, USA, 1951)
(KM)(ROO)

SILVER KNIGHT

SINTON'S STANDARD

SIPKE ARJEN

SIR MATT BUSBY

SMILE GIRL

SNOWFIRE

Snowy Summit

Snowy Summit
Double H2 Trailer
Tube white. *Sepals* long, broad and white. Petals in the fully double *corolla* also white. The medium-sized flowers are freely produced. There is a slight touch of pink when in full sunlight. An excellent 'white' for all types of basket work.
(Stubbs, USA, 1975) (FUC)

Solar Orange
Semi-Double H2 Bush
Tube and *sepals* salmon. *Corolla* petals deep orange. The natural growth is as an upright bush.
(RIV)

Solent Pride
Single H2 Trailer
Tube thin and white, veined slightly pink. *Sepals* white-tipped with pale green on top and pale pink underneath. *Corolla* petals red purple maturing to slightly duller purple. The medium-sized flowers are bell-shaped. Lax growth so will make a good basket.
(deBono, UK, 1980) (STM)

Sombrero
Double H2 Lax Bush
Tube thick and flesh-coloured. *Sepals* light pink on the outside and darker on the underside. *Sepals* large, thick, gracefully recurving. *Corolla* petals brilliant rose. Very large blooms fairly freely produced. Rather lax growth so useful for hanging containers.
(Nelson, USA, 1957) (BRY)(BRI)(RIV)

Sonia Ann Berry
Single H2 Bush
Tubes blush pink. *Sepals*, horizontally held, blush pink. *Corolla* small cup-shaped, has petals of baby pink. Extremely floriferous. Growth is upright and self-branching. Will do well in medium-sized pots.
(Goulding, UK, 1998) (GOU)

Son of Sneezy
Single H3 Bush
Tube and *sepals* red. *Corolla* petals pale mauve. Dwarf-growing bush for the front of a hardy border. This 'sport' of 'Sneezy' has all the attributes of its parent.
('sport' of 'Sneezy')
(Bellcross, UK, 1998) (BEL)

Sophie Louise
Single H2 Bush
Tube medium, thin, greenish white. *Sepals* slender, upswept, white, flushed with red at the base and green-tipped. The petals in the cylindrical *corolla* dark purple blue, maturing to a lighter shade. A bushy, self-branching plant, easy to grow and extremely floriferous.
(Wilkinson, UK, 1999) (KM)

Soroptomist International
Single H2 Bush
Tube and *sepals* waxy white. *Corolla* petals deep pink. The natural growth is as an upright self-branching bush.
(ROU)

Southgate Ann
Single H2 Bush
Triphylla-type. *Tubes* long and pink. *Sepals* pink. *Corolla* petals soft powder pink. Good, strong, upright growth.
(BRI)

South Lakeland
Single H2/3 Bush
Tube creamy white. *Sepals* creamy white, flushed with pink on both sides. *Corolla* petals turkey red but overlaid with a flush of blue when young. Growth is upright and bushy.
(Thornley, UK, 1963) (ROU)(BRE)(RIV)(BRI)(GLE)(ISL)

Sparky
Single H1 Bush
Triphylla-type. *Tubes*, short *sepals* and short *corolla* petals all very dark blood red. The plant has short internodes and a bushy

habit. Makes an attractive but small show plant or conservatory specimen.
(Webb, UK, 1994)
(CL)(FOX)(ROU)(RKY)(BRE)(MO)(EX)(CHA)(WV)(PER)(ROO)(BLA)(RIV)(HYDE)(POT)(ASK)(ISL)

Speedbird
Double H2 Bush
Tube and *sepals* creamy white. *Corolla* petals pinky blue. The natural bushy and self-branching growth will produce a very good plant for the patio tubs.
(RIV)

Spell Binder
Single H2 Bush
Single with paniculate parentage. *Tubes*, recurving *sepals* and flared *corolla*s small and dark red. There are multiple small clusters of blooms. Strongly self-branching and upright. A novelty well worth growing.
(Goulding, UK, 1995) (GOU)(RKY)

Spice of Life
Double H2 Bush
Tube and *sepals* rosy purple. *Corolla* petals violet. A good, strong, upright-growing bush.
(Forward, UK, 1994) (WV)(FUC))(GLE)(ISL)

F. splendens* var. *cordifolia
Single H1 Bush
Species hybrid. *Tube* yellow to amber. *Sepals* green. *Corolla* petals yellow. The *tube* is quite long, flattened and slightly curved. Spreading growth.
(Raiser and crossing unknown) (CL)

Sporty
Single H2 Bush
Tube short, light creamy pink. *Sepals* blush pink with green tips. *Corolla* petals a stronger red but lighter at the base. The flowers are held erect on stiff pedicels. *Foliage* dark green.
(Twigg, UK, 1998) (FEN)(MO)(JAK)

SOPHIE LOUISE

SPARKY

F. SPLENDENS VAR. *CORDIFOLIA*

SPORTY

Sports Knight

Sports Knight
Single H2 Bush
Tube and *sepals* white. *Corolla* petals white with a pink flush. The medium-sized flowers are profuse. Upright and strong growth.
('sport' from 'Tom Knights')
(Newstead, UK, 1987) (WV)

Sporty Anna
Semi-Double H2 Trailer
Tube and *sepals* rose pink. *Corolla* petals pale lilac pink. The natural trailing of this superb plant makes it very useful for growing in hanging baskets.
(Waving, UK, 1998) (SIM)

Spotlight
Single H2 Bush
Tube and *sepals* pink. *Corolla* petals white. Large flowers shaped like a chinese hat.
(Raiser unknown, USA, 1970s)
(BRY)(WAY)(RIV)

Springbells
Semi-Double H2 Bush
Tube and *sepals* bright red. *Corolla* petals clear white. Medium-sized flowers very freely produced. Probably a 'sport' from 'Snowcap' with larger flowers and a much longer flowering period. Growth upright and bushy.
(Kooijman, Holland, 1972)
(STM)(EX)(RIV)

Square Peg
Double H2 Bush
Tube and *sepals* red. *Corolla* petals deep violet blue. Large blooms fairly free for the size of the flower. Square-shaped blooms. Growth upright and bushy.
(Clyne, UK, 1972)
(FOX)(FEN)(ARC)(CHA)
(GLE)

Stadt Malaka
Single H1 Bush
Species hybrid. *Tube, sepals* and *corolla* a mixture of green and plum. A novelty fuchsia that is a bit of fun to grow.
(The species crosses unknown)
(de Boer, Holland, 1992) (PER)

Stals Kevin
Single H1 Bush
Triphylla-type. Single of the terminal-flowering sort. *Tubes* long and thin. *Sepals* short, downward hanging and shorter *corolla* petals dark red. Growth is strong, self-branching and amenable. Tolerance to heat. Ideal in large containers.
(Stals, Holland, 1990) (CL)

Stardust
Single H2 Bush
Tube thin, salmon. *Sepals* salmon pink on the outside and salmon orange underneath. *Corolla* petals orange at the base blending to crimson edges. Small flowers, early and prolific. *Foliage* mid-green with narrow leaves. Growth upright and bushy.
(Handley, UK, 1973) (FEN)(CL)
(STM)(EX)(ARC)(JAK)(BRI)
(CHA)(WV)(BAK)(ROO)(BLA)
(RIV)(BRY)(CLI)(WHE)(GLE)
(ISL)(OLD)(OLI)

Star Eyes
Double H2 Trailer
Tube and *sepals* light rose. *Corolla* petals violet blue. A natural trailer that, with its large flowers, makes a superb basket.
(Lockerbie, Australia, 1968)
(HYDE)

Star Lite
Double H2 Lax Bush
Tube and broad, pointed *sepals* smoky rose. *Corolla* petals a deep shade of lilac rose. Large blooms and free for its size. Unique appearance in that it opens into square-shaped flowers with eight-pointed star-like centre. Growth lax bush or trailer.
(Waltz, USA, 1961) (CLI)

Star Rose
Single H2 Lax Bush
Tube creamy white. *Sepals* creamy white with green recurved tips. *Corolla* opens deep coral red maturing to slightly lighter. The petals have wavy edges. The flowers are of medium size and are freely produced. *Foliage* darkish

green with a lightening of the green on the underside. Small upright although the growth is rather lax and will make a reasonable basket.
(Caunt, UK, 1985) (KM)(CLI)

Steirerblut
Single H1 Bush
Triphylla-type fuchsia. *Tubes* long, thin and dark red. *Sepals* short and dark red. *Corolla* petals have a similar colouring. Flowers are held erect at first. The leaves are large and reddened. Growth upright and vigorous. Best in borders with other plants.
(CL)

Stella Marina
Semi-Double H2 Bush
Tube and long recurving *sepals* crimson. *Corolla* petals violet blue irregularly splashed with crimson and white. Large flowers very free. Growth strong, upright bush.
(Schnabel, USA, 1961) (LOK)

Steretje
Single H2 Bush
Tube and *sepals* pink with a hint of aubergine. *Corolla* petals pale aubergine. The growth is upright, bushy and short-jointed.
('Whiteknight's Ruby' × 'Ting a Ling')
(Weeda, Holland, 1987) (CL)

Stolze von Berlin
Double H2 Lax Bush
Tube and *sepals* bright cerise. *Corolla* petals white with red veining. Lax-type growth. Very similar in appearance to 'Swingtime' and considered to be synonymous with it.
(STM)

Stoney Creek
Double H2 Lax Bush
Medium-sized flowers. *Sepals* and *tube* shell pink. *Corolla* petals also shell pink. Very attractive flowers produced in profusion. The rather lax growth makes it suitable for basketwork.
(Sinton, UK, 1997) (CLI)(FEN)
(ROU)(WAR)(BRE)(PER)(HYDE)
(FUC)(SMI)

SPORTY ANNA

SPRINGBELLS

STARDUST

STAR EYES

STEIRERBLUT

STONEY CREEK

Straat Malakka
Single H2 Trailer
Tube and *sepals* of this small-flowered fuchsia browny red. *Corolla* petals aubergine red. The natural trailing habit and the quantity of flowers produced make this an attractive basket plant.
(de Boer, Holland, 1992) (GOU)(HYDE)

Straat Napier
Single H2 Bush
Tubes and *sepals* dark red with a hint of aubergine. *Corolla* petals very dark violet. Heavily flowered. Good, strong, upright growth. If allowed to develop and trained it would make a good climber on a pergola.
(de Boer, Holland, 1998) (GOU)(ROO)(HYDE)

Strawberry Festival
Double H2 Bush
Tube and *sepals* bright red. *Corolla* petals pale pink, veined with carmine. Large blooms very freely produced. Upright growth. The heavy blooms need support.
(Haag, USA, date unknown) (OLI)

Strawberry Fizz
Double H2 Trailer
Tube and *sepals* clear pink. *Sepals* curl back onto the tube. *Corolla* petals deep pink with picoteed edging. The large blooms are fairly freely produced. *Foliage* dark green. A natural trailer, it will make a good basket.
(Stubbs, USA, 1971) (FOX)(CHA)(HYDE)(SMI)

Strawberry Mousse
Double H2 Bush
Tube and *sepals* white shaded with light pink. The very full petals in the *corolla* are a delightful shade of pink. Large flowers freely produced.
(Pickard, UK, 1995) (VER)

Stuart Joe
Single H2 Bush
Tube and *sepals* pale pink. *Corolla* petals violet blue maturing to violet. Beautiful pastel-shaded blooms on short-jointed growth. Choice show plant.
(Swinbank, UK, 1994) (KM)(WV)(ISL)

Stuart Martin
Single H2 Bush
Tube and *sepals* red. *Corolla* petals intense purple. The natural growth is as an upright self-branching shrub.
(RIV)

Student Prince
Single H2 Trailer
Tube and *sepals* white tipped with green and shading to neyron rose on underside. *Sepals* long and sweeping upwards. *Corolla* petals aster violet veined rosein purple and shading to white at the base. Fairly large flowers and very free-flowering. Growth as a trailer.
(Pacey, UK, 1982) (BRI)(WV)

Sue
Single H2 Bush
Tube and *sepals* cerise. *Corolla* petals cerise and orange. Large flowers carried on an upright and bushy growth.
(Introduced by Holmes, UK, 1986) (FEN)(RKY)(BRE)(EX) (CHA)(PER)(ROO)(HYDE)(FUC) (GLE)(ISL)

Summerwood
Double H2 Bush
Tube and *sepals* red. *Corolla* petals purple. Fairly large flowers freely produced.
(Sinton, UK, 1997) (ROU)(BRE)(WAY)(STM)(EX) (WAL)(ISL)

Sundance
Single H2 Trailer
Tube and *sepals* light rose. *Sepals* long and well held out. *Corolla* petals light burgundy maturing to cerise. The large flowers are very freely produced. They are long and bell-shaped with overlapping petals. *Foliage* pale yellow-green. Growth is as a natural trailer.
(Handley, UK, 1974) (EX)

Sun Dial
Double H2 Bush
Tube and *sepals* light reddish-orange. *Corolla* petals also reddish orange. *Foliage* medium green.
(Paskesson/Storvick, USA, 1987) (EX)

Sunlight Path
Single H2 Bush
Tube and *sepals* pink. *Corolla* petals mauve. The abundant blooms are bell-shaped and upward-looking. Strong-growing upright bush. Best grown in tubs where they can benefit from the extra root room.
(Goulding, UK, 1990) (CL)(FEN)(HYDE)

Sunny Jim
Single H2 Lax Bush
Tube and *sepals* white. *Corolla* petals orange coral. Although growth is strong it is rather lax. It will therefore need support for the medium-sized flowers if grown as a bush.
(EX)

Sunny Skies
Double H2 Lax Bush
Can best be described as a blush white self. *Tubes*, *sepals* and *corolla* petals all blush white. The large, heavy flowers are produced in quantity. Growth is somewhat lax so will only make a good bush with supports but will be useful in hanging containers.
(McLaughlin, USA, 1991) (ISL)(BRI)(SMI)

Sunrise
Single H2 Bush
Tube and *sepals* white. *Sepals* white flushed with rose and tipped with crimson. *Corolla* petals clear scarlet. Medium-sized blooms, early and free. Growth stiff, upright and shrubby.
(Reiter, USA, 1942) (OLI)

STRAAT MALAKKA

STRAAT NAPIER

STRAWBERRY FIZZ

SUE

Supersport
Double H2 Bush
Tube and *sepals* red. *Corolla*
petals white and marbled
occasionally with red and mauve.
The blooms are large and freely
produced. Growth is strong,
spreading, and self-branching.
Makes an excellent plant, with its
quantity of flowers, for the patio
tub or in wall baskets.
(Klein/Garrett, Holland, 1985)
(FOX)(EX)(WAL)(HYDE)(GOU)
(CHA)

Susan
Double H2 Bush
Tube and *sepals* pale rose.
Corolla petals light blue turning
to violet with maturity. Medium-
sized blooms freely produced.
Serrated leaves. Early flowering.
Upright bushy growth.
(Niederholzer, USA, 1948)
(CL)(FEN)(BRE)(ROO)(RIV)
(HYDE)(GLE)(OLI)(BRY)

Susan Arnold
Double H2 Bush
Tube and *sepals* white flushed
pink. *Corolla* petals purple
maturing to reddish purple.
Foliage medium green on the
upper surface and yellowish green
on the lower. Attractive flower.
('Gay Parasol' × 'Torvill and
Dean')
(Bell, UK, 1989) (ASK)

Susan Diana
Single H2 Trailer
Tubes and upturned *sepals* white.
Corolla petals slightly mauve or
pink. The small to medium
flowers are carried in profusion.
Excellent as a basket or as a
weeping Standard. A 'sport' from
'Waveney Gem' with all its floral
characteristics but with a
variegation in the *foliage*.
('sport' from 'Waveney Gem')
(Wye, UK, 1998) (ROO)(HYDE)

Susan Green
Single H2 Trailer
Tube and *sepals* pale pink. *Sepals*
have green tips. *Corolla* bell-
shaped, coral pink. *Foliage*

medium green. Growth is fairly
strong and even with good, self-
branching stems. Superb baskets
can be made with comparative
ease. Worth trying as a weeping
Standard.
(Caunt, UK, 1974) (SIL)(FEN)
(KM)(CL)(BRE)(MO)(WAY)
(STM)(JAK)(CHA)(WV)(BEL)
(ROO)(BLA)(ALD)(RIV)(CLI)
(ASK)(WHE)(FUC)(GLE)(ISL)
(OLD)(OLI)(SIM)

Susan Jill
Double H2 Bush
Tube white with a faint touch of
pink. *Sepals* pale pink on the
upper surface and phlox pink on
the lower. *Corolla* petals
spectrum violet maturing to
imperial purple.
('Paula Jane' × 'Blush of Dawn')
(Tite, UK, 1987) (RIV)

Susan McMaster
Single H2 Bush
Tube and *sepals* claret rose.
Corolla petals a lovely shade of
violet purple maturing to claret
rose. Small flowers but extremely
profuse. Upright and bushy.
(Day, UK, 1986) (LOK)

Susan Young
Double H2 Bush
Tube white. *Sepals* white with a
red-purple base to orchid pink.
Corolla petals purple-lilac – four
quarters with four petals in each
quarter. Medium-sized blooms
and free for a double. Growth
upright and very bushy.
('sport' of 'Blue Pearl')
(Young, UK, 1975) (ASK)

Sutton 21
Single H2 Bush
Tube and *sepals* pink with white
tips. *Corolla* petals white veined
with pink. An upright-growing
bush.
(Originally grown from packet of
seeds) (FEN)(OLI)

Sutton's Summertime
Single H2 Lax Bush
Tube and *sepals* rose. *Corolla*
petals violet-purple. The rather

lax growth makes it suitable for
bushes if given supports or for
use in hanging containers.
(FEN)(WAY)

Suzanna
Single/Semi-Double H2 Bush
Tube short and pinkish red.
Sepals a little darker. *Corolla*
petals blue with small red veins at
the base. Medium-sized flowers
very freely produced. *Foliage*
dark green. Growth strong,
upright and bushy.
(van der Grijp, Holland, 1968)
(EX)

Suzy
Double H2 Trailer
Tube short and medium pink.
Sepals slightly lighter in colouring
being pink tinged with salmon.
Corolla petals lilac to pink. Huge
blooms with some fifteen petals
folding into each other. *Foliage*
large, dark green with red stems.
Growth semi-trailing or lax bush.
(Carlson, USA, 1977)
(HYDE)(SMI)

Swanland Candy
Double H2 Lax Bush
Tube neyron rose. *Sepals* neyron
rose on the top surface and lighter
underneath. *Corolla* petals white.
The flowers are large and are
freely produced with up to three
appearing at each axil. Lax
upright growth so will make a
bush with supports and could also
be used in hanging containers.
('Joy Bielby' × 'Applause')
(Crawshaw, UK, 1989) (FEN)

Swanley Beauty
Single H2 Bush
Tube and *sepals* waxy white.
Corolla petals soft pink. Medium-
sized flowers freely produced.
Growth upright and bushy.
(Lye, UK, 1875) (BRY)

Swanley Pendula
Single H2 Lax Bush
Tube and *sepals* orange pink.
Corolla petals orange vermilion.
(Lye, UK, 187?)
(FOX)(EX)(CHA)(LOK)

SUPERSPORT

SUSAN

SUSAN GREEN

SWANLEY BEAUTY

SUSAN DIANA

Sweetie Dear
Single H2 Bush
Species hybrid. *Tube* and *sepals* red. *Corolla* petals reddish purple maturing to dark rose. *Foliage* dark green on top surface and lighter underneath. Best colour is produced in the flowers with bright but filtered light.
(*F. lycioides* × *F. magellanica* × *F. magdalenae*)
(de Graaffe, Holland, 1988) (FEN)

Sweet Linda
Single H2 Bush
Tube and *sepals* flesh-coloured. *Corolla* petals pink. Smallish flowers but very freely produced. Growth upright and bushy, self-branching and short-jointed.
(Kirby, UK, 1983)
(BRE)(BUR)(ROO)(ALD)(ISL)

Sweet Samantha
Double H2 Trailer
Tube pure white. *Sepals* white flushed with pink on top and pale pink underneath and tipped with green. *Corolla* petals purple splashed with pink and maturing to a lighter purple. Growth is naturally trailing so will make an excellent basket.
(M. Allsop, UK, 1997) (ROO)

Sweet Sixteen
Double H2 Trailer
Tube and upturned *sepals* neyron rose. *Corolla* petals rich pink. Large blooms fairly free for their size. Naturally trailing growth. Excellent for all types of hanging containers.
(Walker and Jones, USA, 1951)
(BRY)(BRI)(LOK)

S'Wonderful
Double H2 Trailer
Tube and *sepals* pink with splashes of darker pink at the base of the buds. *Corolla* petals pale lavender on the inner petals and orchid pink on the outer. Medium-sized blooms, freely carried. Growth is as a natural trailer.
(Castro, USA, 1981) (BAK)(FOX)(EX)(BRI)(CHA)(WV)(ROO)(RIV)(BRY)(LOK)

Syljon
Single H2 Bush
Encliandra-type. *Tube* and *sepals* currant red. *Corolla* petals scarlet. The blooms are medium-sized for an encliandra. *Foliage* dark green with a red flush on the undersides. Growth is small, self-branching and upright. Excellent for use as a bonsai.
(Cox, UK, 1997)
(ROO)

F. sylvatica
Species H1 Bush
Tube pink. *Sepals* small, pink on pale red. *Corolla* crimson to purplish red. The smallish flowers are carried in terminal racemes. *Foliage* medium green. Growth is as a low shrub. Synonymous with *F. atroruba* and *F. nigricans*.
(Bentham, Colombia, 1845)
(KM)(CL)(HYDE)

Sylvia Barker
Single H2 Bush
Tube long and waxy white. *Sepals* that are held well out also waxy white with green tips. *Corolla* scarlet with a slight smoky cast. The blooms are fairly small but are very freely produced. *Foliage* dark green with veins that stand out. Growth is rather lax.
(Barker, UK, 1973)
(FEN)(ROU)(RKY)(WAR)(CL)(LB)(BRE)(MO)(WAY)(STM)(BRI)(WV)(PER)(BEL)(GOU)(ROO)(ALD)(RIV)(HYDE (CLI)(ASK)(ISL)(SIM)

Sylvia Rose
Double H2 Bush
Tubes and *sepals* pale pink. *Corolla* petals white veined with pink. A compact bushy growth.
(Forward, UK, 1994)
(WV)(FUC)(GLE)(ISL)

Sylvia's Choice
Double H2 Bush
Tube and *sepals* white. *Corolla* petals deep purple. The growth is naturally strong, upright and self-branching. The short-jointed growth makes it an ideal plant for the show bench.
(Stiff, UK, 1996)
(BAK)(ROO)

Symphony
Single H2 Bush
Tube and *sepals* pale phlox-pink. *Corolla* petals cobalt violet. Medium-sized blooms freely produced and very gracefully shaped. Growth is tall, upright and naturally bushy.
(Niederholtzer, USA, 1944)
(BAK)(FEN)(WAY)(STM)(WV)(BRY)(ASK)(GLE)(LOK)

Syrie
Semi-Double H2 Lax Bush or Trailer
Tube and *sepals* pink. *Corolla* petals also pink. The natural growth is lax upright so will need staking to make a good bush or will make a plant for a hanging container with weights.
(OLI)

T

Taatje
Single H2 Trailer
Tube and *sepals* light purple. *Corolla* petals open purple and mature to reddish purple. Growth is as a natural trailer. Prefers full sun with best colour in bright light.
('Foolke' × 'La Campanella')
(Bogemann, Germany, 1990) (RIV)

Tabu
Double H2 Bush
Tube pale pink. *Sepals* salmon pink on the inside and pale pink outside, stand straight out on early bloom but reflex as bloom matures. *Corolla* petals magenta rose with pale pink marbling at the base of the outer petals, fading to smoky rose. Medium-sized blooms very freely produced. The natural growth is as an upright, self-branching and bushy plant.
(Paskesson, USA, 1974) (BRI)

SWEET LINDA

SYLJON

S'WONDERFUL

SYLVIA BARKER

F. SYLVATICA

Taco

Taco
Single H1 Bush
Terminal-flowering fuchsia. *Tubes* orange to red. *Sepals* orange with green tips. *Corolla* petals a brighter shade of orange. Growth is strongly upright and, unlike many of the triphylla types, is quite amenable to 'stopping'. Enjoys a good root run so is best when grown in large pots or tubs.
(de Boer, Holland, 1998)
(GOU)(HYDE)

Tamar
Single H2 Bush
Tube and *sepals* white. *Corolla* petals pale blue white with a pansy eye. Upright bushy growth.
(SMI)

Tamino
Single H2 Bush
Tube and *sepals* pink. *Corolla* petals lilac pink. The flowers are large. Growth is medium upright.
(Rapps, Germany, 1983)
(MO)

Tammy
Double H2 Lax Bush
Tube waxy white. The long broad *sepals* are a lovely pink, spreading, twisted and upturned. *Corolla* petals mauve lavender, streaked with rose pink. Large, spreading blooms are free for their size. Flowering is early and continuous. Growth is as a lax bush or trailer and is rather vigorous.
(Erickson, USA, 1962)
(CLI)(EX)

Tantalizing Tracy
Double H2 Trailer
Tube pale pink. *Sepals* pale pink on the top and deep pink with white stripes down the centre of each sepal underneath. *Corolla* petals dark pink and lighter at the base maturing to orange pink splashed with pink. Very free-flowering growth and a natural trailer that will therefore make a good basket.
(M. Allsop, UK, 1996)
(LB)(ROO)

Tanya
Single H2 Bush
Pale pink self. That is, *tube*, *sepals* and *corolla* petals all pale pink. Medium-sized flowers are very freely produced. Growth is upright and of bushy habit.
(R. Holmes, UK, 1975)
(KM)(WV)(LOK)

Tanya Leanne
Semi-Double H2 Bush
Tubes and *sepals* white and rose. *Corolla* petals violet blue. The natural growth is as an upright bush.
(Australia) (WAY)

Tear Fund
Double H2/3 Bush
Tubes and *sepals* scarlet with a waxy texture. *Corolla*s densely petalled, white and red-veined. Growth is sturdy, upright and versatile. *Foliage* dark green. Excellent for the hardy border.
H and S: 2ft 6in (75cm)
(Goulding, UK, 1994)
(RKY)(WV)

Ted Stiff
Semi-Double to Double H2 Lax Bush
Tube and *sepals* pale pink. *Corolla* petals soft mauve. The growth is rather lax for a bush but will do well if given the necessary supports. Excellent for a hanging pot or basket.
(Stiff, UK, 1998)
(PER)(BAK)

T'Einde
Double H2 Trailer
Tube and *sepals* deep pink. *Corolla* petals shell pink. Fairly large flowers are carried on trailing stems.
(Moermann, Germany, 1991)
(BRY)

Tessa Jane
Single H2/3 Bush
Tube and *sepals* pink. *Corolla* petals white, lightly veined with pink. A good plant for the hardy border. H and S: 18in (45cm)
(BRI)

F. e. tetradactyla (Enc)
Single H2 Bush
Encliandra-type. *Tube* and *sepals* red. *Corolla* petals rose scarlet or paler. The flowers are borne solitarily in the leaf axils. *Foliage* bicoloured, dark green leaves with pale green undersides and slightly hairy. Lowish shrub growing to 2ft (60cm) or upwards.
(Lindley, 1846, Guatemala) (LB)

Teupel's Erflog
Single H2 Bush
Tube and *sepals* both red. *Corolla* petals rose shading to red. Medium-sized flowers freely borne. *Foliage* medium green.
(Teupel, Germany, 1926) (FEN)

Texas Star
Double H2 Trailer
Tube and *sepals* dark rose. *Corolla* petals blue streaked with orchid pink. The natural habit is as a trailer, although the growth is rather slow.
(Stubbs, USA, 1990) (EX)

Thalia
Triphylla-type H1 Bush
Tube long and very slender, deep flame red. *Sepals* small and pointed, also flame red. *Corolla* petals very small and orange scarlet. The flowers are produced in great quantity throughout the season in terminal racemes. *Foliage* dark olive green with magenta veins and ribs. The reverse of the leaves is a delightful light purple. Growth is vigorously upright. Early 'stopping' is advised to encourage the plant into the best bushy shape.
(Bonstedt, Germany, 1905)
(SIL)(FOX)(FEN)(ROU)(RKY)(KM)(WAR)(CL)(LB)(BRE)(MO)(BUR)(WAY)(VER)(STM)(EX)(ARC)(JAK)(CHA)(WV)(WAL)(PER)(BEL)(BAK)(GOU)(ROO)(BLA)(RID)(AL)(OAK)(RIV)(HYDE)(POT)(BRY)(CLI)(ASK)(WHE)(FUC)(GLE)(ISL)(SMI)(OLD)(OLI)(SIM)(LOK)

TAMINO

TANTALIZING TRACY

TACO

TED STIFF

THALIA

The Jester

The Jester
Double H2 Bush
Tube pale red. *Sepals* white.
Corolla petals Dubonnet red. The
large blooms are fairly freely
produced. Growth is tall and
strong upright. Frequent pinching
is necessary to get a compact
bush.
(Tiret, USA, 1972)
(BAK)(FEN)(RIV)

The Joker
Double H2 Trailer
Tube and *sepals* red. *Corolla*
petals violet. Medium-sized
blooms with a trailing habit.
(Introduced 1986 – Raiser and
date unknown) (CLI)

The Marvel
Single H2 Bush
Tube and *sepals* white, of a crêpy
texture and tipped with green.
Corolla petals pink with a
lavender sheen. The large, solid
flowers are freely produced. An
upright bush in its growth.
(Vicarage Farm Nurseries, UK,
1968) (BAK)(RKY)

Theo Giessen
Single H2 Bush
Tube and *sepals* dark red.
Corolla petals red. Good, strong,
upward and self-branching
growth.
(Schwab, Holland, 1980) (HYDE)

The Phoenix
Double H2 Trailer
Tube and long *sepals* rosy pink.
Corolla petals lilac. Large
blooms, very full and fairly free.
Growth naturally trailing. Will
make an excellent plant for a
hanging container.
(Tiret, USA, 1967) (WV)

Therese Dupuis
Single H3 Bush
Tube and *sepals* crimson. *Corolla*
petals reddish purple. An early-
flowering plant carrying large
flowers. *Foliage* medium to dark
green. Strong, upright growth. H:
approx. 3ft (90cm)
(Lemoine, France) (SIL)

The Speedbird
Double H2 Bush
Tube and *sepals* pure white.
Corolla petals deep blue. The
very full blooms are freely
produced. Growth is upright and
bushy.
(Rawlins, UK, 1967)
(BRY)(CLI)(OLD)

The Spoiler
Double H2 Lax Bush
Tube and *sepals* white to pink.
Corolla petals blue to plum
purple. Very large blooms that
are fairly free. Growth is as a lax
bush or a trailer.
(Fuchsia La, USA, 1968)
(CLI)(BRI)(RIV)

The Tarns
Single H3 Bush
Tube short and pale pink. *Sepals*
very long pale pink with a rose
reverse. Long, narrow and
reflexing. *Corolla* violet blue
paling to rose at the base of the
petals. The medium-sized flowers
are very freely produced. *Foliage*
dark green, small, narrow and
heavily serrated. Growth is very
strong, upright and hardy. H and
S: 3ft–4ft (90–120cm)
(Travis, UK, 1962)
(SIL)(RKY)(KM)(STM)(EX)
(ARC)(WV)(BAK)(RIV)(HYDE)
(BRY)(ASK)

Thilko
Single H3 Bush
Species hybrid. Possibly
F. magellanica × *F. lycioides*.
Naturally occurring in Chile.
Hardy.
(KM)

Thistle Hill
Semi-Double H2/3 Bush
Tube and *sepals* red. *Corolla*
petals white. *Foliage* variegated
cream and greyish. 'Sport' from
the good old faithful 'Snowcap'.
(KM)(MO)

Thumbelina
Single H2 Bush
Tube short and carmine rose
lined with green. *Sepals* are

crêped, carmine rose outside and
crimson rose inside. *Corolla*
beetroot purple with empire rose
at the base of the petals and
crimson veins. Small flowers but
very profuse. The four neat
petals form a natural bell.
Foliage mid- to lightish green.
Growth medium upright and
bushy.
(Eamer, UK, 1976)
(RKY)

Tiara
Semi-Double H2 Lax Bush
Tube and *sepals* pale pink.
Corolla petals a very light shade
of pink salmon in the centre
changing to lavender blue on the
outer petals. The medium-sized
flowers are freely produced. The
growth is rather lax and will
therefore be suitable for bushes
with supports or in hanging
containers.
(Martin, USA, 1965)
(BAK)

Tiffany
Double H2 Trailer
Tube white. *Sepals* white on the
upper side but palest pink on the
underside. Petals in the full
corolla pure white. The large
blooms are borne in clusters.
Foliage dark green and provides a
fitting backcloth to the flowers.
Resistant to heat and a natural
trailer in its growth. Will make a
superb basket.
(Reedstrom, USA, 1960)
(BAK)(RKY)(RIV)

F. tilletiana
Single H1 Bush
Species. An apetalous (without
petals) species. *Tube* long,
tapering and pink. *Sepals*
upturned, curling well back, also
pink. The long, pink stamens are
tipped with yellow anthers.
Foliage medium green but rather
sparse although pinching of the
growing tips will often courage
the growth of three branches
from each node. Compact bush
growth for a species.
(Berry, USA, 1979) (KM)

THE TARNS

THERESE DUPUIS

THISTLE HILL

Tillingbourne
Double H2/3 Bush
Tube and *sepals* pink. *Corolla* petals purple and pink. The flowers are large for a hardy. Strong upright growth. H and S: up to 2ft (60cm)
(CL)(SIM)

Tillmouth Lass
Single H2 Bush
Tube thin and striped pink. *Sepals* rhodamine-pink underneath and a paler colour on the upper surface. They twist and curl around the tube from an early stage. *Corolla* petals are lavender fading to purple, with slight veining at the base of the petals. Medium-sized flowers, well-shaped, and quite free. Growth medium upright bush.
(Ryle, UK, 1975)
(KM)(BRE)(BRY)(CLI)(ASK)

Timothy Titus
Single H1 Bush
Single of the terminal-flowering (triphylla) type. *Tubes* short and dusky orange. *Sepals* also dusky orange. *Corolla* petals orange with a hint of brown. Growth is upright, sturdy and self-branching. Should make its name on the show bench.
(Goulding, UK, 1998)
(GOU)(HYDE)

Tina Head
Double H2 Bush
Tube and *sepals* rose pink. *Corolla* petals white, overlaid with rose pink. Medium-sized flowers and very prolific. Very attractive golden *foliage*. Growth upright, bushy and self-branching.
(Head, UK, 1981) (BRI)

Tina's Teardrops
Double H2 Trailer
Tube deep pink. *Sepals* deep pink, lined with red and have green tips. *Corolla* petals deep violet and red at the base, maturing to purple and red. The blooms are very compact and attractive and the natural habit of the plant is as

a trailer. Should make an excellent basket with its profuse flowering.
(M. Allsop, UK, 1997) (ROO)(LB)

Tinkerbell 1
Single H3 Bush
Tube and *sepals* red. *Corolla* petals white. The small flowers are very freely produced. *Foliage* dark green. Growth is very dainty and arching achieving a height of about 6–9in (15–23cm).
(Tabraham, UK, 1976)

Tinkerbell 2
Single H2 Lax Bush or Trailer
The long *tube* and spreading *sepals* are white to pink. The inside of the *sepals* is a soft pink. *Corolla* petals white veined with soft pink. The fairly large and long flowers are freely produced. Lovely soft colouring carried on stems that are inclined to be trailing.
(Hodges, USA, 1955)
(BAK)(FOX)(ROO)

T'Jinegara
Single H2 Trailer
Tube and *sepals* dark rose. *Corolla* petals rose. This delightful colour combination is carried on trailing stems that will rapidly fill a good basket.
(de Boer, Holland, 1997)
(CL)(HYDE)

Toby Summers
Single H2 Bush
Tube and fully recurved *sepals* pink. *Corolla* petals bluey mauve. The bell-shaped flowers are produced on short bushy growth. Very floriferous and will suit small pot work or for growing as a Standard.
(Summers, UK, 1994) (BLA)

Tom Boy
Single H2 Bush
Tube and *sepals* cerise. *Corolla* petals purple lilac with pink veining at the base. The medium-sized blooms are produced on upright and bushy growth.
(Introduced by Holmes, UK, 1986) (RIV)

Tom Coulson
Double H2 Trailer
Tubes short and red. *Sepals* pink and sweep up at the tips. *Corolla* petals dark salmon orange with pink marbling. Growth is spreading and very strong. Will make a good plant for a large basket.
(Goulding, UK, 1999)
(GOU)

Tom H. Oliver
Double H2 Trailer
Tube short, thick and rose-coloured. *Sepals* claret rose on top and light rose underneath. *Corolla* petals a deep ruby red with light rose bases. The edges of the petals are serrated. The largish blooms are freely produced. Natural trailer so will make an excellent basket.
(Pennisi, USA, 1972)
(BAK)(RIV)

Tomma
Single H2 Lax Bush
Tube and *sepals* red. *Corolla* petals also red. *Foliage* dark green with red stems. The natural growth is as a lax bush or a trailer.
(Bogemann, Germany, 1987) (EX)

Tom West
Single H2 Bush
Tube small and red. *Sepals* short and broad, also red. *Corolla* purple, small and compact. *Foliage* (for which the plant is usually grown) variegated pale greyish/green and cream. The leaves are of medium size. Growth is rather lax but self-branching. The best foliage colour comes with fresh young shoots; regular 'stopping' provides a very colourful plant.
(Meillez, France, 1853)
(SIL)(FOX)(FEN)(ROU)(RKY)
(KM)(WAR)(CL)(LB)(BRE)(MO)
(WAY)(VER)(STM)(EX)(ARC)
(JAK)(CHA)(WV)(PER)(BEL)
(BAK)(GOU)(ROO)(BLA)(RID)
(ALD)(OAK)(RIV)(HYDE)
(BRY)(CLI)(ASK)(WHE)(FUC)
(GLE)(ISL)(SMI)(OLD)(OLI)
(SIM)(LOK)

TIMOTHY TITUS

TINKERBELL 2

TINA'S TEARDROPS

TOM WEST

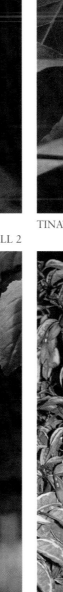

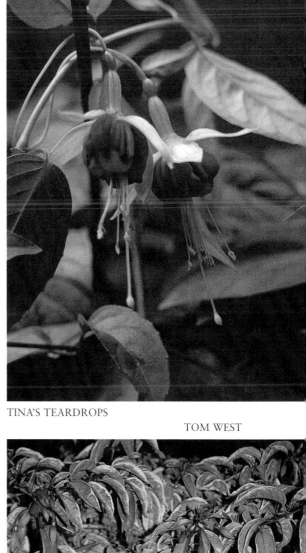

Tony Alcock

Tony Alcock
Double H2 Bush
Tube and *sepals* pale pinky aubergine. *Corolla* petals aubergine and rather frilly. Strong, upright growth making a compact self-branching bush.
(EX)

Tony Galea
Single H2 Bush
Tube and *sepals* waxy white. *Corolla* petals light purple. Good, strong, bushy growth. *Foliage* medium green. Early and floriferous.
(R. Holmes, UK, 1996) (CL)(RIV)(CLI)(OLD)

Tony Porter
Semi-Double to Double H2 Bush
Tube and *sepals* crimson. *Corolla* petals pale aster mauve with crimson veins. This plant produces both semi-double and double flowers. Very floriferous.
(Hall, UK, 1997) (MO)(JAK)(ROO)(HYDE)(ISL)

Tony's Treat
Double H2 Bush
Tube and *sepals* candy pink. *Corolla* petals royal purple. The upright and self-branching growth builds into a very attractive plant.
(Raiser unknown, 1996) (POT)(EX)

Toos
Single H2 Lax Bush
Tube short and cream. *Sepals* creamy rose, rather narrow and held horizontally with reflexed tips. *Corolla* petals rose pink. The medium-sized flowers are freely produced. Growth is as a rather lax bush.
(van Suchtelen, Holland, 1980) (FOX)(EX)(CHA)(ROO)(RIV)

Top Score
Semi-Double H2/3 Bush
Tube short and cerise. *Sepals* brilliant cerise and reflex back to the tube. *Corolla* petals rich violet and cerise at the base. The large blooms are of good substance and will take full sun. *Foliage* dark green. Upright, strong growth and self-branching. Should make a good plant for the hardy border.
(Handley, UK, 1980) (WV)(GLE)

Tosca
Double H2 Trailer
Tube and *sepals* rose pink. *Corolla* petals blush pink with deep pink at the base of the petaloids. Large fluffy blooms and fairly free, flaring but fading quickly. Naturally trailing in growth, this cultivar will make a good basket.
(Blackwell, UK, 1965) (FUC)(GLE)

Toskve (Sometimes written Tvoske)
Single H2 Trailer
Variegated foliage 'sport' from 'Auntie Jinks'. *Foliage* yellow and green. Very attractive and not too difficult. The flowers are similar to 'Auntie Jinks' in that they have pink-red *sepals* and purple *corolla* petals with white shading. The natural habit is as a trailer.
('sport' from 'Auntie Jinks') (Finder and date unknown) (ISL)(FEN)(RKY)(BRE)(WAY) (ARC)(CHA)

Tourtonne
Single H1 Bush
Single of the triphylla-type. *Tube*, long thin and light crimson. *Sepals*, long and pointed with horizontal spread, also light crimson. Petals in the well-exposed *corolla* light crimson but lighter at the base. *Foliage* medium green and quite small for the large flowers. Upright and vigorous. Needs extra warmth to safely overwinter.
(F. van Suchtalen, Holland, 1968) (BRY)

Trabant
Single H2 Bush
Tube ivory white. *Sepals* ivory white tipped with green and with blush pink on the undersides. *Corolla* petals pinkish lavender with white at the base of the petals. The small flowers are held semi-erect. Growth is self-branching upright bush.
(Gotz, Germany, 1991) (ROO)

Tracid
Semi-Double H2 Bush
Tube short and red. *Sepals* red, broad and upturned. *Corolla* petals pale pink with darker pink at the base. Medium-sized blooms. Growth upright and bushy.
(Colville, UK, 1980) (SIL)(BAK)(LOK)

Trade Winds
Double H2 Lax Bush
Tube white. *Sepals* white and pink. *Corolla* white with pink at the base of the petals. The small blooms are very freely produced. *Foliage* medium green. The growth is rather lax so is useful in hanging containers.
(Fuchsia La, USA, 1968) (SMI)

Tranquility
Double H2 Trailer
Tube and *sepals* pink. *Corolla* petals purple overlaid and splashed with rose. The petals change to ruby red and pink with maturity. Beautiful colouring carried on large flowers. Excellent trailing cultivar for use in baskets.
(Soo Yun, USA, 1970) (CLI)(BRI)(SMI)

Traviata
Double H2 Bush
Tube and *sepals* pink. *Corolla* petals white. A free-flowering and very attractive bush plant.
(ISL)(CHA)(FUC)(GLE)

Treasure
Double H2 Bush
Tube pale rose. *Sepals* neyron rose. *Corolla* petals pale silvery violet pink. Large full blooms very freely produced. Growth is upright and bushy.
(Niederholzer, USA, 1946) (BAK)(BRI)(BRY)(OLI)

216

TOOS

TONY PORTER

TOSCA

TRADE WINDS

TREASURE

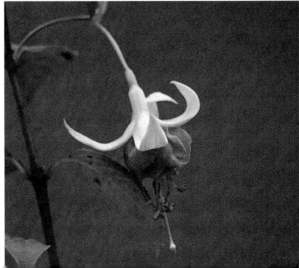

Très Long
Single H2 Lax Bush
Single of the intermediate type. *Tubes* very long, thin and orange. *Sepals* green and drooping. *Corolla* petals pale orange. Growth is weakly upright. Requires some support but dislikes being 'pinched'. Care needed with watering.
(Van der Post, Holland, 1990) (GOU)

Tricolori
Single H3 Bush
Tube and *sepals* crimson. *Corolla* petals purple, cerise at the base. Small flowers very freely produced. *Foliage* variegated with creams, greens and a pink flush. Growth is upright, bushy and hardy.
(Potney, UK, date unknown) (ROU)(KM)(WV)(BAK)(RIV) (POT)(ASK)

Trimley Bells
Single H2 Bush
Tube and *sepals* red. *Corolla* petals lavender. Growth is strongly upright and self-branching. Will make a very good show plant.
(Stiff, UK, 1996) (BAK)(ROO)

Tring
Single H2 Bush
Tube and *sepals* deep pink. *Corolla* petals reddish aubergine. Good, strong, upright and self-branching bushy growth.
(BRI)

Trio
Double H2 Bush
Tube and *sepals* lavender pink. *Corolla* petals rose pink. The medium-sized flowers are very prolific, especially for a double. *Foliage* pale green and the strong, compact, bushy growth makes this a good candidate for the show bench.
(E. Holmes, UK, 1981) (LOK)

Trisha
Double H2 Bush
Tube and *sepals* near white and tipped with green. *Corolla* petals

burgundy splashed with rose and magenta. The large blooms are free for the size. Growth upright, bushy and quite strong.
(Antonelli, USA, 1965) (BLA)

Trish's Triumph
Single H3 Bush
Tube and *sepals* red. *Corolla* petals white. *Foliage* delightfully variegated. Well worth growing in the hardy border.
(BRE)(GLE)

Tromba
Single H1 Bush
Species derivative of *F. fulgens rubra grandiflora* with slimmer flowers and without green tips. *Foliage* large, velvety and similar to *F. fulgens*.
(BEL)

Troon
Single H2 Bush
Tube long and light red. *Sepals* spear-shaped, long and recurving also red. *Corolla* petals white with pink overtones and heavily streaked with red veining. *Foliage* is yellow with red veins. Upright and bushy growth.
(Goulding, UK, 1986) (CLI)(FEN) (RKY)(CHA)(WV)(BEL)(RIV) (ASK)(FUC)(GLE)(ISL)

Troubadour
Double H2 Trailer
Tube and wide *sepals* brilliant crimson. *Corolla* petals dark lilac purple with splashes of crimson at the base. The large blooms are free for the size and have long, pointed buds. *Foliage* dark green. The growth is naturally trailing so will make a good basket.
(Waltz, USA, 1963) (WAY)(LOK)

Troutbeck
Single H2/3 Bush
Tube short and salmon. *Sepals* creamy white, flushed pink and tipped with green. *Corolla* aster violet. The flowers are quite short and are very freely produced. The plant is capable of taking full sun. Growth is upright and bushy.

('Dorothea Flower' × 'Hawkshead')
(Thornley, UK, 1967) (RIV)

Truly Treena
Double H2 Trailer
Tube white striped with pink. *Sepals* red and curl and twist like a bow. *Corolla* petals are deep violet fading to deep pink at the base. The petals are veined with red and curl around. Fast-growing self-branching trailer. Excellent for baskets.
(M. Allsop, UK, 1996) (LB)(ROO)

Tumbling Water
Double H2 Trailer
Tube and reflexed *sepals* dark crimson outside and light crimson on the inner. *Corolla* petals cyclamen purple. The blooms are medium to large and are fairly freely produced. A natural trailer, this unusual colour combination will make a superb basket.
(Reiter, USA, 1954) (VER)(RIV)

Tutti Frutti
Double H2 Trailer
Tube and reflexed *sepals* pale pink. *Corolla* petals iridescent magenta-rose. The medium-sized blooms are freely produced. The four centre petals and well-defined auxiliary petals are marbled rose pink. Growth is naturally trailing for this is a very long-jointed plant.
(Schnabel/Paskesen, USA, 1966) (CLI)(WHE)(LOK)

Twinkletoes
Single H2 Bush
A fine flower with a nice white bell-shaped *corolla*. *Tube* crimson. *Sepals* pale carmine rose becoming nearly white at the fly-away tips. Upright growth and self-branching. A very nice and dainty flower that seems to dance on a well bushed plant. (This should not be confused with another plant carrying the same name that is correctly called 'Waltz Jubelteen'.)
(Hall, UK, 1998) (FEN)(MO)(FUC)

TRÈS LONG

TRIMLEY BELLS

TRISH'S TRIUMPH

TRULY TREENA

Twinny
Single H2 Bush
Sepals deep pink. *Corolla* petals white with a pink blush. Very short-jointed, self-branching and readily forms a compact bush shape. The small single flowers are carried in profusion. Undoubtedly a winner for the show benches.
(Gordon, UK, 1998)
(LB)(BRE)(MO)(PER)

Twirling Square Dancer
Double H2 Trailer
Tube and *sepals* ivory. *Corolla* petals light rose and light red purple. If you like large doubles then this is the one for you. As it is naturally trailing, it will make an excellent basket and will be the envy of your neighbours.
(Stubbs, USA, 1991) (ISL)(FOX)(CHA)(BLA)(RIV)(HYDE)(SMI)

Twister
Single H2 Trailer
Tube and *sepals* rose. *Corolla* petals pale orchid. Long and twisted flowers, small but freely produced. Naturally a trailer, it will produce an eye-catching basket.
(Niederholzer, USA, 1944)
(RIV)(OLI)

Twist of Fate
Semi-Double–Double H2/3 Bush
Tube short and deep pink. *Sepals* fully curled and slightly twisted also deep pink. *Corolla* petals purple shading to pink at the base. An upright-growing bush that has already proved itself hardy in the south Midlands. Attains a height of about 2ft (60cm) in a season.
(Rolt, UK, 1996) (KM)

U

Ultra Light
Single H2 Trailer
Tube and *sepals* rose. *Corolla* petals red with a lighter base fading to purple to the edge and maturing to red. Waxy petal edges. A trailing plant that will make a good basket. Best colour in bright light as it prefers full sun.
(de Graaff, Holland, 1988) (BRY)

Uncle Jinks
Single H2 Trailer
Tube and *sepals* pink. *Corolla* purple with a little white shading. The small or medium-sized blooms are produced in profusion. *Foliage* small, mid-green with pointed leaves. Growth is pendulous so will make a superb basket quite easily. The flowers are similar to but larger than its parent 'Auntie Jinks'.
(Wilson, UK, 1985)
(ISL)(ROO)(RIV)(HYDE)(OLI)

Uncle Mike
Double H2 Trailer
Tube and *sepals* white. *Corolla* petals lipstick red, maturing to wine red. Large blooms fairly free for their size. Growth is naturally trailing.
(Tiret, USA, 1962)
(EX)(RIV)(OLI)

University of Liverpool
Single H2 Trailer
Tube and *sepals* white. *Corolla* petals red. A very floriferous plant. Naturally trailing so will make an excellent subject for use in hanging pots or baskets.
(D. Clark, UK, 1998) (MO)(ROU)(STM)(ARC)(JAK)(BLA)

U.X.B.
Double H2 Bush
Tube and *sepals* light red. *Corolla* petals purple. The natural growth is as an upright bush.
(RIV)

V

Vailant
Single H2 Bush
Tube and *sepals* scarlet. *Corolla* petals purple veined with scarlet.
Strong, upright and self-branching growth.
(Jennings, UK, 1850) (BAK)

Valda May
Double H2 Bush
Tube and *sepals* bright red. *Corolla* petals deep purple. Medium-sized blooms fairly produced.
(E.C. Smith, Australia, 1970s) (WV)

Valentine
Semi-Double H2 Trailer
Tube and long *sepals* white flushed rose. *Corolla* petals deepest imperial purple. Large flowers freely produced. Growth is as a semi-trailer.
(Reiter, USA, 1948)
(FEN)(BRI)(BAK)

Val's Pink Ice
Single H2 Bush
Tube and *sepals* white tinged pink. *Corolla* petals open light purple maturing to magenta. Petals fold to create a novel form. Medium-sized flowers freely produced.
(Luther, UK, 1995)
(WV)(HYDE)

Vanessa
Double H2 Bush
Tube pink. *Sepals* long, pink, curling upwards. *Corolla* petals pale lavender blue. Very full blooms, medium-sized and freely produced. *Foliage* lightish green. Growth upright and bushy.
(Colville, UK, 1964)
(LOK)(EX)

Variegated Auntie Jinks
Single H2 Trailer
The flowers are normal for the parent plant. *Foliage* variegated with green, cream and pinks. (*See* also 'Toskve'.)
(HYDE)

Variegated Dancing Flame
The flowers are normal for the parent plant. *Foliage* variegated with greens, creams and pinks.
(FEN)(RKY)

TWINNY

UNIVERSITY OF LIVERPOOL

UNCLE JINKS

VAL'S PINK ICE

VARIEGATED AUNTIE JINKS

Variegated Echo
Single H2 Bush
Tube and *sepals* bright pink.
Corolla petals red/mauve. Upright
bushy plant with variegated
foliage.
(FEN)

Variegated *fulgens*
The same long flowers. *Foliage*
variegated.
(FOX)(CHA)(PER)

**Variegated *fulgens rubra
grandiflora***
The flower type and qualities are
the same as *fulgens rubra
grandiflora. Foliage* is a delightful
variegation.
(BEL)

Variegated La Campanella
Foliage variegated on plants
carrying the usual coloured
flowers.
(WHE)

Variegated Lottie Hobby (Enc)
Crimson self small flowers. *Foliage*
green, yellow and red. Slow to
start at beginning of season.
(CL)(BRE)(FOX)(PER)(GOU)
(ADD)(HYDE)(ISL)

Variegated Mag Alba
The same flowers and growth as
magellanica var alba *Foliage* bright
cream and green.
(ROO)

Variegated Pixie
Single H3 Bush
Tube and *sepals* cerise. *Corolla*
petals rosy-mauve. *Foliage*
variegated pale yellowish green
with cream and gold markings. H:
3ft (90cm)
(Russell, UK, 1960) (MO)

Variegated *procumbens*
The flowers are the same as the
parent plant. *Foliage* edged with
cream.
(Breary, UK, 1996)
(FOX)(PER)(CHA)(LOK)

Variegated Snowcap
The description of the flowers and
the type of growth is the same as
'Snowcap'. *Foliage* variegated.
(WHE)

Variegated Superstar
Tube and *sepals* phlox pink.
Corolla rose purple. *Foliage*
variegated green, cream and pink.
(ROU)

Variegated Vivienne Thompson
Semi-Double H2 Bush
Tube and *sepals* rhodamine pink.
Corolla white. *Foliage* variegated
green, cream and pink.
(FOX)(BRE)(ROU)(CHA)(PER)

Variegated Waveney Sunrise
Single H2 Bush
Tube and *sepals* pale pink. *Corolla*
red. *Foliage* variegated green,
cream and pink.
(Burns, UK, 1986) (BUR)

Varty's Pride
Double H2 Trailer
Tube white, flushed with rose.
Sepals white, flushed rose and
tipped with green. *Corolla* petals
white with slight flush of rose
under the sepals. Medium-sized
blooms with red stamens. *Foliage*
lighter than 'Swingtime' and red-
veined. Growth as a trailer.
Throws two sets of flowers from
each leaf axil.
('sport' of 'Swingtime')
(Varty, UK, 1979) (BRI)(WV)

Veenlust
Double H2 Trailer
Tubes and recurved *sepals* white.
Corolla petals scarlet with white
splashes on the outer petals.
Spreading growth. Looks well in
mixed baskets or in garden tubs.
(Jansink, Holland, 1995)
(LB)(MO)(GOU)(HYDE)(FUC)
(ISL)

F. venusta
Single H1 Bush
Fuchsia species. An orange self.
The long, tapering *tubes*, short
sepals tipped with green, and
spreading *corolla* petals all orange.
The blooms are very striking.
Foliage a glossy dark green.
Growth is upright but lax.
(Humboldt, Bonpland and Kunth,
Colombia, 1823)
(SIL)(KM)(CL)(EX)(BAK)(GOU)

F. venusta (CL 02)
The description is as given above
except that the flowers are red and
foliage slightly darker. (CL)

Verity Edwards
Single H2/3 Bush
Triphylla-type. *Tube* long, thin and
cardinal red. *Sepals*, held below the
horizontal are also cardinal red.
Corolla petals start plum purple
blotched with cardinal red at the
base and mature to ruby red.
Foliage green with deep red stems.
Perhaps the first triphylla-type to
be considered slightly hardy.
('Thalia' × 'Lady Boothby')
(H. Dunnet, UK, 1985) (FEN)

Versicolor
Single H3 Bush
Tube and *sepals* red. *Corolla*
purple. A good, strong, upright-
growing bush with variegated
foliage. Extremely hardy.
('Magellanica Versicolor')
(FEN)(WHE)

Vespa
Double H2 Lax Bush
Tube and *sepals* rose pink. *Corolla*
petals purple overlaid with rose
pink. Large blooms that are freely
produced. Lax bushy growth that
makes it a very versatile plant for
training.
(Dresman, UK, 1987) (RIV)

Vicki Putley
Single H2 Lax Bush or Trailer
Tube and *sepals* white, flushed
with carmine. *Corolla* petals rich
crimson red. Medium-sized flowers
freely produced.
(Putley, UK, 1964) (RIV)

Victoria Smith
Single H2 Bush
Tube and *sepals* pale pink. *Corolla*
petals deep red. Upright-growing,
self-branching plant. (FEN)

VARIEGATED LOTTIE HOBBY   VARIEGATED *PROCUMBENS*
VARIEGATED VIVIENNE THOMPSON   VEENLUST

F. VENUSTA   VERSICOLOR

Victory
Semi-Double H2 Trailer
Tube and long recurved *sepals*
carmine. *Corolla* petals rose
madder. The long flowers, which
have a globular shape, are very
freely produced. Natural growth is
as a trailer so will make an excellent
plant for use in hanging containers.
('Suzanne Pasquier' × 'San
Francisco')
(Reiter, USA, 1942) (FEN) (BAK)
(RKY)

Vielliebchen
Single H3 Bush
Tube and *sepals* shining red.
Corolla petals deep purple
changing to red purple with
maturity. Small to medium flowers
very freely produced. *Foliage* small,
medium green.
('Charming' × *magellanica* var.
gracillis)
(Wolf, Germany, 1911)
(SIL)(BRE)(RIV)(RKY)

Vincent van Gogh
Single H2 Bush
Tube, *sepals* and *corolla* of this
medium-sized single flower all the
same delightful pink. *Foliage*
medium green. The natural growth
is as an upright bush.
(Van der Post, Holland, 1984)
(MO)(FOX)(RKY)(BRE)(EX)
(CHA)(GOU)(RIV)(HYDE)

Violacea
Double H2 Trailing
Tube and *sepals* white. *Corolla*
petals orchid pink. Fairly free-
flowering. Naturally trailing
growth.
(Fuchsia La, USA, 1968) (SMI)

Violet Gem
Semi-Double H2 Bush
Tube and *sepals* carmine. *Corolla*
petals are deep violet. Large
spreading flowers freely produced.
Growth upright and bushy.
(Niederholzer/Waltz, USA, 1949)
(LOK)(OLI)

Violetta
Single H2 Bush
Tube and slim curved *sepals* ivory
white. *Corolla* petals Bishops violet
with a light blotch at the base of
each petal. Long, bell-shaped
flowers fairly free and continuously
produced. Growth upright and
vigorous.
(Schnabel, USA, 1952) (BRY)

Virginia Curryer
Single H1 Bush
Triphylla-type fuchsia. The long
tube and short *sepals* orange
scarlet. *Foliage* variegated. A
variegated form of 'Thalia'.
(Curryer, UK, 1998)
(ARC)(HYDE)

Vivien Davis
Single H1 Bush
Triphylla-type fuchsia. *Tube*, *sepals*
and *corolla* petals all pink. Growth
is upright and very strong. Will
need early pinching to create a
good bush.
(Stannard, UK, 1993) (ROO)

Vivien Harris
Single H2 Bush
Triphylla-type. *Tube* long, thick,
waxy and turkey red. *Sepals* are of
the same colouring. *Corolla* petals
a deeper shade of turkey red. Long
flowers of the triphylla-type, very
free. Growth upright and bushy.
(Harris, UK, 1977) (WAY)(BRI)

Vivienne Colville
Single H2 Bush
Tube narrow and pink. *Sepals*
orange, narrow and upturned.
Corolla petals start with deeper
orange than the *sepals* edged with
red. Petite flowers profusely
produced.
(Colville, UK, 1980) (BRI)

Vivienne Thompson
Semi-Double H2 Bush
Tube medium-sized, rhodamine
pink. *Sepals* also rhodamine pink
with edging of neyron rose.
Corolla white with neyron rose
veins at the base. The blooms are
of medium size. *Foliage* medium
green. Self-branching upright
growth that will produce a very
acceptable bush.
('Tolling Bell' × 'Border Queen')
(Reynolds, UK, 1983)
(BUR)(WAY)(ARC)(WAL)
(RIV)(HYDE)(CLI)(ISL)

Vogue
Double H2 Trailer
Tube and *sepals* ivory white,
tipped with green. Petals in the
corolla are campanula-violet fading
to Bishop's violet. Largish blooms
rather sparse. Natural trailer.
(Fuchsia La, USA, 1959)
(BAK)(BRI)(CHA)(RIV)(BRY)

F. vulcanica var. hitchcockii
Single H1 Lax Bush
Tubes long, thin and orange.
Sepals shorter, green. *Corolla*
petals orange. *Foliage* held in
whorls. Its habit of growth is
rather spreading. Does best when
growing in hanging containers.
(Edouard André, Colombia,
1888) (CL)

Vuurwerk
Single H2 Bush
Tubes orange with copper tints.
Sepals short and green. *Corolla*
petals like burnished brass. It has
a self-branching habit and tends
to flower continuously. Quite
challenging – a real novelty plant.
(De Graaff, Holland, 1988)
(RKY)(EX)

W

Waconda Queen
Semi-Double H2 Bush
Tube and *sepals* dark rose.
Corolla petals dark reddish
purple. Vigorous upright
growth.
(Springer, UK, 1988) (EX)(RID)

Wagtails White Pixie
Single H3 Bush
Tube and *sepals* carmine red.
Corolla petals white-veined
carmine. Smallish flowers like a
miniature 'Snowcap'. *Foliage* light
to medium green, shading darker
at tip with red veins and stems.
H: 12in (30cm)
(Saunders, UK, 1966) (SIL)(BAK)

VIELLIEBCHEN

VINCENT VAN GOGH

VIVIEN DAVIS

VIVIENNE THOMPSON

VIOLETTA

Waldfree
Single H3 Bush
An encliandra-type fuchsia with small pink to dark pink flowers. *Foliage* small and the willowy growth will make this a good candidate for use with all types of small structures.
(Travis, UK, 1973) (RKY)

Wally Yendell
Double H2 Trailer
Tubes and horizontally held *sepals* ivory white. *Corolla* petals many pleated and clover pink. Growth is strong and spreading. Best grown in wall baskets.
(Goulding, UK, 1998)
(GOU)

Walstraw
Single H2 Bush
Tube and *sepals* waxy white, veined with rose bengal. *Corolla* petals Bishop's violet maturing to mallow purple. Good, strong, upright bush.
(CLI)

Walton Jewel
Double H2 Bush
Tube and *sepals* creamy white. *Corolla* petals lavender blue. Strong, upright and self-branching bushy growth. Another super plant from a well-respected hybridizer.
(Stiff, UK, 1996)
(BAK)(PER)(ROO)

Waltraud
Semi-Double H2 Bush
Tube and *sepals* white. *Corolla* petals purple. Large-sized blooms. Makes an excellent plant for the patio tub.
(ARC)

Walz Banjo
Single H2 Lax Bush
Tube long, azalea pink. *Sepals* mandarin red. *Corolla* petals scarlet. The lax growth makes this plant suitable for use either as a bush or as a basket.
(Waldenmaier, Holland, 1987)
(EX)

Walz Bienard
Double H2 Lax bush
Tube white. *Sepals* rose. *Corolla* petals dark rose. The lax growth makes this suitable for bush or basket use.
(Waldenmaier, Holland, 1987)
(RIV)

Walz Bulunkous
Single H2 Trailer
Tube and *sepals* rose pink. *Corolla* petals bright orange. A natural trailer that will make a good basket.
(Waldenmaier, Holland, 1988)
(RKY)

Walz Duimelot
Single H2 Lax Bush
Tube and wide *sepals* neyron rose with green tips. *Corolla* petals red/purple. *Foliage* medium green. A lax upright or stiff bush. A very profuse bloomer.
(Waldenmaier, Holland, 1985)
(HYDE)

Walz Epicurist
Single H2 Bush
Tube and *sepals* crimson. *Corolla* petals blue to light purple. The flowers are produced in great quantity.
('Fascination' × 'Vogue')
(Waldenmaier, Holland, 1987)
(EX)

Walz Estafette
Double H2 Trailer
Tube long, thin and white. *Sepals* horizontally held, white on the upper surface and white flushed rose underneath. *Corolla* petals medium purple and mature to imperial purple. A natural trailer will make an excellent basket.
(Walz Bruintje ×)
(Waldenmaier, Holland, 1985)
(HYDE)

Walz Fanfare
Single H2 Lax Bush
Tube long, red. *Sepals* red on top, orange underneath. *Corolla* petals are orange red. The blooms are of the triphylla-type. *Foliage* is very dark green on top and dark red

underneath. Growth is as a lax bush.
('Whiteknights Ruby' × 'Fanfare')
(Waldenmaier, Holland, 1987)
(ROO)

Walz Fluit
Single H2 Lax Bush
Tube and *sepals* orange. *Corolla* petals also orange. The flowers are of medium size. *Foliage* dark green.
(Waldenmaier, Holland, 1988)
(FOX)(PER)(FUC)(HYDE)

Walz Klaroen
Single H2 Bush
Tube azalea pink. *Sepals* wide, scarlet with green tips. *Corolla* petals signal red/orange. *Foliage* is dark yellow/green. Good strong upward growth – for best colour of flower filtered light is preferable.
(Waldenmaier, Holland, 1987)
(HYDE)

Walz Nugget
Single H2 Bush
Tube claret rose. *Sepals* chartreuse green. *Corolla* petals neyron rose maturing to crimson. *Foliage* is dark green on the upper surface and lighter on the lower.
(Waldenmaier, Holland, 1987)
(HYDE)

Walz Pauk
Double H2 Bush
Tube carmine rose. *Sepals* carmine rose on the upper surface, scarlet shaded orange on the lower. *Corolla* petals scarlet shaded with orange, maturing to crimson shaded with orange. *Foliage* dark green.
(Waldenmaier, Holland, 1987)
(EX)

Walz Toeter
Single H2 Bush
Tube dark rose. *Sepals* dark rose with large, yellowish green tips. *Corolla* petals red with smooth edges. *Foliage* large, medium green.
(Waldenmaier, Holland, 1988)
(HYDE)

WALZ DUIMELOT

WALZ ESTAFETTE

WALZ FLUIT

WALZ NUGGET

Walz Trompet
Single H2 Bush
Tube long, thin, claret rose.
Sepals also claret rose. *Corolla*
petals purple. *Foliage* is dark
green on the upper surfaces but
lighter green on the lower. Strong
upright grower.
(Waldenmaier, Holland, 1987)
(HYDE)

Walz Wipneus
Single H2 Bush
Tube and *sepals* pinkish white.
Corolla petals deep reddish violet.
Flowers fairly small but prolific.
(Waldenmaier, Holland, 1987)
(ARC)(ROO)(HYDE)

Walz Xylophone
Single H2 Trailer
Tube salmon. *Sepals* dawn pink
on the upper surface and azalea
pink on the lower. *Corolla* petals
azalea pink. A natural trailer
that will make an excellent
basket.
(Waldenmaier, Holland, 1987)
(HYDE)

Wapenfeld's 150
Single H2 Bush
Semi-paniculate with 'perfect'
flowers. *Tubes*, recurved *sepals*
and *corolla* are all lavender hued.
Growth is strong, self-branching
and upright. One for large tubs
or conservatories.
(Kamphuis, Holland, 1993)
(MO)

War Dance
Semi-Double H2 Bush
The short *tube* and flared *sepals*
white. *Corolla* petals dianthus
purple with coral pink marbling,
fading to reddish-purple. The
large blooms are freely produced.
Large *foliage*. Growth upright
and very bushy.
(Kennett, USA, 1960) (BRI)(WHE)

Water Nymph
Single H2 Bush
White and crimson. Grown and
cultivated in the Netherlands
under the name of 'Deutsche
Perle'. Sometimes confused with

'Wassernymph' that has *tube* and
sepals of the palest pink whilst
the petals in the *corolla* are
salmon orange. A good, strong,
upright-growing plant.
(Story, UK, 1859)
(BRY)(FEN)(ROU)(RKY)(BRE)
(EX)(RIV)(FUC)(OLI)(LOK)

Wee One
Double H2 Bush
Tube and outside of *sepals* pale
pink, the inside being a lovely
soft pink. *Corolla* petals also a
lovely soft pink. The small to
medium-sized blooms are very
freely produced. Growth is
upright and willowy.
(Tiret, USA, 1951) (RIV)

Wendy
Double H2 Lax Bush
Tube white. *Sepals* coral pink on
the upper surface and tipped with
green, pinkish orange underneath.
Corolla pinkish orange splashed
with orange. The medium-sized
blooms are fairly full. *Foliage*
medium green. Growth is rather
lax so can be used for hanging
containers or as a bush if given
supports.
(Dresman, UK, 1986)
(CLI)(EX)(RIV)(OLD)
(*See* photograph on page 231.)

Wendy van Wanten
Single H2 Bush
Tube and *sepals* very light pink.
Corolla petals white with bright
red anthers. The smallish but
prolific flowers are held out
horizontally from the plant.
(Geerts, Belgium, 1995)
(FEN)(MO)(ROO)(HYDE)(ISL)

Wessex Hardy
Single H2/3 Bush
Tube and recurving *sepals* red.
Corolla petals start purple and
pink at the base and mature to a
slightly lighter purple with
turned-under smooth edges.
Medium-sized flowers. Upright
self-branching growth. Hardy in
most areas.
(Luther, UK, 1986) (WV)
(*See* photograph on page 231.)

Wessex Jubilee
Double H2 Lax Bush
Tube and *sepals* light pink.
Corolla petals lavender. A lax
upright variety producing masses
of full, heavy blooms.
(Forward, UK, 1995)
(BRE)(FUC)(GLE)(ISL)

Westham
Single H2 Bush
Tube and *sepals* rosy pink.
Corolla petals purple to magenta.
Prolific number of small flowers.
Vigorous grower that will fill a
6in pot in the first season. Show
quality.
(Wilson, UK, 1994) (CL)(ISL)(SIM)

Westray
Double H2 Bush
Tube and *sepals* of this medium-
sized flower are red. *Corolla*
petals are a bluish purple.
Upright, self-branching growth.
(Weston, UK, 1997) (SIM)

W.F.C. Kampionen
Single H2 Bush
Tube and *sepals* white. *Corolla*
petals violet. The medium-sized
blooms are carried on strong,
upright-growing bushes.
(Krom, Germany, 1989)
(WAY)(ARC)(BRY)

Whickham Ann
Double H2 Bush
Tube and *sepals* red. *Corolla*
petals crimson. Small double
flowers produced on compact
bushes.
(Bainbridge, UK, 1989) (CLI)

Whickham Girl
Single H2 Bush
Tube and *sepals* of this attractive
medium-sized flower pink.
Corolla petals also pink. Upright,
self-branching growth.
(Bainbridge, UK, 1990) (CLI)

Whickham Rosa
Single H2 Bush
Tube and *sepals* pink. *Corolla*
petals rose with darker edges.
Good, strong, upright growth.
(Bainbridge, UK, 1990) (CLI)

WALZ WIPNEUS

WALZ XYLOPHONE

WENDY VAN WANTEN

WESSEX JUBILEE

WESTHAM

WESTRAY

White Blue Veil
Double H2 Trailer
Tube and *sepals* white. *Corolla* petals also white. The large flowers are freely produced.
(OLI)(HYDE)

White Bouquet
Double H2 Bush
Tube thick, greenish and white. *Sepals* spiky, tapering, held horizontally, ivory white with pink underneath and tipped with green. *Corolla* petals ivory white with pink veining. Rather bold medium-sized blooms with folded scalloped petals of heavy texture. *Foliage* mid-green with slight serration to the edges. Medium upright, strong and bushy.
(Gadsby, UK, 1970)
(CLI)

White Eyes
Single H2 Bush
Tube and *sepals* red. *Corolla* petals white. Good, strong, upright and bushy growth.
(FOX)(CHA)(OLI)

White General Monk
Double H2 Bush
Tube and *sepals* cerise rose. *Corolla* petals white, veined with rose. A compact and self-branching bush that proudly presents its medium-sized flowers.
(FOX)(CHA)(OLI)

White Gold
Single H2 Lax Bush
Tube and *sepals* white, tipped green and pink at the base. *Corolla* petals white with pale pink shading at the base. The medium-sized flowers are fairly freely produced. *Foliage* variegated golden, white-tipped and ageing to green. Needs sunny spot to produce best foliage colouring. Growth is as a lax bush. Not easy.
(York, USA, 1953)
(BAK)

Whitehaven News
Single H2 Bush
Tube and *sepals* white with slight pink cast. *Corolla* petals white.
Medium-sized, crisp blooms. Versatile plant that does well as a Standard.
(Fleming, UK, 1991)
(HYDE)

White Heidi (White Ann)
Double H2/3 Bush
Tube and *sepals* crimson cerise. *Corolla* petals white. Good, strong-growing bush.
('sport' from 'Heidi Ann')
(Wills/Atkinson, UK, 1972)
(FOX)(CL)(WAY)(CHA)
(WV)(ROO)(RID)(BRY)(CLI)
(FUC)(GLE)(LOK)

White Henry
Double H2 Lax Bush
Tube and *sepals* white to pink. *Corolla* petals white shading to pink with pink base. Medium to large blooms are produced in rather lax growth. Will make a bush with supports but might be best in hanging containers.
(Intro. by Holmes, UK, 1986)
(WV)

White Lace
Double H2/3 Bush
Tube and *sepals* deep red. *Corolla* petals white, veined with red. The large and full double blooms are freely produced. *Foliage* is dark green and helps to enhance the colouring of the flowers.
(Tabraham, UK, 1976)
(RIV)

White Marshmallow
Double H2 Lax Bush
Tube white. *Sepals* pink. *Corolla* petals are white. Medium to large flowers carried profusely.
(UK, 1989)
(RIV)

White Princess
Single H2 Bush
Tube short, waxy and white. *Sepals* waxy, curving downwards, cream on top with a pink flush on the undersides. *Corolla* has rather short petals of rosy cerise shading to orange at the base. The small flowers are produced
abundantly. *Foliage* small and bronzy-green.
('White Queen' ×)
(Gray, UK, 1973) (RIV)(SIM)

White Veil
Double H2 Bush
Tube and *sepals* white. *Corolla* petals also white with some pale pink. Flowers are of medium size and prolific.
('sport' from 'Blue Veil')
(ISL)(BRI)(WV)

Whitton Pride
Double H2 Bush
Tube and *sepals* glossy red. *Corolla* very full with bright white, well-shaped petals. The flowers are very large, similar in size to 'Swingtime' and are produced quite freely. Strong upright-growing plant.
(Tickner, UK, 1994)
(JAK)

Wibke
Single H2 Bush
Tube pink. *Sepals* pink with green reflexed tips. *Corolla* petals pink with wavy edges. *Foliage* medium green with reddish green veins. Medium-sized flowers but freely produced. Self-branching, small upright.
(Leverkusen ×)
(Bogemann, Germany, 1987)
(ROO)

Wickham Blue
Single H2 Bush
Tube and *sepals* white. *Corolla* petals are bright blue. The natural growth is as an upright bush.
(Bainbridge, UK, 1990)
(JAK)(FEN)

Widow Twanky
Double H2 Trailer
Tube and *sepals* red. *Corolla* petals red purple at first, maturing to light purple. The large blooms are produced freely. Naturally trailing, this cultivar will make an excellent hanging container.
(Forward, UK, 1993)
(WV)(RIV)(FUC)(GLE)(ISL)

WENDY

WESSEX HARDY

WHITEHAVEN NEWS

WIDOW TWANKY

Wiebke Becker

Wiebke Becker
Single H2 Trailer
Tube long and *sepals* pale pink.
Corolla petals white. The natural
trailing qualities of the plant make
it useful for hanging containers.
(Strumper, Germany, 1991)
(KM)(ARC)

Wigan Pier
Double H2 Bush
Tube pale pink, darker at the
base. *Sepals* white flushed pale
pink. *Corolla* petals white. The
small flowers are produced on a
stiffly upright, self-branching
plant.
(Clark, UK, 1988)
(WAR)(BRE)(MO)(BUR)
(WAL)

Wilfred C. Dobson
Single H2 Spreading Bush
Tubes and spiralling *sepals* pink.
Corolla petals dark aubergine to
aubergine. Flowers are bell-
shaped. The habit is rather
spreading and the plant is
therefore ideal for use in hanging
containers. Some protection from
strong winds is suggested.
(Goulding, UK, 1996)
(CHA)(RIV)(PER)(HYDE)

Willbet
Double H2 Bush
Tube and *sepals* cream, flushed
with pink. *Corolla* petals are dark
blue speckled with pink. The
medium-sized flowers are freely
produced on a strong, upright
and self-branching bush.
(Delaney, UK, 1995) (BLA)

Will Gibbs
Double H2 Trailer
Tube and *sepals* dark rose and
pink. *Corolla* petals open light
purple, veined with red and
mature to purple. Largish flowers
that twist and curl – very
attractive.
(Roach, USA, 1977) (ISL)

William Grant
Semi-Double/Double H2 bush
Tubes and flyaway *sepals* pink.
Corolla petals are dark aubergine

to ruby red. Growth is strong and
versatile. Ideal as a container
plant or for growing as a
Standard.
(Goulding, UK, 1999)
(GOU)

William Jay
Double H2 Lax Bush
Tubes and *sepals* ivory, the *sepals*
having a pink flush on the
underside. *Corolla* petals magenta
with pink marbling. Growth is
strong and very versatile. Will
make a good weeping Standard
or a basket.
(Goulding, UK, 1996)
(RKY)(HYDE)

Willie Tamerus
Single H2 Trailer
Tube long, narrow and pale
salmon. *Sepals* also pale salmon.
Corolla petals rose orange. A
natural trailer, this plant will
show off its medium-sized flowers
well when grown in a basket.
(Tamerus, Holland, 1981)
(ROO)(HYDE)

Wilma's Versloot
Single H2 Trailer
Tube rose. *Sepals* rose/red.
Corolla petals purple fading to
red. A natural trailer, this one
does well in a hanging pot.
(Stoel, Holland, 1989)
(PER)

Wilson's Colours
Single H2 Bush
Tube dark rose madder. *Sepals* a
shade lighter but with much
darker edges. *Corolla* petals
campanula violet with white
bases. Growth is very strong,
upright and self-branching. An
excellent plant for the patio
tubs.
(Wilson, UK, 1975)
(POT)(FEN)(RKY)

Win Pettener
Single H2 Bush
Tube and *sepals* carmine rose, the
latter curving very attractively
upwards. *Corolla* petals amethyst
violet shading to mallow purple

at the base of the petals. The
medium-sized flowers are very
freely produced. Growth strong,
upright and short-jointed, making
the plant ideal for the show
bench.
(Pacey, UK, 1983)
(WV)(FEN)

Winter's Touch
Single H2 Bush
Tube and *sepals* are white, tinged
with pink. *Corolla* petals white.
Foliage medium to dark green,
quite small. Ideal plant for
growing in the smaller pots.
(Fleming, UK, 1996)
(BRE)(BLA)(CLI)(ISL)

Wise Choice
Single H2 Bush
Tube and *sepals* light pink.
Corolla petals mallow purple.
The natural growth is as an
upright, self-branching bush.
(Holmes, UK, 1989)
(RIV)

Woodside
Double H2/3 Bush
Tube and *sepals* rose red, the
latter being slightly lighter on the
undersurface. *Corolla* petals mid-
lilac with smooth edges. Large
double blooms fairly freely
produced. Considered to be
hardy. *Foliage* dark green.
(Dawson, UK, 1985)
(SIL)(BRY)

W.P. Wood
Single H3 Bush
Tube and *sepals* scarlet. *Corolla*
petals violet blue, scarlet at the
base. Small to medium-sized
flowers very freely produced but
rather late in appearing. *Foliage*
darkish green. Upright, strong,
bushy growth. Hardy. H: 2ft
(60cm)
(Wood, UK, 1954)
(SIL)(RKY)(RIV)(ASK)

WILFRED C. DOBSON

WILLIE TAMERUS

WILMA'S VERSLOOT

WINTER'S TOUCH

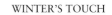

F. wurdackii
Species H1 Bush
The single flowers are produced
fairly prolifically in bunches,
terminally. *Tube* long and trumpet-
shaped orange to red. *Sepals* quite
small and of similar colouring.
Corolla petals red. *Foliage* fairly
large, the leaves are dark green and
hairy. Growth is upright and
bushy. A relatively easy species to
grow in larger pots.
(Northern Peru)
(SIL)(KM)(HYDE)

X

X. Bacillaris
Single H2 Bush
Encliandra-type fuchsia with very
small red and pink flowers.
Foliage very petite. The plant will
make an ideal subject for growing
as hoops or any other type of
fuchsia topiary.
(*F. microphylla* ssp. *microphylla* ×
F. thymifolia ssp. *thymifolia*)
(OLI)

Xmas Tree
Single H2 Bush
Tube and *sepals* white. *Corolla*
petals smoky blue. Growth is
naturally bushy.
(FEN)(BRE)(EX)(BRI)(BLA)(CLI)
(ASK)

Y

Yme
Single H2 Bush
Tube and *sepals* pink. *Corolla*
petals a lovely shade of lavender.
Foliage a very attractive light
green/yellow. The blooms are of
medium size. Growth is lax bush
and is quite suitable for growing in
hanging containers.
(Stiff, UK, 1993)
(MO)(PER)(BAK)(RIV)(OLI)

Ymje
Single H1 Bush
Terminal-flowering fuchsia with
single flowers. *Tube* long, thin and
orange. *Sepals* and short petals
also orange. Flowers are
copiously produced in terminal
corymbs. Growth is upright and
moderately self-branching. Best
grown in pots for a conservatory
display.
(Van den Berg, Holland, 1994)
(CL)(MO)(BRI)

Yvonne Priest
Single H2 Bush
Tube and *sepals* crimson. *Corolla*
petals cyclamen purple. Growth
is as an upright bush.
(R. Holmes, UK, 1995)
(RIV)

Yvonne Schwab
Single H1 Bush
Species hybrid? Flowers a bit like
F. denticulata. Growth is strong
upright.
(Schwab, Holland, 1995)
(ROO)

Z

Zara
Single H2 Bush
Tube and *sepals* light rose.
Corolla petals flame-orange. The
small flowers are borne in great
profusion. Growth is upright,
self-branching and bushy.
(Porter, UK, 1981)
(SIL)(BRY)(STM)(EX)(ROO)
(CLI)(WHE)

Zellertal
Single H2 Trailer
Tube and *sepals* white. *Corolla*
petals a vivid pink. Growth is lax
bush or trailing so will make a
bush with supports or a reasonable
hanging container.
(Gotz, Germany, 1989)
(EX)

Zets Bravo
Single H2 Bush
Tube and *sepals* are white. *Corolla*
petals orange. The flowers are a
delightful shape and are carried on
fairly strong, upright-growing
plants.
(Stoel, Holland, 1993)
(FOC)(BRE)(CHA)(PER)(GLE)

Zulu King
Single H2 Trailer
Tube and *sepals* deep carmine.
Corolla blackish purple. *Foliage*
dark green. The growth is
naturally trailing. The colour
and form of the medium-sized
flowers is retained right through
maturity.
(de Graaff, Holland, 1990)
(ARC)(BLA)(BRY)(OLI)(EX)
(GOU)(ROO)(BRI)

Zwarte Dit
Single H2 Spreading Bush
Tubes short and dark red. *Sepals*
also dark red and flyaway.
Corollas saucer-shaped with
petals that are almost black
aubergine. The branches spread
horizontally. Best seen in
hanging baskets or pots.
(de Graaff, Holland, 1995)
(PER)(ROO)(HYDE)

Zworte
Semi-Double H2 Trailer
This plant could be described as
an aubergine self. *Tube, sepals*
and *corolla* petals all have the
same delightful and attractive
colouring. Good, strong, trailing
growths that make it ideal for
hanging containers.
(de Graaff, Holland, 1995)
(RKY)

F. WURDACKII

XMAS TREE

YME

YMJE

ZETS BRAVO

ZULU KING

Nursery Addresses – 2000

(Please remember that when requesting copies of catalogues two or three first-class stamps would be appreciated.)

(ALD) ALDERTON PLANT NURSERY.
Pam Hutchinson, Spring Lane, Alderton, Towcester, Northants NN12 7LW (01327 811253) (no postal service).

(ARC) ARCADIA NURSERIES.
Brass Castle Lane, Nunthorpe, Middlesbrough, Cleveland TS8 9EB (01642 310782) (postal service).

(ASK) ASKEW NURSERIES.
South Croxton Road, Queniborough, Leicester LE7 3RX (01664 840557) (postal service).

(BAK) B. & H.M. BAKER.
Bourne Brook Nurseries, Greenstead Green, Halstead, Essex CO9 1RJ (01787 472900) (no postal service).

(BEL) BELLCROSS NURSERIES.
Howden, Goole, East Yorkshire DN14 7TQ (01430 430284) (no postal service).

(BLA) BLACKWELL FUCHSIA NURSERY.
Woodbine Cottage, Blackwell, Nr. Shipston on Stour, Warwickshire CV36 4PE (01608 682531) (postal service).

(BRE) BREACH LANE NURSERY.
Breach Lane, Wootton Bassett, Swindon, Wiltshire SN4 7QR (01793 854660) (no postal service).

(BRI) BRIGADOON FUCHSIAS.
25 King's Way, Lyme Regis, Dorset DT7 3DU (01297 445566) (postal service only).

(BRY) BRYNAWEL GARDEN CENTRE (FISHER FUCHSIAS).
Sully Road, Penarth CF64 3UU (02920 702660) (postal service).

(BUR) BURNSIDE FUCHSIAS.
Parsonage Road, Blackburn, Lancs BB1 4AG (01254 249203) (postal service).

(CHA) CHASE FUCHSIAS.
Pye Green Road, Hednesford, Cannock, Staffs WS12 4LP (01543 422394) (postal service).

(CL) CLAY LANE NURSERY.
Ken Belton, 3 Clay Lane, South Nutfield, Nr Redhill, Surrey RH1 4EG (01737 823307) (no postal service).

(CLI) CLIFTON PLANT CENTRE.
Clifton, Morpeth, Northumberland NE61 6DG (01670 515024) (postal service).

(EX) EXOTIC FUCHSIAS.
Pen-y-banc Nurseries, Crwbin, Kidwelly, Dyfed SA17 5DP (01269 870729) (postal service).

(FEN) FENLAND FUCHSIAS.
Cyril and Jenny Waters, Old Main Road, Fleet Hargate, Spalding, Lincs PE12 8LL (01406 423709) (no postal service).

(FOX) DAVID FOX, NURSERYMAN (FINE FUCHSIAS).
Mail Order to: 34 Cottrell Road, Eastville, Bristol BS5 6TJ (0117 951 8819) (postal service).

(FUC) FUCHSIAWORLD PLANT CENTRE.
Cedar Nursery, Birdham Road, Chichester, West Sussex PO20 7EQ (01243 776822) (postal service).

(GLE) GLENACRES NURSERY.
Wimborne Road West, Stapehill, Wimborne, Dorset BH21 2DY (01202 872069) (postal – wholesale – service).

(GOU) GOULDINGS FUCHSIAS.
Link Lane, Bentley, Nr Ipswich, Suffolk IP9 2DP (01473 310058) (postal service).

(HYDE) HYDE & SON.
The Nursery, New Road, Ruscombe, Reading, Berkshire RG10 9LN (0118 934 0011) (postal service).

(ISL) ISLAND GARDEN NURSERY.
Church Street, Upwey, Weymouth, Dorset DT3 5QB (01305 814345) (Mail Order Enquiries:- Beacon Fuchsias, 32 Markham Avenue, Bournemouth BH10 7HN).

(JAK) JACKSON'S NURSERIES. Clifton Campville, Nr. Tamworth, Staffs B79 0AP (01827 373307) (no mail order).

(KM) KATHLEEN MUNCASTER FUCHSIAS. 18 Field Lane, Morton, Gainsborough, Lincs DN21 3BY (01427 612329) (limited postal service).

(LB) LITTLE BROOK FUCHSIAS. Carol Gubler, Little Brook, Ash Green Lane West, Ash Green, Nr Aldershot, Hampshire GU12 6HL (01252 329731) (no postal service).

(LOK) C.S. LOCKYER (FUCHSIAS). 70 Henfield Road, Coalpit Heath, Bristol BS36 2UZ (01454 772219) (postal service).

(MO) MIKE OXTOBY FUCHSIAS. 74 Westgate, North Cave, Brough, East Yorkshire HU15 2NJ (01430 423049) (postal service).

(OAK) OAKLEIGH NURSERIES LTD. Petersfield Road, Monkswood, Alresford, Hampshire SO24 0HB (01962 773344) (postal service).

(OLD) OLDBURY NURSERIES. Brissenden Green, Bethersden, Ashford, Kent TN26 3BJ (01233 820416) (postal service).

(OLI) OLI-BEE NURSERY. Pegmire lane, Aldenham, Watford, Herts WD2 8DR (01923 853117) (postal service).

(PER) PERCIVAL'S FUCHSIAS. Hill Farm, Bures Road, White Colne, Colchester CO6 2QA (01787 222541) (postal service).

(POT) POTASH NURSERY. (Mike Clare) The Cottage, Cow Green, Bacton, Nr Stowmarket, Suffolk IP14 4HJ (01449 781671) (limited postal service).

(RID) FUCHSIA VALE NURSERIES. (John Ridding) Worcester Road, Torton, Kidderminster, Worcs DY11 7SB (01299 251162) (limited postal service).

(RIV) RIVERSIDE FUCHSIAS. (Puddefoot), Gravel Road, Sutton at Hone, Dartford, Kent DA14 9HQ (01322 863891) (postal service).

(RKY) ROOKERY FARM NURSERY. 5 Rookery Road, Wyboston, Beds MK44 3AX (01480 213506) (postal service).

(ROO) ROOSTER FUCHSIAS. 7 Accommodation Road, Boxted, Colchester, Essex CO4 5HR (01206 272232) (no postal service).

(ROU) ROUALEYN FUCHSIAS. 'Roualeyn', Trefriw, Conwy, North Wales LL27 0SX (01492 640548) (postal service).

(SIL) SILVER DALE NURSERIES. Shute Lane, Combe Martin, North Devon EX34 0HT (01271 882539) (postal service).

(SIM) WARRENORTH FUCHSIAS (Peter and Marian Simmons) East Grinstead Road, North Chailey, Lewes, East Sussex (01825 723266) (postal service).

(SMI) JOHN SMITH AND SON. The Fuchsia Centre, Thornton Nurseries, Thornton, Leicestershire LE67 1AN (01530 230331) (postal service).

(STM) ST MARGARET'S FUCHSIA NURSERY. St Margaret's Lane, Titchfield, Fareham, Hampshire PO14 4BG (01329 846006) (no postal service).

(VER) VERNON GERANIUM NURSERY. Cuddington Way, Cheam, Surrey SM2 7JB (0208 393 7616) (postal service).

(WAL) WALTON NURSERIES (FUCHSIA SPECIALIST). 54 Burford Lane, Lymm, Warrington, Cheshire WA13 0SH (01925 759026) (postal service).

(WAR) WARD FUCHSIAS. 5 Pollen Close, Sale, Manchester M33 3LS (0161 282 7434) (postal service).

(WAY) WAYSIDE FUCHSIAS. Chester Road, Acton, Nantwich, Cheshire CW5 8LD (01270 625795) (postal service).

(WHE) WHEELER, A.D. & N. Pye Court, Willoughby, Rugby CV23 8BZ (01788 890341) (no postal service).

(WV) WHITE VEIL FUCHSIAS. Verwood Road, Three Legged Cross, Wimborne, Dorset BH21 6RP (01202 813998) (postal service).

Glossary

Anther The pollen-bearing part of the stamen.

Apetalous A flower without petals, that is, without a corolla.

Axil The angle formed by the junction of the leaf and stem from which new shoots or flowers develop.

Berry The fleshy fruit containing the seeds; the ovary after fertilization.

Biennial The term used for the process of growing a plant one year to flower the following year.

Bleeding The loss of sap from a cut or damaged shoot of a plant.

Break To branch or send out new growth from dormant wood.

Bud Undeveloped shoot found in the axils of plants; also the developing flower.

Callus The scab formed during the healing process of a cut surface. It also forms at the end of a cutting before rooting commences.

Calyx The sepals and tube together; the outer part of the flower.

Cambium A layer of activity; dividing cells around the xylem or wood.

Chlorophyll The green colourant present in plant tissue which contains magnesium. It traps blue and red light (energy), and is responsible for photosynthesis.

Chromosomes Thread-like bodies consisting of a series of different genes arranged in linear fashion. They occur in the nucleus of every plant cell.

Clear stem The amount of stem free of all growth. It is measured from the soil level to the first branch or leaf. It is of importance when growing standards or bushes.

Compost A mixture of ingredients specially prepared for the growing of cuttings, plants, or the sowing of seeds.

Cordate Heart-shaped.

Corolla The collective term for the petals; the inner part of the flower.

Cultivar A cultivated variety: a cross between two hybrids or species and a hybrid. Normally written cv.

Cutting A piece from a plant encouraged to form roots and thus produce a new plant. This is vegetative reproduction, and plants produced by this method are true to their parental type.

Cyme An inflorescence where the central flower opens first as in *F. arborescens*.

Damp down Raising the humidity of the atmosphere in the greenhouse by spraying plants, benches or paths with water.

Damping off The collapse and possible death of cuttings or seedlings usually due to attack at ground level by soil-borne fungi.

Double A fuchsia with eight or more petals.

Elliptic An oval shape, with pointed or rounded ends.

Emasculation The process of removing immature stamens from a host plant to prevent self-pollination, during the cross-pollination of two plants.

Etiolation The blanching of leaves and the lengthening of the stems that occurs when plants are grown in the dark or when the light intensity is not sufficient for adequate growth.

Fasciation The growing together, or fusion, of different parts of a plant. Leaves and flowers occasionally fuse together.

238

Feeding Applying additional plant nutrients to the compost in an effort to enhance growth or remedy compost deficiencies.

Fertilization The union of male and female cells.

Fibrous roots The white roots produced from the main fleshy roots vital for the taking up of water and nutrients essential for healthy growth.

Filament The stalk of the stamen.

Final stop The last removal of the growing tip which a plant receives before being allowed to grow to flowering stage.

First stop The removal of the growing tip of a rooted cutting to encourage branching into the required shape.

Genus The name given to a group of closely related species, for example *Fuchsia*.

Hermaphrodite Flowers which have both male and female parts.

Hybrid A cross between two species.

Hypanthium The correct term for the tube.

Inflorescence Of flowers – usually arranged around a single axis, as in *F. paniculata* or *F. arborescens*.

Internode The portion of the stem between two nodes. Rooting from this section is described as internodal.

Lanceolate Lance-, or spear-shaped.

Mutation Departure from the normal parent type, or sport.

N.A.S. The abbreviation used by show judges to indicate that an entry in a class is not according to the schedule. Exhibits so marked cannot be considered for an award within the show.

Node Part of the stem from which a leaf or bud arises. When taking cuttings, roots form most readily from this point.

Nutrients The food used by the plant from the growing medium, necessary for sustained and healthy growth.

Ornamental A term used to describe those plants which have decorative foliage. The foliage can be variegated or of a colour other than the usual green.

Ovary The part containing the ovules which, after fertilization, swells and encloses the seeds.

Ovate Egg-shaped.

Overwintering The storage of plants during the resting period, the winter months, so that the tissue remains alive though dormant.

Panicles A branched inflorescence consisting of a number of racemes.

Pedicel The flower stalk.

Petal A division of the corolla.

Petaloid Normally used to describe the smaller outer petals of the corolla.

Petiole The leaf stalk.

Photosynthesis The process carried out by the plant in the manufacture of plant food from water and carbon dioxide, using the energy absorbed by the chlorophyll from sunlight.

Pinch To remove the growing tip.

Pistil The female part of the flower, consisting of the ovary, stigma and style.

Pot-bound When the plant container is full of roots to such an extent that the plant will become starved of nutrients.

Pot on To transfer the plant from one size of pot to a larger one so that there will be a continuous supply of nutrients.

Potting up Transferring a seedling or rooted cutting from its initial seedbox or propagator into a plant pot.

Propagation Increasing of stock by means of seeds or by rooting cuttings.

Glossary

Pruning The shortening of laterals or roots to enhance the shape of the plant or to remove a damaged portion.

Raceme A flower-cluster with the separate flowers attached by short equal stalks at equal distances along a central stem.

Rubbing out The removal of unwanted side growths, for example on a standard stem, usually in early bud stage.

Self-pollination The transference of pollen from anther to stigma of the same flower or another flower on the same plant.

Semi-double A fuchsia with five, six or seven petals.

Sepals The outermost part of the flower; four sepals and the tube form the calyx.

Shading The exclusion of some of the rays of the sun by the use of blinds, netting or a glass colourant.

Shaping To grow a plant into a definite shape by means of training the laterals or by selective pinching out of the growing tips.

Siblings Offspring of the same female and male parents.

Single A fuchsia with only four petals.

Species The smallest unit of classification. Individuals in a species are assumed to have emanated from a single original genetic source and are sexually compatible with each other.

Sport A shoot differing in character from the typical growth of the parent plant, often giving rise to a new cultivar, which must be propagated vegetatively.

Stamen The male part of the flower comprising the filament and anther.

Stigma The part of the pistil to which the pollen grain adheres.

Stop To remove the growing tip.

Striking a cutting The insertion of a prepared cutting into a suitable rooting compost.

Style The stalk carrying the stigma.

Sub-species A partially differentiated group within a species.
Systemics Insecticides or fungicides taken up by the roots and carried into the sap of the plant, thus causing it to become poisonous to sucking insects or protected from the attack of viruses. Can also be absorbed through the foliage if applied in spray form.

Terminal At the extremities or ends of the branches.

Ternate Arranged in threes; of leaves or flowers at a joint.

Trace elements Nutrients required by a plant to maintain steady and healthy growth (boron, copper, manganese, molybdenum and zinc).

Tube The elongated part of the calyx, correctly called the hypanthium.

Turgid The condition of the plant cells after absorption of water to full capacity.

Turning The term used to describe the turning of a plant daily in an effort to achieve balanced growth from all directions.

Variety Botanically a variant of the species, but formerly used to denote what is now more commonly called a cultivar.

Virus An agent causing systemic disease. It is too small to be seen other than with powerful microscopes, but is transmitted very easily.

Whip A term given to a single stem of a plant being grown with a view to producing a standard.

Wilt Drooping caused by a lack of moisture within the plants. Can also be caused by disease or toxins.